HYPERACTIVE CHILDREN

HYPERACTIVE CHILDREN

Diagnosis and Management

Daniel J. Safer, M.D., and Richard P. Allen, Ph.D.

University Park Press

BALTIMORE • LONDON • TOKYO

UNIVERSITY PARK PRESS
International Publishers in Science, Medicine, and Education
233 East Redwood Street
Baltimore, Maryland 21202

Copyright © 1976 by University Park Press
Second printing, October 1977
Third printing, August 1980

Typeset by The Composing Room of Michigan, Inc.
Manufactured in the United States of America
by Universal Lithographers, Inc.,
and The Maple Press Co.

Library of Congress Cataloging in Publication Data

Safer, Daniel
Hyperactive children.

Includes bibliographical references and index.
1. Hyperactive children. I. Allen, Richard P.,
joint author. II. Title.
RJ506.H9S24   618.9'28'58   76-7366
ISBN 0-8391-0757-9

Contents

Foreword

The legitimacy of both the diagnosis and the treatment of hyperactivity in children has become a topic of strident public debate in the last few years. An issue that was once the limited concern of a few physicians and educators has become a major preoccupation in medicine, education and public policy. There are those who argue that the condition is the result of brain malfunction, who regard it as widespread and who recommend a vigorous program of medical and educational management for its remediation. There are others who contend that it is a myth invented by those who "medicalize" behavioral deviance; these critics stress the consequences of "labeling" and dismiss the proposed "treatment" as an altogether inappropriate response to normal or even "creative" variability. Between these polemical camps are others (among whom must be included the authors of this book) who believe that there is a set of behavioral phenomena which require attention but who recognize the hazards of a unitarian view. They can expect (and will receive) assaults from both sides.

Much of the debate centers on the shibboleth: behavior control. Critics object alike to drugs and operant conditioning. Both methods (for which our critics prefer the term "technologies") are condemned because they are effective, within limits, in controlling behavior. What matters in determining the legitimacy of control is the purpose for which it is to be used. If control per se is the end in mind, then I am prepared to join in condemning it on medical as well as libertarian grounds. The extent to which we simply make the child less troublesome will be the extent to which we will no longer trouble to help him. Used in that way, technical means are bastardized just as if we were to use aspirin to control the headache from a brain tumor without trying to identify and extirpate the tumor. Stimulant drugs and behavior therapy have been shown to lengthen attention span. Well and good. But the whole point in increasing attention is to enable the child to profit from instruction. That instruction has to be available at a level the youngster can assimilate or there is no point to the whole exercise in the first place. Drugs, in particular, carry with them the hazard that they are so easy to prescribe and so relatively inexpensive that they may be used without the other components of a remedial program. That is clearly wrong. What is wrong is the misuse of medication, not the medication itself.

Is hyperactivity a "myth" or is it "real"? The answer depends upon the definition of clinical reality. "Diseases" are concepts that medical science evolves through successive stages of study. Alert clinicians note the concurrence of a set of signs and symptoms which characterize a group of patients. They denote this constellation as a "syndrome" when the natural history of the condition shows a degree of coherence which can be anticipated upon recognizing the initial collection of findings (i.e., the physician can cast a prognosis). When further study identifies changes in the structure or function of body organs, the syndrome becomes a "disease." If additional research clarifies causal agents and specifies successful therapeutic interventions, we are satisfied that we "understand" the nature of the disease process. That understanding is always partial and incomplete; new knowledge leads to modified concepts. A disease is not an entity "out there" (like a tree or a house) but an alteration in human physiology and psychology. The clinical condition is a complex final resultant of the interaction among biological, psychological and social factors.

Hyperactivity is in none of these senses a "disease." As it is described in this monograph, it is a collection of signs and symptoms that approaches the status of a "syndrome." That is, it distinguishes a group of children who differ from others, not only at the time when the diagnosis is made but when they are followed up five or ten years later, and who are at increased risk for both present and later academic, social, and behavioral problems. Indeed, it is probable that we are dealing with several syndromes (which we have not yet learned to distinguish reliably) rather than a single condition. The diagnostic problem is made complex by the ability of other known conditions (anxiety, hypoglycemia, etc.) to mimic the clinical features of hyperkinetic disorders. Interesting hypotheses have been put forward about possible underlying derangements (abnormalities in central neurotransmitters, sensitivity to food additives, deviant embryologic development, cerebral anoxia during pregnancy or parturition, and the like) but none have been proved; conversely, each may hold true for some unknown fraction of cases.

What is undeniably "real" is the fact that there are children whose manifest activity and attention pattern provide a problem to their parents, to their teachers, to their peers, and to themselves. What seems equally "real" is that one-sided formulations, whether medical or social, neither account for the problem fully nor make it go away.

It is true that labeling can have invidious effects. Tagging a child creates in his parents and his teachers a nexus of expectation which may bring about the fulfillment of the prophecy by shaping the child's behavior. It would be a mockery to call "treatment" a regime imposed upon a child after an inappropriate diagnosis. It is equally absurd to refuse to recognize the existence of a problem for fear of its definition. What is called for is careful attention to the clinical phenomenology, the use of tentative diagnostic formulations and the design of remedial programs based upon identifying each child's strengths and weaknesses as well as the measures likely to be helpful in fostering healthy development. A medical label that implies more than the scientific knowledge we have *can* be misleading, especially to lay persons with undue respect for medical opinion.

Twenty years ago, it was conventional wisdom in pediatrics and psychiatry that hyperkinetic syndromes diminished with age and that the principal task was to stand by the parents in the difficult early years while reassuring them that the youngster would outgrow his disability. In the last five years, systematic study of the subsequent school careers of these youngsters has called attention to persisting problems in academic attainment, social adaptation, and emotional development. Looking from the other direction, a number of clinicans have identified impulsive character disorders in adults with a history indicative of hyperkinetic behavior disorders in childhood. If we were unduly optimistic a generation ago, we have to guard against unwarranted pessimism at present. Some of the follow-up studies have not distinguished hyperkinesis from other co-existent behavior disorders and from the disadvantages of lower social class. At present, the information we have warrants regarding this disorder as one that requires continuous educational and medical supervision, our best efforts at therapeutic intervention, and further study to determine which combination of methods is most effective. It is simply too soon to make an accurate prediction about the course in the absence of treatment or to be certain about the efficacy of available treatments.

After a quarter of a century of clinical experience, I find it difficult to dismiss as a myth a set of problems repeatedly brought to me by distressed and overwhelmed parents. I am fully aware of how little I understand about the cause and the mechanism of these problems; yet, like my colleagues, I have seen the benefit that existing empirical remedies can offer these troubled families. Indeed, a substantial part of today's medical armamentarium used for the treatment of conditions far better defined and understood than hyperactivity is based upon little more than empiricism. Which one of us, when ill, would disdain a remedy that offers relief because the mechanism by which it is produced is obscure or unknown?

It is, of course, important to ask whether the cure is worth the cost. While the evidence that benefit exceeds cost in the short run seems quite clear in the treatment of hyperactivity, in this condition, like many others that are chronic, we will need more and better information on long term outcome before a complete assessment can be made. Most of the fears that have been expressed have been based on hypothetical predictions, not data. For example, some are alarmed by the possibility that the prescription of stimulant drugs may lead to drug addiction. The information that we have belies this concern and the basis for the prediction itself seems dubious. In general, addiction is based upon a craving for the psychological effects a drug produces. Children given stimulants are more likely to report dysphoria than euphoria. They seem no more likely to become "addicted" than epileptics given anticonvulsants or diabetics given insulin under appropriate medical supervision. If anything, the uncorrected adolescent behavioral outcome of the hyperactive syndromes seems more likely to create a personality pattern at risk for addiction than the provision of a well planned treatment program *if* it is successful in diminishing the stresses and dissatisfactions associated with the initial disorder.

The fact that a treatment may be effective and appropriate when prescribed thoughtfully provides no guarantee against its abuse by thoughtless and incompetent physicians. That state of affairs is hardly unique to the group of disorders under consideration here. To argue from cases of abuse to a condemnation of appropriate use would be to remove from patients the availability of most existing medical and surgical treatments since almost all can be and have been abused. The logical conclusion from the possibility of abuse is to stress the importance of better education for physicians, psychologists, educators and parents on the limitations as well as the uses of current diagnostic and therapeutic procedures.

That is precisely what this monograph provides. Drs. Safer and Allen have compiled in one scholarly and practical book a meaningful synthesis of current information. It stresses, more than any other monograph on the topic I am familiar with, the practical details of daily clinical management. No one who reads this book with care is likely to be cavalier either in assessing or prescribing for this group of children. This is in no sense, nor was it intended to be, a definitive work. No matter how thoroughly the literature is searched, there remain too many unanswered questions to conclude a study of this subject with the feeling that we have more than preliminary answers to many important questions. What this book reflects, as it should, is the state of the art in 1976. The next edition, and I am confident that there will be a next edition, will differ substantially from its predecessor. Some of the things which appear to be true as of the present will have been shown to be false; some of the hypotheses will have been abandoned; better treatments will be recommended to replace some currently in use. We will know more than we now know about long term outcome as we learn the results of follow-up studies now in progress.

We may even have some better idea about a number of very puzzling features of the prevalence of this disorder. It seems much less common in England than in the United States, although it is recognized and diagnosed by psychiatrists in many different countries. From the reports of early visitors to the People's Republic of China, it seems to be even rarer there, though it should be acknowledged that we have only the slimmest anecdotal evidence. Many observers have commented on the differential prevalence by social class in this country and have used this observation to argue that the label reflects class bias. Yet, as the authors' own studies have indicated, drug treatment, the major bugaboo in this field, is less often provided to lower-class than middle-class children. Will we have moved beyond arguments in favor of parent counseling *or* drugs *or* behavioral management *or* remedial education? I hope so. There is enough evidence now to support the authors' conclusion that a *combined* "multimodal" coordinated plan of management makes the most sense. Either-or formulations do violence to clinical reality. A significant feature of this book is its skillful synthesis of multiple approaches into a comprehensive plan of care for children very much in need of our help. It is clear to me that the book is a major contribution. I wish there had been something like it when I began my training. I am delighted that it is now available for professionals in child care.

Leon Eisenberg, M.D.
Maude and Lillian Presley Professor
of Psychiatry
Harvard Medical School

Senior Associate in Psychiatry
Children's Hospital Medical Center
Boston, Massachusetts 02115

Preface

Over the past seven years, we have been providing community mental health services to children. Nearly all of our professional time in this effort has been spent in the School Child Mental Health Services of the Baltimore County Department of Health, and in the Division of Child Psychiatry of The Johns Hopkins University School of Medicine. Early in our work at these two institutions, we became aware of the limitations of traditional psychotherapy for children classified as hyperactive and searched for more successful methods of intervention. As a result, we tried family therapy, psychotropic medication, behavior therapy, consultation, and collaborative school programs. We left the office increasingly and spent more and more time in schools. Based upon our broader clinical experiences, our evaluative studies, and the reports of others, we concluded that for hyperactive (HA) children: 1) the school is a vital area for management intervention, 2) multiple modes of intervention are generally more valuable than unidimensional efforts, 3) some professional approaches (e.g., stimulant medication and behavior therapy) are more efficacious than others. The evidence supporting these views is presented in this book.

Another orientation which underlies our presentation is the view that hyperactivity (HA) is a deviant developmental characteristic which customarily has its onset in early childhood and begins to fade in the early teens. It is not an irreversible fault, as implied by the term "brain damage," and it is not a symptom of situational stress, as implied by the term "restless." It is a persistent temperamental and behavioral pattern most prominent during the primary school years. For simplicity *only,* we refer to this developmental deviation as HA.

As we wrote the chapters, our attempt to communicate *uniformly* to a diverse student and professional audience proved difficult. After discussing the problem with the publishers, we decided to keep the chapters relatively uncomplicated and to place details in "notes" sections following each chapter. The notes sections were designed to be self-contained units—to be read as a group—so as to alleviate the need for conscientious readers to page back and forth. In the body of the chapters, we have used alphabetic letters to refer to these notes, and numbers to refer to the Literature Cited.

This book was not written to be a guide for parents. We like *Raising a Hyperactive Child* (1) for that. Although we have included three chapters which review the field and emphasize diagnosis, this book was not primarily written to make scientific readers aware of the numerous dimensions of the hyperactive condition; Paul Wender's book, *Minimal Brain*

Dysfunction in Children (2), did that. Rather, this book was designed to stress clinical management; its main purpose is to present practical methods to help professionals more successfully manage HA children.

LITERATURE CITED

1. Stewart, M., and Olds, S. Raising a Hyperactive Child. New York: Harper and Row, 1973.
2. Wender, P. Minimal Brain Dysfunction in Children. New York: Wiley, 1971.

Acknowledgments

We wish to acknowledge the continued administrative support we have received in our work over the last 7 years from Dr. Mehdi Yeganeh of the Baltimore County Department of Health and Dr. Alejandro Rodriguez of The Johns Hopkins University School of Medicine. Helpful program support has also come from: Drs. Ron Heaton, Gene Ostrom, Ted Toulan, Jack Arthur, Paul Wender, John Krager, Phil Young, Charles Lawrence, and from Mr. Nick Spinnato, Mr. Bill Brown, Mrs. Evelyn Barr, Mrs. Virginia Homberg, Mrs. Joy Unglesbee, and Mrs. Dorothy Reidt.

Making valuable textual suggestions were: Dr. John Guthrie, Mrs. Sharon Goldberger, Mrs. Kathleen DeLever, Mrs. Linda Fabizak, Dr. John Gaynor, and Mr. Frank Funderburk.

Mrs. Lilian Burke, as usual, did her excellent job of typing (and correcting) the manuscript.

Graphs and forms reprinted from published sources were obtained with permission. These were obtained from the American Orthopsychiatric Association, *Journal of Learning Disabilities, Pediatric Clinics of North America, American Journal of Psychiatry, American Journal of Orthopsychiatry,* Scott, Foresman and Co., The Society for the Experimental Analysis of Behavior, Inc., and from Drs. S. Cohen, W. L. Brown, C. Keith Connors, T. F. McLauglin, J. Malaby, John Werry, Lauretta Bender, James Satterfield, and Mark Stewart.

This book is dedicated to our parents

Mendel and Belle Safer
Dean and Gretchen Allen

HYPERACTIVE CHILDREN

Chapter 1 _____The Historical Background

Hyperactivity in children has become an issue of popular concern only since the late 1960's, even though the clinical pattern has been noted in scientific writing since the 1920's and has been recognized in all areas of the world. (*1*). It was not, however, until the last two decades that investigators separated the learning and behavior problems of hyperactive (HA) children from others who failed in school or misbehaved in group settings. This was particularly apparent in follow-up studies of children first evaluated in the 1930's and 40's (*2, 3*).

During the early part of this century, literate society was only beginning to be concerned about the needs and rights of slow learners, mental retardates, epileptics, criminals, and the seriously emotionally ill. Extreme deviants were still placed in colonies (e.g., colonies for the retarded, for epileptics, for the insane) and those with minor handicaps were given no compensatory assistance from schools or government agencies.

In 1915, when the child guidance movement began in the United States, it also showed relatively little concern for learning-impaired and misbehaving children. Despite a marginal concern then about delinquents (*4*), child guidance clinics as a group shifted quickly in the 20's and 30's to a focus on neurotic behavior and dynamic, insight-oriented therapy (*5, 6*). When serious behavior problem children were seen by psychiatrists, they were customarily diagnosed and then referred to social workers and social agencies. On occasion, when outpatient psychological treatment was tried for such a child, an attempt was made to convert the behavioral difficulties into a neurotic dilemma so that psychoanalytically oriented treatment could be utilized (*7*). A cursory review of the literature suggests that even when psychiatrists dealt with learning impairments (in children of normal intelligence), they focused on the hypothetical construct of a "neurotic block" to learning (*8*).

From the 1930's to the late 1950's, American middle and upper-middle class society developed in strength and became increasingly concerned about children's education and development. Correspondingly, mental health professionals focused increasingly on the successful management of learning impairments and behavior deviance. Family and group therapies were tried, amphetamine drugs were explored (9, 10), residential treatment was made more flexible, and remedial education was made more precise (11). Nonetheless, during this period, treatment services for those children now recognized as hyperactive were few and utilized primarily by the well-to-do.

Beginning in the late 1950's, public health and public education services for children with learning and behavior difficulties began in earnest in the United States. In the mental health arena, the expansion of services was spurred largely by the impact of drug treatment successes with (psychiatric) outpatients from state hospitals. By the late 1960's, also because of successful experiences (a), the use of medication in psychiatry expanded to include hyperactive children (focusing a great deal of attention on the disorder). With the increased demand for psychiatric services, waiting lists for both children and adults became untenable and crisis intervention came to be utilized as a standard mode of psychotherapeutic treatment for those in distress (12). Then, in the late 1960's and early 1970's, behavior modification as a treatment caught on, particularly in child psychology, and systematized a historic avenue of psychological intervention.

In public education, particularly at the elementary school level, the changes of the last two decades have been more gradual, except in the field of special education. In the early 1960's, special educational assistance for children's specific learning disabilities was minimal except in some wealthy suburban areas (13). However, in just one decade, spurred by public demand (and then federal funds), these services became increasingly available in public schools: first in the suburbs, next in the cities, and last in rural areas. Now, nearly 200,000 United States public school children are enrolled in learning disability classes (13).

For education in general, one major change has been the gradual but persistent public demand for high school graduation. In 1900, only 10% of school children graduated from high school; in 1950, this rose to 50%, and in 1975, it stands at over 70% (b). With this increasing demand for high school graduation, all educators were made less comfortable when they failed misfits routinely and were forced to consider alternative modes of response (throughout the grade levels) that would allow a goodly share of them to graduate.

In the mid-1970's, there is now a clear, although still relatively modest, public commitment to aid the disadvantaged child. The general public has become upset about the battered child, somewhat aware of the malnourished child, and increasingly sympathetic to the learning-impaired child. Concern for the behaviorally deviant child is still nascent. It is hoped that, in time, as the adult population senses that childhood difficulties in learning and temperament result in *community,* as well as family, problems, greater public efforts will be forthcoming.

Thus, over the last half-century, as increasing and more structured attempts have been made to manage learning and behaviorally deviant children, categories and subcategories of deviance have evolved. Of these categories, one of the largest has turned out to be the hyperactive problem. It was always there.

NOTES

a. The availability of a viable treatment for a disorder can increase the frequency with which it is diagnosed. This occurred in relation to manic-depressive psychoses after the initiation of lithium treatment and certainly occurred for hyperactivity after stimulant treatment came into prominent use.

b. In other words, in 1915 the average American left school at age 15, in 1935 at 17, and in 1965 at 19 (*14*).

LITERATURE CITED

1. Report of the conference on the use of stimulant drugs in the treatment of behaviorally disturbed young school children. Psychopharm. Bull. 7: 23–29, (July) 1971.

2. Robins, L. Deviant Children Grown Up. Baltimore: Williams & Wilkins, 1966.

3. Morris, H., Escoll, P., and Wexler, R. Aggressive behavior disorders of childhood: A follow-up study. Am. J. Psychiat. 112: 991–997, 1956.

4. Healy, W. The Individual Delinquent. Boston: Little, Brown and Company, 1915.

5. Witmer, H. (Ed). Psychiatric Interviews with Children. New York: Commonwealth Fund, 1946.

6. Lowrey, L. Trends in therapy. Am. J. Orthopsychiat. 9: 669–706, 1939.

7. Eissler, K. (Ed). Searchlights on Delinquency. New York: International Universities Press, 1949.

8. Pearson, G. Psychoanalysis and the Education of the Child. New York: W. W. Norton, 1954.

9. Bradley, C. The behavior of children receiving benzedrine. Am. J. Psychiat. 94: 557–585, 1937.
10. Korey, S. The effects of benzedrine sulfate on the behavior of psychopathic and neurotic juvenile delinquents. Psychiat. Quart. 18: 127–137, 1944.
11. Orton, S. Reading, Writing and Speech Problems in Children. New York: Norton, 1937.
12. Parad, H. (Ed). Crisis Intervention. New York: Family Service Association of America, 1965.
13. Dunn, L. An overview, in L. Dunn (ed.), Exceptional Children in the Schools: Special Education in Transition, 2nd Ed., pp. 3–62. New York: Holt, Rinehart and Winston, 1973.
14. Jencks, C. Inequality: A Reassessment of the Effect of Family and Schooling in America. New York: Basic Books, 1972.

Chapter 2   Hyperactivity
in Children

Before addressing the issues of management, it seems useful to introduce in some detail the hyperactive child and the issues involved in diagnosis. Such a description would be fairly routine and simple for many clinical entities, but for the much abused concept of hyperactivity, defining this behavioral pattern becomes testy and complicated. Some have argued that hyperactivity as a category is so general or so poorly defined as to be useless. Others have been so impressed with the significance and specificity of this category as to call it a syndrome. Neither position seems correct. On one hand, hyperactive children present a diversity of symptoms so wide that diagnosis can be difficult and at times can appear almost arbitrary; on the other hand, the diagnosis is generally useful for treatment.

It is the purpose of this chapter to introduce the reader to hyperactivity in children: its characteristics, history, prevalence, and prognosis. In the process, the basis for the diagnosis will be presented. The nuts and bolts of systematically gathering the information helpful for the diagnosis are, however, delayed for detailed description in Chapter 4.

DIAGNOSTIC TERMS FOR DEVELOPMENTAL HYPERACTIVITY

A certain amount of the confusion regarding hyperactivity stems directly from problems inherent in the terminology. In diagnoses, two terms are commonly used, often interchangeably. The first diagnostic term is "hyperactivity" itself. It is used synonomously with the more sophisticated medical label, hyperkinetic behavior pattern. Hyperactivity (HA) is simply defined as a long term childhood pattern characterized by excessive restlessness and inattentiveness. It is a developmental disorder which begins in early to midchildhood (ages 2–6), and begins to fade during adolescence *(1; a)*. During childhood, the pattern is consistent year after year; i.e., it is not observed for one year but absent the next two.

The second diagnostic term that pertains to hyperactivity is "minimal brain dysfunction." It is known commonly by its initials, MBD. MBD is generally based on a learning or perceptual impairment, usually associated with hyperactivity and inattentiveness (*b*). A behavioral difficulty is sometimes added as a diagnostic feature of MBD (2).

Despite the interchangeable use of MBD and HA in public discussions, the two categories are not identical. For one, MBD children are not always hyperactive, although most are (*c*). Secondly, hyperactive children do not always have a learning or perceptual disability, although most do. In this book, the term HA will be used henceforth for the developmental hyperactive pattern, and the term MBD only when specific emphasis is placed on the learning disability aspects of HA.

LIMITATIONS IN TERMINOLOGY

Further confusion regarding hyperactivity is created by the limited applicability of certain terms commonly related to HA. For example, consider the not uncommon reference to "brain damage." That term is usually used inappropriately since more than 95% of hyperactive children have no evidence of an injured area in the brain. It seems most likely that hyperactivity does not reflect an anatomical lesion, but rather a minimal dysfunction associated with a selective lag in the maturation of the central nervous system (*3, 4; d*).

A second term that is somewhat limited is the term hyperactivity itself. Hyperactive children have no more total daily body activity than nonhyperactive children (*5, 6*). In many settings, they have a normal activity level (*7; e*). However, when they are expected to sit quietly at their seats and pay attention in the classroom, they are unusually active. Thus a better way of viewing the activity problem these children have is to state that they have difficulty modulating their activity level, particularly when they are expected to perform an abstract academic task.

A third term that is limited in its application to hyperactivity is the term "syndrome" (*f*). Physicians often speak of the "hyperkinetic behavior syndrome." A syndrome implies a set of coexisting characteristics, such as those which occur together in rheumatic fever or measles. The clinical signs and symptoms of developmental hyperactivity, however, have only a modest degree of inherent unity, not enough at this time to technically merit the tag "syndrome" (*g*). The major reason for this is that HA children share no specific learning or perceptual-cognitive problem (*5, 8, 9*). A child could qualify as learning disabled for inclusion in the MBD category with perceptual-cognitive problems in any of a number of areas, e.g., auditory memory, directionality, the visual-motor sphere. Such variability in learning disabilities does not mean, however, that there are no syndromes among children who are hyperactive. There are indeed. One, in fact, is that subgroup of hyperactives who have mongoloid-type features (*10*). Another might be a group with a history of perinatal difficulties who evidence choreiform movements (*11*). In the next 10–20 years, as the HA entity becomes more thoroughly explored, a number of other hyperactive syndromes no doubt will be identified.

THE ESSENTIAL FEATURE OF THE HA PATTERN

The only necessary feature of the HA pattern is developmental hyperactivity. Hyperactivity is best determined by history. It is the *persistent* pattern of *excessive* activity in situations requiring motor inhibition. Persistent means consistently, year after year. Excessive means extreme (i.e., the most restless 3–5%).

Hyperactivity is most clearly brought out in the classroom, but it is also notable at the meal table, during visiting, in church, and whenever attention and the sedentary position are expected. The child may be hyperactive in a gross way, as when he leaves his assigned seat constantly to meander around the classroom. Or he may be able to stay in his seat (for example, while watching cartoons on television), but he will show his restlessness by fidgeting constantly. Both qualify.

THE MAJOR FEATURES:
THOSE MOST CLOSELY ASSOCIATED WITH HA

For purposes of order and simplicity, four of the most prominent characteristics commonly associated with HA will be viewed as the major features of the disorder.

The most prominent of the major features of HA is *inattentiveness,* i.e., the inability to maintain attention (*12; h*). Teachers report inattentiveness by these descriptive phrases: short attention span and short interest span. Psychologists say that the child is unable to persist at an abstract task. Parents report that the child doesn't listen to stories for any length of time and that he frequently changes activities.

The second major feature of HA is a *learning impediment.* About one-third of HA children have a prominent learning impairment, and another 40–50% have a notable academic lag (*13–16; i, j*). A learning disability is usually assumed when there is a clear discrepancy between the child's mental and/or chronological age and his age-expected academic achievement (*k*). Most feel that a retardation greater than 15% (or 2.8 years) in achievement indicates a prominent learning defect and that a child should be at least 10% (or 2 years) retarded academically to be considered for this category (*17, 18*). The 15% figure, using mental and chronological age, would mean that a child of 10 with an I.Q. of 100 would have to be achieving below the mid-third grade level to merit the tag (*l, m*).

Academic deficits, however, can be greatly influenced by cultural factors. In fact, in large urban areas, approximately 30% of sixth graders are 2 or more years behind the national norms in achievements (*19; n*). Since an estimated 8–15% of children nationally have a learning impairment (*17*), presumably only one-third to one-half of urban children with academic delays of 2 or more years would actually be classified as learning impaired.

One partial means of sorting out the learning impaired from within the population of poor achievers has been to use area norms as the reference standard. Another has been to use I.Q. as a correction factor since I.Q. tests show less cultural bias than achievement measures. With area norms, only the most impaired children would then remain as 2 years academically retarded. With the I.Q. correction, only those most underachieving relative to expectations would remain.

The learning difficulties of the HA child are usually appraised with respect to the three areas of information processing: receptive, integrative, and expressive. These terms respectively refer to the child's ability to grasp sensory detail, organize this input, and utilize or express this information (*o*). These dimensions of learning can be viewed as intake, integrative, and output spheres, and are often described using simply one term, "perceptual." That term is technically misleading and the term "perceptual-cognitive" is better. Examples of perceptual-cognitive disorders are: the child having difficulty retaining spoken words, sentences, or letters ("auditory memory"); deciphering sounds ("auditory discrimination"); and duplicating designs ("visual-motor integration skill") (*p*). The majority of children with notable academic deficiencies have perceptual-cognitive deficits (*17, 20, 21*).

As a rule, HA children with learning impediments have great difficulty grasping abstractions, although they may be successful on concrete tasks. Frequently, they have trouble with phonics; they can identify the letters but cannot pronounce them correctly. Their spelling is frequently poor. They often add numbers well on their fingers, but do poorly on paper and pencil subtraction. They may memorize their multiplication tables, but do poorly on division. In effect, they have trouble incorporating new information and applying it in the realm of ideas.

Behavior problems are the third most common feature of the hyperactive pattern. Misconduct is notable in over 80% of hyperactive children (*22, 23; q, r*). The behavior difficulties occur most prominently in the classroom situation. Teachers report that the child disturbs others, speaks out of turn, makes disruptive noise, and often gets into fights. Parents usually stress belligerence, fighting, sibling quarrels, and disobedience.

The fourth most common feature of HA children is *immaturity*. Nearly all HA children operate on a less sophisticated level than do their age-mates. This is reflected in their wishes, their choice of younger friends, their interests, their difficulty in coping with environmental changes, their frequent temper outbursts, and their low frustration tolerance. Their drawings of people are simplistic even if one considers and corrects for the visual-motor problems which many of these children have. They have a mild tendency to cry more easily, to persist longer in baby talk, and to be more afraid. Although immaturity is a subjective and often nebulous term, those who see hyperactives routinely recognize this dimension. In fact, even in their teenage years, 70% of hyperactives were characterized by their parents as immature (*14, 24; s*).

MINOR FEATURES: THOSE LESS CLOSELY ASSOCIATED WITH HA

A number of emotional and behavioral features occur fairly often in hyperactive children, but less often than the major features of the disorder. One is *impulsivity*. This is common in hyperactives. It is apparent in tasks (*25*). When the HA child is asked to follow a path on a maze test, he goes headlong into blind alleys without stopping to meditate (*25*). Likewise, in a play room, he darts from one activity to another without much forethought (*t*).

Peer difficulties are also fairly common for hyperactives. This is in part because their restlessness bothers their classmates (*u*) and in part because learning-impaired children generally tend to be unpopular (*18*). In games, their low frustration tolerance, impulsiveness, and short interest span adversely influence their ability to cooperate (*22*). Many HA children also have *low self-esteem* (*26*). Low self-esteem particularly characterizes learning-impaired children, so it is by no means a peculiar characteristic of HA.

As a group, HA children also tend to have more emotional deviance and anxiety than do nonhyperactive children (*13, 27–30*). The nature of the relationship of these symptoms to HA is somewhat unclear. Are many HA children different emotionally because of their hyperactivity, or are they hyperactive as a result of their emotional deviance? Alternatively, are the hyperactivity and emotional deviance separate entities, or are they part of the same basic illness? Each HA child is different, so these questions cannot be answered simply. However, certain general statements can be made.

First, it can be said with assurance that HA children on average are immature, low in frustration tolerance, more sensitive to stress, and more prone to respond to stress with anxiety. Their learning difficulties particularly predispose them to anxiety under academic stress (31). In these respects, then, their emotional differences are part of the clinical picture. Second, although it has been reported that anxiety can cause hyperactivity, there is no evidence to support that it causes *developmental* hyperactivity, i.e., persistent hyperactivity since early childhood. Third, it has been documented that children with central nervous malfunction have, on average, a 5–6 times greater risk of an emotional impairment (27), and that learning-impaired children, too, are at greater risk for anxiety and emotional disability (32–35). For many separate and possibly overlapping reasons, then, HA children as a group have a higher degree of emotional deviance (v).

Table 1 gives data for the frequency of occurrence of behavioral symptoms in HA children compared with non-HA children.

CO-OCCURRENCE OF THE MAJOR HA FEATURES

The hyperactive behavior pattern which has been described is customarily the combination of developmental hyperactivity and associated major features: inattentiveness, a learning or perceptual-cognitive disability, a conduct problem, and immaturity (w). However, each of the major features of HA may occur without HA and, in fact, HA may occur without any of the major features of the pattern. Table 2 presents the prevalence of the four major features which are commonly associated with HA. Columns 3 and 4 present percentages of relative occurrence of each feature and HA; column 5 presents the natural occurrence of each feature in the elementary school population.

The first major feature is inattentiveness. Although approximately 85% of hyperactives are inattentive (12), only about 13% of children who are inattentive have HA. Inattentiveness is particularly associated with learning disability. Over 80% of children with a learning handicap are viewed by their teachers as having a short attention span (18).

The second major feature of HA is learning disability; 70–80% of HA children have a learning disability and approximately 30–45% of learning-impaired children have HA (*24, 28, 36–43;* Table 3). Thus, the coexistence of these two impediments is high.

The third major feature is misconduct; 75% of HA children reportedly fight or are defiant in school (*22, 23*) and approximately 38% of the children who show this misconduct in school are HA (Table 1). Moreover, 40% of elementary school children who are suspended are HA (*44*).

Thus, like learning disability, the finding of a serious conduct disorder, although not diagnostic, clearly raises developmental HA as a strong possibility. When a child has either a learning impairment or serious school misconduct, there is a 35–40% likelihood that he is also hyperactive (Table 1). When the child developmentally exhibits both a serious learning and conduct problem, the figure can go as high as an 80% likelihood of HA.

For the fourth major feature, immaturity, there is insufficient data available to make any statement beyond that previously noted, namely that 70% of HA children are immature.

HISTORICAL AND DEVELOPMENTAL FINDINGS ASSOCIATED WITH HYPERACTIVITY

There are a number of historical and developmental features that are significantly associated with (or positively correlated with) hyperactivity. These are items in the history that occur more for hyperactives than for nonhyperactives. Except for restlessness and inattentiveness in the preschool years, these features are *not* in the history of most hyperactives.

During pregnancy, the mother of the hyperactive child is more likely to experience vaginal bleeding (*45, 46; x*) and preeclampsia (*45, 47*) (which is characterized by swelling, high blood pressure, and protein in the urine). The hyperactive baby's birth weight is more likely to be below normal or premature (*45–51*). Technically, prematurity means that the newborn is under 5.5 pounds, or is the product of a pregnancy of less than 38 weeks (38–42 weeks is considered normal). Prematurity averages 5–15% in the population (*52, 53*) and varies greatly with socioeconomic conditions. In hyperactives, prematurity rates average 10–25% (*46, 54, 55*). During the period after delivery, hyperactives have a more frequent history of respiratory distress (*45, 54*). This means difficulty breathing, with a likelihood of some cyanosis or blueness. The breathing difficulty after delivery can also be associated with a slowing of the heart rate. Such perinatal difficulties have been quantified in what is called an Apgar score (*56; y*). Thus, medically, one can say that hyperactive children tend to

Table 1. Percentage of occurrence of behavioral symptoms for HA and control children from two data sources

	Data from Satterfield[a] et al. (23)		Data from Stewart et al. (22)		
Behavior	7.8 years[b] control (n = 14)	7.8 years[b] HA (n = 14)	Behavior	6.7 years[b] control (n = 33)	7.6 years[b] HA (n = 37)
Unusually active	14	86	Overactive	33	100
Unable to sit through school period	21	86	Can't sit still	8	81
Rocks, jiggles legs	14	86	Fidgets	30	84
Dances, wiggles hands	14	86	Leaves class without permission	0	35
Leaves doctor's office	14	64	Can't accept correction	0	35
Unable to take correction	0	86	Temper tantrums	0	51
Temper tantrums	7	71	Fights	3	59
Fights with peers	7	93	Defiant	0	49
Defiant	14	71	Doesn't complete project	0	84
Does not complete projects	7	71	Doesn't stay with games	3	78
Unable to follow directions	7	79	Doesn't listen to whole story	0	49
Difficult to get to bed	7	79	Moves from one activity to another in class	6	46

Item		Item	
Hard to get to to sleep	7 71	Doesn't follow directions	3 62
Wakes early	7 71	Hard to get to bed	3 49
Poor relationship with peers	0 71	Unpopular with peers	0 46
		Talks too much	20 68
		Wears out toys, furniture, etc.	8 68
		Gets into things	11 54
		Unpredictable	3 59
		Destructive	0 41
		Unresponsive to discipline	0 57
		Lies	3 43

[a] Matched for I.Q. (mean for both groups was about 110).
[b] Mean age.

Table 2. Relative occurrence of major features of HA

Feature	Data source	Probability (HA/feature) %[a]	Probability (feature/HA) %[b]	Natural occurrence of feature (%)
1. Developmentally hyperactive	Teacher rating, 3 consecutive years	100[c]	100[c]	5[c]
2. Restless or overactive	Teacher rating, 1 year	14	100	35
3. Inattentive	Teacher report	13	85	33
4. Learning impairment	School data (Achievement <88% of expected level)	39	78	10
5. Misbehavior: classroom fights or defiance	Teacher report	38	75	10
6. Immaturity	Parent report		70	

[a]Percentage of children with feature who are hyperactive.
[b]Percentage of hyperactive children with the feature.
[c]HA is defined as developmental hyperactivity.

Table 3. Percentage of learning disabled children reported to be hyperactive

Authors	Number learning impaired	Number hyper-active[a]	% hyper-active	Characteristics of each population
Hertzig et al. (40)	90	19	21	Educationally designated as "brain damaged"
Dykman et al. (24)	82	29	35	Learning disabled
Shain (37)	40	17	43	Learning disabled
Grant (38)	91	44	48	Learning disabled
Eaves et al. (39)	25	11	44	Learning impaired
Hinton and Knight (36)	67	23	35	Academically retarded
Denckla (41)	50	17	34	Language disabled
Keele et al. (42)	23	9	39	Learning disabled
Kenny and Clemmens (43)	100	42	42	Learning disabled

Median = 39%

[a]Since nearly all of these children were evaluated on the basis of parent, school, psychologist, and physician data, it is assumed that their diagnosis of hyperactivity refers to developmental HA as defined in this text.

have a low Apgar score. At birth, they also tend to have more congenital disorders (55), i.e., physical defects present at birth.

In infancy, these children have a greater incidence of colic (22). Furthermore, their activity level in the first year of life tends to be extreme (22, 57, 58); that is, they can be unduly passive and unresponsive, or they can be restless. Some, particularly those with a serious learning impairment, have a history of delayed developmental milestones (22, 48, 54). This means that they first learn to walk at an age beyond a year and a half, speak in words after age 2, and speak in sentences over age 3. (Language delays are far more common than motor lags.) Hyperactive children also tend to have a history of strabismus (cross-eyedness) (22), and a speech impediment, particularly an articulation disorder lasting beyond age 6 (22, 47, 51). Parents often report, too, that these children have difficulty getting to sleep and that they talk excessively (22, 23).

Hyperactives tend to have a greater history of brain malfunction. For example, they have a greater incidence of seizures (with and without fever), a history of encephalitis, of brain injury, and of cerebral palsy (51,

54). In two of these conditions particularly, there is a high frequency of hyperactivity. Nearly one-third of children with seizure disorders (*28, 59–61*) and one-fifth of children with cerebral palsy have a clinical history of hyperactivity (*62*). Thus, whereas a small portion of hyperactives have clear and major evidence of cerebral malfunctioning, those children with clear-cut brain irregularities have a high risk for hyperactivity.

Hyperactives tend to have a family history of learning difficulty, behavior difficulty, and hyperactivity. Around 20–35% of the fathers of hyperactives have a history of hyperactivity or repetitive behavioral difficulties in their childhood, a higher percentage than that of nonhyperactives from the same social circumstances (*51, 63–65*). This information, plus adoptive studies (*55, 66*), supports the contention that genetic influences constitute a major causative factor in the development of hyperactivity (*z*).

Children with more than one known developmental correlate of HA have an increased likelihood of becoming hyperactive. Thus, children with a low birth weight, a congenital disorder, and a positive family history are more likely to be hyperactive than others with low birth weight alone (*55; aa*). In the developmental history obtained from the parent, it is, therefore, important to ask about the pregnancy, the neonatal period, the early childhood developmental patterns, the medical history, and the family history. Positive reports in one or more of these areas do not make the diagnosis. The diagnosis is based on the presence of hyperactivity and is supported by the coexistence of the major features of HA. However, correlates in the pre- and perinatal periods and in infancy add additional support for the diagnosis.

More important than perinatal historical difficulties for the diagnosis of HA is a history from the preschool period, that is, when the child is age 2–5. During this period, most HA children are usually described by their parents as being excessively restless, temperamental, meddlesome, and disruptive. They constantly get into things (*bb*) and frequently shift from one activity to another. They often destroy toys by tinkering repeatedly with them, and bed wetting at night is also fairly frequent for them (*51, 58*). A careful history reveals that *most* hyperactives have a preschool history of restlessness and inattentiveness, the essential and the most frequently associated major feature of HA (*cc*).

Observant parents also report that in the immediate preschool years and in midchildhood, many of these children have learning difficulties. The children rapidly forget academic material that has been memorized. They have difficulty learning to tell time and putting on the "right" shoe. They have more spelling irregularities than could be expected for their age.

Not uncommonly, they continue to have reversals in writing and in words after ages 6 (for girls) and 7 (for boys). Examples of reversals are: "b" for a "d," a backwards "7," or "saw" for "was." The children often have difficulty grasping number concepts. Most are delayed in skills requiring good fine motor coordination (22), such as buttoning buttons, tying shoelaces, holding a pencil properly, drawing a person, and copying a design. A history of early and midchildhood learning difficulty is particularly helpful to obtain because it constitutes evidence of a major feature of the disorder.

DIAGNOSTIC PRIORITIES

To make the diagnosis of HA, it is most important to obtain a detailed and accurate history. The school history is usually best in these respects, although a detailed parent history is nearly as useful. The combination of school *and* parent data is, of course, ideal.

The most important school information includes the present teacher's behavioral report and behavioral comments from previous teachers (which are usually in the school folder). The present teacher's report can be nicely presented in the form of a check list, indicating degrees and types of restlessness, inattentiveness, etc. If that is not available, a detailed anecdotal account may supply the needed information. If previous teachers' comments are not available from the school folder, report cards from earlier years are helpful. Two particular items are helpful from old report cards: one is the conduct grade; the other is the grade for study habits. Both of these are consistently poor for hyperactive children not on medication.

The parental report of the child's developmental history is helpful but generally not as useful as school reports because hyperactivity reaches its peak in a sit-down, all-day classroom situation, an experience routinely observed only by the teacher. Also, the parent may not be an accurate reporter of past events, since she depends on a recall from years back. The doctor's judgment of hyperactivity, based upon his observation of the child in his examining room, although more reliable than chance (67), offers little to the diagnosis because it is based on a one-to-one involvement with the child, and this often does not bring out a child's hyperactivity (dd).

After a detailed review of available information, one is usually able to categorize children with the major features of HA as having from excellent to fair (or borderline) evidence of the disorder. The borderline or fair evidence cases can present some difficulty for the clinician. If this diagnostic question is not resolved, the clinician may be in a quandary whether to treat the hyperactivity or not. In these cases, a number of reports or measures can be reviewed to clarify the matter. The first is the teacher's itemized and scaled account of the child's classroom restless and inattentive behavior. The second is previous teachers' reports. To establish good evidence of HA, these must indicate a prominent degree of restlessness and inattentiveness, apparent presently and since the first grade. The third is the history or the finding of a learning or a perceptual-cognitive difficulty. Fourth, misconduct since first grade certainly helps the diagnosis. Fifth, a reliable preschool history of the child's restlessness is useful. Available data from the school folder should help to elucidate most of these matters. Essentially, the consistency and, to a lesser extent, the degree of these reports conveys the message. Children who begin their school problems in the third grade are not developmentally HA children.

The point deserves further stress. Most late-elementary and junior high students who exhibit prominent school misbehavior show their serious classroom behavior and school work difficulties initially in the third to fifth grades. The hyperactive children in the school misconduct group, by contrast, have a consistent record of disruptive behavior and inattentiveness dating back to the first grade (or before). Thus, with comprehensive reliable data, the diagnosis can be made relatively easily; without it, uncertainty often prevails.

CLINICAL SUPPORT FOR THE DIAGNOSIS

The clinical examination by a psychologist, pediatric neurologist, child psychiatrist, or pediatrician can clearly support the diagnosis. Particularly helpful for the diagnosis would be findings of a perceptual-cognitive or learning impediment.

One finding from a clinical evaluation is that of a visual motor impediment. This is usually obtained through the Bender Gestalt Test (ee). In this test, the child is asked to duplicate graphically a series of geometric designs. Approximately 75% of HA children score 1 year or more below their age level on this test, whereas only about 20–40% of nonhyperactive children do as poorly (25, 68). Furthermore, hyperactives tend to rotate their designs and have great difficulty with angles, often winging them (69). An abnormal Bender test is not diagnostic of hyperactivity. However, it presents good evidence for eye-hand incoordination, a perceptual-cognitive disorder (ff).

A second clinical procedure is the electroencephalogram (EEG). An abnormal EEG supports the diagnosis because approximately 50% of HA children have abnormal EEG's, whereas only around 15–20% of nonhyperactive children have such irregularities (70–72). Usual EEG abnormalities in HA children are an excessive degree of slow waves and epileptiform spikes in the temporal-occipital regions (gg). The EEG is not used frequently as a clinical test for hyperactivity because it adds only little support to the diagnosis and is costly and time consuming (70). It is indicated primarily when one suspects the hyperactive child also has a seizure disorder.

A third clinical investigative procedure is the pediatric-neurological examination. The clinical finding of soft neurological signs adds a fair degree of support to the diagnosis of HA because one-third to one-half of hyperactive children have a few of these findings; they are infrequently found in nonhyperactive children (73, 74; hh). Soft neurological signs are usually minor irregularities and maturational delays, whereas hard neurological signs pertain to clear defects in sensory function, strength, reflexes, gait, or intellectual capabilities (75). Most soft neurological signs reflect impaired fine motor coordination relative to age-expected ability. Impairment is in areas of rapid finger movement, finger flexion and extension, finger-thumb coordination, and pronation and supination (73; ii). Another impaired area for some is motor impersistence; this is, some hyperactive children do not persist in an activity, such as as keeping their hands still, or sticking out their tongues, or standing on one foot for 30 or 60 seconds, whereas nearly all nonhyperactives can succeed in these tasks (76). A third category of soft neurological signs is choreiform movements. Irregular, jerky limb movements can often be brought out by having the child keep his limbs outstretched (11) or by his hanging his hands down between his knees from a seated position (77) for 30 seconds (11). About one-third to one-half of hyperactives show this sign, whereas only about 10% of nonhyperactives do (11, 77, 78).

Upon physical examination of hyperactives, one occasionally finds mongoloid-related features (jj). These include: an epicanthal fold on the nasal side of the eye lid, a cross palm midline groove, widely spaced eyes, an inwardly curved little finger and little toe, a high arched palate, low lying ears, fine hair, an unusual head circumference, and a long third toe (46; kk).

A fourth clinical procedure is the I.Q. test. A low I.Q. offers some support to the diagnosis because hyperactives tend to have an I.Q. about 10 points below that of children in their neighborhood (ll). Thus, in upper-middle class suburbia, hyperactives have an average I.Q. of 105, compared with the 115 I.Q. of their classmates (22, 23, 79). Like the EEG, an individual I.Q. test is generally not worth the time or money for its value in supporting the diagnosis of hyperactivity (*mm*). Individual I.Q. test scores, however, can be useful in the appraisal of learning disability. Also, Weschler Intelligence Scale for Children (WISC) I.Q. subtest scatter and verbal vs. performance scores, although of little value in the diagnosis of hyperactivity or "organicity" (*5, 80–82*), can be useful to appraise learning disability.

A fifth clinical procedure to evaluate the HA child is to measure his academic level. Prominent academic retardation can be measured informally by teacher estimates, or formally by a standard achievement test. When a number of the child's achievement scores are available from school material, it is usually not necessary for the clinician to readminister these tests. In the absence of school information, the child's level of academic achievement can be approximated by the experienced clinician using graded standard word lists (*83*) and the like. Alternatively, it can be requested that school personnel administer a simple achievement test to the child (as the Wide Range Achievement Test). It is important to obtain a general measure of the degree of academic underachievement in HA children because it represents a major feature of the disorder (*nn, oo, pp*).

LABORATORY MEASURES OF HYPERACTIVITY

Although laboratory measures of hyperactivity have scientific value and hold some promise in the future, they are far less valid and less generally reliable than are the classroom ratings of independent observers or of teachers (*84*).

One of the better laboratory measures for hyperactivity is the stabilimetric cushion, which records seat movement while the child sits on the cushion (the cushion being located on top of a small chair) (*85*). This measure is sensitive only when the child is doing an attention task. That is, developmentally hyperactive children, when attempting to pay attention, e.g., on a prolonged surveillance task, have measurably more seat movements than nonhyperactive children (*86*).

A second major laboratory measure for HA is a test of prolonged attention, which is known as a vigilance test. The most used of these is the Continuous Performance Test or CPT. In this test, different letters are presented on a screen at the rate of one every 1–2 seconds and the child is instructed to press a button for every occurrence of a specific letter sequence, such as "X" followed by "A." In this task, hyperactive children as a group have more misses, less accuracy (*87–89*), and slower reaction times (*25*) than do nonhyperactives.

These tests in combination can be useful in studies because they are modeled after a major classroom expectation, that the child sit in his seat and pay attention.

PREVALENCE OF HA

What is the prevalence of the features of HA and of the HA pattern? Well, if one goes from door to door and asks parents of children ages 6–12 if their children are restless, the parents report that 35–50% of their boys and 20–25% of their girls indeed are (90, 91). Teachers likewise report that approximately 40% of their students are restless and that over a third are inattentive (92–94). If these descriptions are taken at face value, then nearly one-third of the boys and one-fifth of the girls in elementary school would qualify as hyperactive-inattentive children. However, when teachers are asked, instead, to identify only those children who have a prominent degree of hyperactivity and inattentiveness and have had it since they began school, then the number of hyperactives is reduced to a total of 5–10% of the elementary school population. If learning disability is added to the criteria, along with a positive preschool history as a factor deserving consideration, then the total is reduced to about 5%. Since boys have more HA than girls, in a ratio of 3 or 4:1 (qq), the prevalence comes to about 8–9% in elementary school boys and 2–3% in elementary school girls (79, 95, 96). In a classroom of 30 students, then, an average of 1–2 children would qualify as having clear HA features. This rate of HA does not appear to be prominently influenced by socioeconomic factors, although there is a tendency for more HA to occur in lower socioeconomic class families (35, 96–98; rr).

In a child guidance clinic, 30–40% of the children who are evaluated have HA (98–102). This is because the major reasons for mental health clinic referral of children are behavior and learning problems (103). Thus, the most common child psychiatric disability is HA. As with child guidance clinics, pediatric clinics also see many children with HA (104). In fact, approximately 10% of their regular client caseloads are also children with HA.

OUTCOME

Children with hyperactivity generally manifest their symptoms throughout their elementary school years. From ages 13–15, their hyperactivity begins to lessen (ss). In the mid-junior high years, hyperactive students are better able to remain in their seat during class periods (*105*). However, their fidgetiness still makes them identifiable in the junior high classroom (*106*). Inattentiveness also declines in the junior high school period; however, unlike hyperactivity, it persists as a notable problem throughout the teens (*14, 24*). The children's perceptual-cognitive impairments also remain throughout the teens (*105*), although in the junior high school years many HA children become mature enough to cope with simple abstract material, such as phonics, and/or they learn to successfully compensate for their cognitive limitations. Nonetheless, late teenagers with a history of learning handicaps can still be picked out of junior or senior high classrooms (*107*). Relative to their age-mates, those with reading delays are still poor spellers. Likewise, those with earlier problems in auditory discrimination, figure-ground perception, and visual-motor coordination still show signs of their defect (*24, 108, 109*).

The school misconduct pattern which these children regularly show fades in the teens (*24*) in approximately half of the cases (*105*). It is also of note that whereas approximately one-third to one-half of elementary students with serious misconduct problems have HA, only about 20% of junior high school students with multiple suspensions for misconduct have a hyperactive pattern or history (*110*).

Hyperactive children have a great risk of school grade failure and suspensions (*tt*). Their rate of academic nonpromotion is 2–3 times that of neighbor children their age (*105, 111*). They tend to drop out of school more often and they have juvenile court records far more often than do nonhyperactives (*26, 105, 112; uu*). In fact, it has been estimated conservatively that 1 in 6 boys seen in juvenile court has an identifiable hyperactive behavior pattern (*113; vv*).

Hyperactive children as a group retain additionally (at least until their late teens) their greater degree of emotional deviance. Minde et al. (*13*) reported that 21% of hyperactives who were followed up in their teens were strikingly maladjusted as judged by specific social, sexual, and behavioral criteria. Likewise, Laufer (*112*) reported that 35% of 66 hyperactive children needed psychiatric therapy in their teens. However, the risk of psychosis among hyperactives has been less clear. Menkes et al. (*108*) reported that 22% of 18 psychiatrically ill hyperactive children became psychotic during the follow-up period, and Laufer (*112*) reported that 6% of 66 hyperactive outpatients needed psychiatric hospitalization in their teens or early 20's. On the other hand, Weiss et al. (*14*) and Shelley and Riester (*109*) reported, respectively, that none of 64 and none of 16 HA children developed a psychosis over the 5–10-year period between the time of diagnosis and follow-up (*ww*).

The long term behavioral outlook for these children in influenced, of course, by factors other than the hyperactivity. A major one is the family support factor. Hyperactives from advantaged, cohesive, supportive families usually do fairly well behaviorally in their late teens and in young adulthood (*13*). Children from disadvantaged, disorganized homes who are hyperactive have just one more strike against them. The family variable appears to be one of the most significant in the outcome of hyperactive children (*xx*). Drug treatment, by contrast, appears to be at most a minor long term outcome variable (*13, 105, 114*). Variables that have an adverse influence on outcome are a low I.Q., grade repeats, poor reading skill, and poor emotional adjustment (*13*).

The high school and post high school educational outcome of HA children has not been the subject of much investigation to date. In two studies, the rate of high school graduation was good (*109, 112; yy*). If the rate of educational progress of children with HA is similar to that of those with learning disabilities, one could generally assume that their rate of learning improvement increases during and following the junior high school years. For the most part, learning-disabled children who possess an average I.Q. become adequate readers and graduate from high school (*115*), even though they go through in a low track class and are commonly overage in the process.

NOTES

a. Hyperkinetic reaction of childhood is defined in *The Diagnostic and Statistical Manual of Mental Disorders (DSM-II)* (*1*) as a disorder "characterized by overactivity, restlessness, distractibility, and short attention span, especially in young children; the behavior usually diminishes in adolescence" (*1*). The developmental nature of impulsivity associated with short interest span has been supported strongly by recent data collected by Kagan (*116*). He reported that 60% of infants who were impulsive at 13—27 months of age remained so at age 10, whereas almost none of the clearly nonimpulsive infants became impulsive.

b. MBD was defined by a Public Health Service Committee headed by Clements (*2*):

> This term as a diagnostic and descriptive category refers to children of near average, average or above average intellectual capacity with certain learning and/or behavioral disabilities ranging from mild to severe, which are associated with deviations of function of the central nervous system. These deviations may manifest themselves by various combinations of impairment in perception, conceptualization, language, memory and control of

attention, impulse or motor function. These aberrations may arise from genetic variations, bio-chemical irregularities, perinatal brain insults, or other illnesses or injuries sustained during the years critical for the development and maturation of the central nervous system.

c. Some MBD children are even said to be hypoactive (*48, 117*). At present, however, the hypoactivity described in some MBD children is a relative term having little research verification (*118*).

d. The concept of a maturational lag as a basis for HA has most recently been supported by the EEG investigations of Buchsbaum and Wender (*3*), Satterfield et al.(*4*), and Shetty (*119*). Buchsbaum and Wender (*3*), particularly, stress that EEG patterns of MBD children show patterns characteristic of chronologically younger children.

e. The terms 'restlessness' and 'hyperactivity' overlap somewhat in this book; generally, hyperactivity is used to refer to a developmental pattern characterized by undue restlessness, particularly when the sedentary position is expected. Pope (*6*) separates the terms, defining hyperactivity as excessive motor activity, and restlessness as the proportion of time spent in motion.

f. The term 'syndrome' has been defined as "a group of symptoms and signs which when considered together characterize a disease or lesion" (*120*). Such a definition allows Wender (*121*) and Stewart et al. (*22*) to consider the HA picture a syndrome, and Werry (*8*) and Schulman et al. (*5*) to consider it a behavior pattern.

g. Even though the HA pattern does not constitute a discrete syndrome, hyperactivity is still a most useful entity for clinical purposes. Children referred to as *developmentally hyperactive* are, by definition, restless from early childhood. The vast majority of such children retain the hyperactive behavioral pattern throughout their elementary school years (*122, 95*) and teachers can reliably identify the features of the disorder (*123*).

Diagnostic categorizing in child mental health varies from the specific (e.g., elective mutism) to the relatively nonspecific (e.g., adjustment reaction). It also varies from being therapeutically valuable (e.g., school phobia) to being of little benefit (e.g., unsocialized aggressive reaction). Developmental hyperactivity is more specific than such child psychopathological entities as adolescent turmoil, group delinquent reaction, depression, and overanxious reaction, but it is less precise than such categories as educable mental retardation and early infantile autism. Likewise, the diagnostic classification of HA assists therapy planning more than using groupings as neurotic, sexually deviant, withdrawing reaction, and obese, but it is less useful than such diagnostic labels as nocturnal enuresis and Tourette's syndrome.

Thus, HA is not a myth. It is a rather specific and moderately useful diagnostic entity in an often subjective field.

h. Distractibility is often viewed as a feature of the hyperactive behavior pattern (*124*). However, in the laboratory, responses to distracting stimuli do not distinguish hyperactive children from nonhyperactive control subjects (*5, 88, 125–128*) and the response of hyperactive children to distraction is not influenced by stimulants (*129*). In the classroom, decreasing distraction does not appear to benefit the HA child academically (*130*). Some data, in fact, suggest that HA children become more attentive when exposed to multiple and varied sensory stimuli (*131*). Because of these largely negative research findings, distraction cannot be recognized at this time as a distinct feature of HA.

i. The association between learning disability (and/or a delay) and hyperactive behavior is striking statistically, and important to all researchers in the field. The relationship is particularly borne out by follow-up studies (*24, 101, 112*). Laufer (*112*), in a follow-up of 20 HA children, found that the "only characteristic common to all was poor school performance despite adequate intellect." Ambrosino and Del Fonte (*132*), in their treatment report of 30 HA children, likewise state: "Although none of the children had been referred for their learning difficulties, almost all of them required remediation." Conners (*69*) perhaps overstated the relationship when he wrote: "The one cardinal criterion for the recognition of MBD is the failure to learn despite adequate general intelligence." Wender (*133*) stressed the relationship clearly when he wrote: "In the presence of normal intelligence, reasonably normal family environment and grossly adequate teaching, the single most important cause of school underachievement is MBD." Likewise, the report on MBD by the Health, Education and Welfare Committee on Medical and Health-Related Services (*134*) reads as follows: "It is child's failure to meet an age dependent level of expectancy in learning and behavior which eventually singles him out."

Learning delays common to HA children cannot primarily be attributed to small differences in average I.Q. between them and non-HA children. Their learning difficulties go beyond this (*135, 136*).

j. A number of authors speculate that the academic difficulty most HA children experience is due to their inattentiveness (*124, 137*). Although inattentiveness is usually associated with an academic handicap, the evidence increasingly suggests that the cognitive difficulties experienced by many HA children account for the greater degree of their scholastic deficiencies (*8, 13, 15, 125, 126, 138, 139*). Even when learning-impaired children receive medication, which in large measure corrects their attentional deficit, they still show a learning lag (*140*). Furthermore, when HA children receive stimulant medication for years, the academic lag persists (*13, 24, 114*).

k. Learning-disabled children as a group have been said to "manifest an educationally significant discrepancy between estimated academic potential and actual level of academic functioning" because of dysfunctioning in the learning process (*141, 142*).

l. Because the correlation between attained and expected achievement for one's mental age is only 0.4–0.6 (*19*, *24*), I.Q. corrections which assume that a perfect (1.0) relationship exists between them are mathematically incorrect. Thus, formulas have been devised to consider mental and chronological age in a more accurate relationship to achievement. The Mykelbust and Boshes (*17*) formula arrives at age-expected achievement by combining mental, grade, and chronological age, essentially, then giving one-third weight to mental age. Their formula is: expectancy age = chronological age + grade age + mental age ÷ 3. Akin to this is Harris's (*143*) formula: reading expectancy age = 2 X chronical age + mental age ÷ 3. A more precise but far more complicated formula was devised by Yule (*144*). He predicts expected reading comprehension by the following equation: 23.44 + (1.15 X short WISC Total Scale Score) + (0.79 X chronological age in months).

m. One problem in using mental age as a correction factor in the estimation of expected reading achievement is that I.Q. does not appear to be fully independent of reading disability. As the reading impaired child gets older, his verbal WISC I.Q. tends to drop (*24*), possibly in part because of the reading deficit (*145*).

n. In suburbia, the percentage of children this far below the average reading achievement is only 3–6% (*19*). When comparing socioeconomic areas, one has also to consider large area differences in I.Q. In upper middle class areas, I.Q.'s average 115. In poor areas, they average 90–95. These group differences in I.Q. are influenced by many factors, one of which appears to be genetic (*146*).

The discrepancy in the average reading achievement scores of youth from different geographic areas suggests influences of a biological nature. Rutter and his associates (*147*) reported that reading delays in association with perceptual-cognitive deficits were twice as prevalent for inner city youth than for their peers residing in outlying areas. Studies by Amante (*148*) also support this position.

o. Receptive or intake skills include understanding spoken words, noises, facial expression, and other visual and auditory cues. Integrative or associational skills include sorting, selecting, coding, retaining, and retrieving. Expressive or output skills include speaking, writing, spelling, calculating, gestures, and facial expression (*149*).

p. Other perceptual-cognitive skills include: auditory decoding, the ability to understand spoken words or sounds; auditory sequencing, the ability to recall in correct sequence and detail prior auditory information; visual figure ground discrimination, the ability to identify meaningful figures within a broader visual input; visual-motor memory, the ability to reproduce, motorically, prior visual experiences (*142*); vocal encoding, the ability to use coherent sentence structure (in speech); and, intersensory integration, the ability to utilize more than one modality in learning.

q. Satterfield et al. (*23*) report that nearly 90% of hyperactive children have notable conduct problems. Stewart et al. (*22*) report that only 60% of hyperactive children seriously misbehave. We feel that the 90% figure is more representative of child guidance clinic caseloads.

r. Since the association between behavior and HA is as striking as that between learning disability (or delay) and HA, one might wonder why misconduct is given a lower diagnostic priority (Table 1). This is quite a legitimate issue. The reason is that misconduct is an even more diffuse, more variable entity than learning delay. This is supported by follow-up studies which reveal that the behavioral adjustment of HA children is less predictable than their learning outcome (24, 150).

s. Of course, too, learning-impaired children are generally viewed as immature (17, 138).

t. Like misconduct, impulsivity is also correlated to low socioeconomic status (151) and environmental disadvantage (152).

u. Hyperactives as a group are generally socially involved. In fact, they seek out the company of others (12). Although unpopularity could lead some to social isolation, this is not the case for hyperactives.

v. The coexistence of behavior difficulty and hyperactivity appears as etiologically intertwined as the relationship between emotional deviance and hyperactivity. Hyperactive children frequently behave in an unacceptable manner because by temperament they find it difficult to sit still, they are usually impulsive and easily frustrated, and they often are immature in their responses. Environmental difficulties can easily exaggerate this behavior pattern. In an educational environment, the children's commonly occurring learning and coordination difficulties readily lead to frustration, depression, and irritability. At home, their restless-intrusive behavior often leads their parents to respond punitively, a reaction which customarily intensifies misconduct. In time, nature and nurture interlock to such an extent that a disentanglement of factors becomes quite difficult.

w. Most researchers in the field operationally base their definition of hyperactivity on the DSM-II criteria (1). For studies on hyperactivity, they select nonretarded, nonpsychotic children who exhibit hyperactivity and inattentiveness (or distractibility). The group headed by Stewart also require that the child have 5 or more of 28 teacher-identified associated characteristics (79). Conners et al. (54) require the basic criteria plus a learning disability, a behavior problem, and at least one neurological, "perceptual," academic, or developmental delay or disability. Satterfield et al. (70) require teacher and parent identification of the basic two criteria plus both impulsivity and excitability.

x. The time of this increased tendency to bleeding in pregnancy is not clear. Pasamanick et al. (45, 153) stress the last trimester, whereas Rapoport et al. (46) stress the first trimester.

y. The Apgar score is an index of distress in the newborn. It includes a measure of heart rate, respiratory effort, skin color, muscle tone, and response to physical stress. It is recorded 1 and 5 minutes after birth (56).

z. Learning difficulty, particularly reading disability, also frequently has a clear genetic component. There is, however, a strong tendency for reading disability to pass genetically from the father (*154*), whereas the inheritance of hyperactivity appears to emanate from either parent (*155*).

aa. The combination of factors (pre- and perinatal) which increase the risk of hyperactivity is also known to increase the risk of behavior and learning difficulties (*156–158*). This fits with Pasamanick's concept of a continuum of reproductive casualty (*159*), which is, the more intense or widespread the biological insult to the developing fetus or newborn, the more serious and diffuse the consequences.

bb. Their restless, meddlesome, tinkering behavior probably explains their accident-proneness and their high rate of accidental poisonings (*160*). It also explains why so many parents of HA children report they have trouble retaining their baby sitters.

cc. A sizeable minority of hyperactive children are first viewed as having hyperactive difficulties when they enter school at age 5 or 6 (*161*). This is either because their restlessness was not noted or reported as a home problem by the parents, or because the restlessness only became noticeable in the classroom atmosphere.

dd. In the study by Zrull et al. (*162*), teacher ratings of HA children's behavior were highly correlated to parent ratings, but only poorly correlated to psychiatrist ratings. The authors therefore concluded for HA behavior that: 1) only parent-school reports have a significant agreement and 2) clinical observations are not useful. Sleator and von Neumann (*163*) found likewise that office evaluations were not diagnostically useful for this disorder. Although individual interviews are usually not useful and playroom observations are only slightly better (*163, 164*), naturalistic home observations have been reported to correlate fairly well with teaching ratings (*165*). Another evidence for the superiority of teacher ratings is their high correlation to objective recordings of hyperactivity (*66, 167*).

ee. Bender-Gestalt deviations in children with perceptual-cognitive impairments include rotated drawings, crude reproductions of circles and dots, gross distortions of gestalten, perseverations, difficulty with acute angles, and poor overall planning of the figures on the page (*69*).

ff. Norms of simple visual-motor skills are available. Most children can draw a circle at age 3, a cross at age 3–4, a square at age 5, a triangle at 6, a diamond at age 7, and a hexagon at age 8 (*168*). The Goodenough Draw-A-Person Test (*169*) is of some value also, in this respect, although poor skill on the drawing may reflect one or more of the following: emotional immaturity, low intellectual ability, and a perceptual-cognitive disability. Generally, children of 3–4 draw a face with arms and legs sticking out from it. At 4–5, they draw a stick figure, and at 5–6, they draw a crude, nonstick figure of a person with appropriately placed features and limbs.

gg. Studies have shown group differences between hyperactives and control subjects in specific EEG dimensions. This has been reported with respect to evoked potentials (*3, 4*) and alpha rhythms (*119*). Shetty (*170*) furthermore found that 11 of 36 hyperactive children had an EEG "driving response" to photic stimulation and that all such abnormalities were eliminated with the intravenous injection of amphetamine. However, this finding was not replicated by Milstein and Small (*171*). Another EEG study of interest was that of Laufer and Denhoff (*124*). They administered Metrazol to HA children and to controls and simultaneously flashed a stroboscope at a fixed frequency as they recorded EEG's. They found that HA children had a lower photo-Metrazol threshold on the EEG than did non-HA children of the same age. They further reported that amphetamines raised the EEG threshold for hyperactives to within the normal range.

hh. The biological and genetic correlates for hyperactive behavior are striking and suggest that the major etiologies of the disorder are organic. With one-third seriously learning impaired, one-tenth having a seizure history, one-third having a positive genetic history, one-half showing abnormal EEG's, and one-third to one-half showing signs of neurological delays, the conclusion is hard to resist. Further evidence for an organic etiology comes from the fact that some physical conditions can create the problem. Four known physical causes of hyperactivity are asphyxia in infancy (*172*), encephalitis (*173*), lead poisoning (*174*), and head injury (*175*).

The possibility that psychological factors account for the hyperactive pattern is reviewed by Wender (*121*), who concludes that although the evidence is weak, social deprivation could account for the pattern. However, a careful analysis of the characteristics of the parent-separated child as described by Bowlby et al. (*176*), Rutter's latest review (*177*), and a recent study on the effects of institutional rearing (*65*) give the deprivation theory no support. Harlow and Harlow's excellent studies (*178*) using monkeys as an animal model to measure the effects of early deprivation on social learning would also argue against a maternal deprivation etiology of developmental HA.

Even though psychological factors do not appear to cause the disorder, they can prominently influence hyperactive characteristics. One group of investigators reported that hyperactive children who had punitive or emotionally ill parents and/or experienced poor parent-child relationships had, on follow-up, more behavioral and adjustment problems than did other initially comparable hyperactive children (*13*).

Two conditions which occasionally overlap HA, familial mental retardation and severe reading backwardness, although constitutional in etiology can be likewise strongly influenced by the environment. An intellectually supportive adoptive or foster home can impressively raise the I.Q. of a retarded child (*179*). Also, prominent reading backwardness, although not caused by neurotic conflicts, can be profoundly exaggerated by poor motivation and negativism (*180*).

ii. Peters et al. (*181*) have devised an abbreviated pediatric neurological examination for MBD children. It consists of 12 items, 10 of which significantly differentiate HA from non-HA children. The items are head rotation passive; imitate finger movement; hop on one foot; skip; finger-thumb; alternating movements of the hands; index finger-thumb; associated movements for the above items; right-left confusion; eye tracking; speech dysfluencies; and writing to dictation.

Another neurological battery that has successfully distinguished groups of HA children from controls is the Lincoln Oseretsky Test (*26*). The administration of the entire test is clinically impractical because it takes too long; however, a reliable short form of the test has been devised (*27*). The short form consists of 12 items: 1) walking backwards about 6 paces; 2) crouching on tip-toe; 3) standing on one foot; 4) touching nose with index finger, eyes closed; 5) touching the fingertips with the thumb of each hand; 6) standing heel to toe, eyes closed; 7) closing and opening the hands alternately, eyes closed; 8) catching a squash ball with one hand; 9) tapping (making dots on paper); 10) sorting match sticks from one box to another; 11) drawing vertical lines between sets of parallel horizontal lines; 12) placing 20 coins in a box.

jj. Rapoport et al. (*46*) estimate that hyperactive children with an abnormal number of these physical anomalies comprise as many as one-third of seriously hyperactive children. Furthermore, they report that such children (compared with others) have a high plasma level of dopamine beta-hydroxylase, a greater family history of hyperactivity, and a history of more complications of pregnancy.

kk. A number of investigators divide hyperactives into two categories based on the presence or absence of organic (EEG, neurological, psychometric, perinatal, and developmental) findings (*182–185*). The group with those findings is labeled the true or organic HA group and the other is called the situational, emotional, or reactive group of hyperactives. Those who categorize in this way note that the groups tend to respond differently to stimulant medication (*182, 184, 185*). However, the fact that many HA children with no 'organic' features respond less dramatically to stimulants does not constitute evidence that their disorder is emotionally based. (Likewise, the absence of organic findings does not make schizophrenia a functional or emotionally based illness.)

ll. Statistically, there is a strong inverse relationship between I.Q. and restlessness. Rutter et al. (*27*) found that fidgety behavior ranges from a 35% rate of prevalence in those with I.Q.'s under 80 to a 9% rate in those with I.Q.'s of 120 or more. Similarly, Shaffer et al. (*186*) reported a significant inverse relationship between activity and I.Q., and Maccoby et al. (*7*), reported that the ability to inhibit activity correlated significantly with I.Q.

mm. The total I.Q. score is usually not of much value in the appraisal of an individual child's specific learning disability because usually the total I.Q. score is within the average range (*115*). Nonetheless, the individual subtests of the WISC I.Q. test can be useful to pinpoint problem areas in learning.

nn. Medical laboratory investigations at this point have little applicability to the diagnosis of hyperactivity. Coleman (*187*) reported that serotonin levels are abnormally low in hyperactive retardates, but Campbell et al. (*188*) found that whereas low I.Q. indeed was related to low serotonin levels, hyperactivity as such was not. Likewise, Rapoport et al. (*189*) reported that there were do differences between hyperactives and control subjects with respect to platelet serotonin. Rapoport et al. (*46*) also reported that although a subgroup of hyperactive boys with physical anomalies had higher plasma levels of dopamine beta-hydroxylase, than the children without such anomalies, this was not related to behavioral ratings.

There is no doubt that lead poisoning can cause organic brain dysfunction and hyperactivity. Furthermore, there is some evidence that children who do not have symptoms of lead poisoning but have abnormal blood levels of lead (over 50 micrograms %) have an increased risk for HA (*190*). However, the evidence that children with lead levels within the normal range are at risk for hyperactivity is weak. In the only study on this issue, the differences in lead levels between the HA and non-HA children averaged only 4 micrograms % (26.2 vs. 22.2 micrograms %) (*191*).

Eisenberg (*192*) and Walker (*193*) suggest that hypoglycemia (low blood sugar) can cause hyperactivity. Unfortunately, blood sugars over time have not been systematically evaluated for hyperactive children and control subjects. Epstein et al. (*185*) reported that dextroamphetamine is excreted to a greater degree and more rapidly in organic than in nonorganic hyperactives. This measurement is too complicated to be obtained clinically, and, unfortunately, no attempt has been made to replicate this finding. Webb and Oski (*194*) found iron deficiency more characteristic of behavior-disordered adolescents than control subjects and suggested that the finding relates to hyperactivity.

As would be expected, some have reported that megavitamins help the disorder (*195*) and that food additives cause it (*196*). Also, as would be expected, anecdotal case summaries document these reports. In the only controlled study on the effect of food additives on HA (*197*), the teacher-rated results of this treatment were essentially negative.

Physiological laboratory measures have also been employed to identify hyperactives. Satterfield et al. (*23, 198*) reported contradictory findings on skin conductance levels of MBD children. Yoss and Moyers (*199*) found that 20–25% of hyperkinetic children showed narcoleptic-like electronic pupillogram patterns, and some data suggest that evoked potentials discriminate HA from non-HA children (*3, 4*).

Because of evidence that some HA has a genetic basis, chromosome studies have been done on HA children. So far, the results of these analyses have been negative (*200*).

oo. Nutritional deficiencies have not been linked directly to hyperactivity in studies, but rather primarily to intelligence and learning (*201*).

pp. The neurochemistry and the neurophysiology of the hyperkinetic disorder are at present interesting speculations with minor supporting evidence. Many investigators suggest that catecholamine (CA) levels are low (*202*) or that re-uptake of CA is low in hyperactive children and that stimulants by increasing CA uptake normalize the system (*203*). A second popular theory cluster is that hyperactive children have certain underaroused centers in the hypothalmus or the midbrain (*70, 204*) which, when activated by stimulants, become normalized (*205*), inhibiting HA "dyscontrol" (*206*). The two theories mesh nicely.

qq. The approximate 3–4:1 male-female ratio is also characteristic of a number of other disorders of childhood, such as reading disability, behavior deviance, and delayed speech development. These developmental differences between the sexes are not the result of social factors, but rather reflect in these respects (at least) the biological superiority of women (*207*).

rr. The features of the hyperactive behavior pattern are more common for children in lower class circumstances and from disrupted homes (*93*). However, the prevalence of the developmental disorder does not vary to that degree.

ss. A few hyperactive children settle down in their late childhood (age 8–10). However, this is uncommon.

tt. School grade retention (or nonpromotion) is much more common than is acknowledged. In elementary schools, the rates have averaged 2–5% per year during the last 10 years (*208*). Since boys are not promoted more often than girls by a 2:1 ratio, this means that the male rate is 3–7% annually. With the annual rate averaging 5% for boys, their cumulative risk for one nonpromotion (in grade) during the elementary school years comes to at least 30%.

Nonpromoted boys commonly tend to be poor, rowdy, restless, immature, and reading delayed (*209*). Thus, the risk of nonpromotion for hyperactives is high. In fact, most are retained during their elementary school years. Although only 1 of 12 boys is hyperactive, approximately 1 in 4 or 5 elementary school nonpromotions involves a hyperactive child.

uu. The risk of a hyperactive child maintaining his behavior problem is not small. In follow-up studies, most hyperactive children in their teens are still judged by their parents to be behavior disordered (*24, 105*).

vv. Some evidence to date suggests that the persistence of misconduct into the teens by hyperactives is related more to family variables than to the level or degree of childhood hyperactivity (*13*). A persistence of misbehavior by a hyperactive child into the teens merits an individual appraisal to evaluate the possible causative factors involved. Prominent possibilities include: a continued high degree of restlessness; an antagonistic defeatist character pattern;

and on-going parental reinforcement of a misconduct pattern. All could be involved simultaneously.

ww. Although the findings presented on psychosis are inconclusive, there is probably a greater risk of this disorder for hyperactives. Robins (*210*), in her 30-year follow-up of behavior disordered children referred for diagnosis and treatment, found that the incidence of later psychosis was 11%. The increased risk of psychosis for misbehaving children presumably also applied to the hyperactives, who comprised approximately one-third to two-fifths of that population.

xx. The genetic factor appears to be interwoven with the psychosocial (family) factor in the etiology and persistence of hyperactivity *and* misconduct. Mendelson et al. (*105*) reported that hyperactive children whose fathers were hyperactive and had learning and/or behavior problems in their childhood had more children who had the same problems.

yy. Only two authors thus far have reported on the rate of high school graduation by HA children. Laufer (*112*), in a 10-year follow-up of cases from his private practice, noted that 13 of 39 formerly HA children were then in college. In Shelley and Riester's follow-up (*109*), all of the 16 young adults in military service who were hyperactive as children were listed as high school graduates. From this and other information, it can be assumed that social class influences the rate of high school graduation (*211, 212*) far more than does a history of hyperactivity.

LITERATURE CITED

1. Diagnostic and Statistical Manual of Mental Disorders, p. 50, 2nd Ed. Washington, D.C.: American Psychiatric Association, 1968.
2. Clements, S. Minimal Brain Dysfunction in Children, NINDB Monograph No. 3, Washington, D.C.: United States Public Health Service, 1966.
3. Buchsbaum, M., and Wender, P. Average evolved responses in normal and minimally brain dysfunctioned children treated with amphetamine. Arch. Gen. Psychiat. 29: 764−770, 1973.
4. Satterfield, J., Lesser, L., Saul, R., and Cantwell, D. EEG aspects of the diagnosis and treatment of minimal brain dysfunction. Ann. N.Y. Acad. Sci. 205: 274−282, 1973.
5. Schulman, J., Kaspar, J., and Throne, F. Brain Damage and Behavior: A Clinical-Experimental Study. Springfield, Ill.: Charles C Thomas, Publisher, 1965.
6. Pope, L. Major activity in brain-injured children. Amer. J. Orthopsychiat. 40: 783−794, 1970.
7. Maccoby, E., Dowley, E., Hagen, J., and Degerman, R. Activity level and intellectual functioning in normal preschool children. Child Develop. 36: 761−770, 1965.
8. Werry, J. Studies on the hyperactive child. IV. Empirical analysis of the minimal brain dysfunction syndrome. Arch. Gen. Psychiat. 19: 9−16, 1968.

9. Routh, D., and Roberts, R. Minimal brain dysfunction in children: Failure to find evidence of a behavioral syndrome. Psychol. Rep. 31: 307–314, 1972.

10. Waldrop, M., and Halverson, C. Minor physical anomalies and hyperactive behavior in young children, in J. Hellmuth (Ed.), Exceptional Infant, Vol. II: Studies in Abnormalities, pp. 343–380. New York: Brunner/Mazel, 1971.

11. Prechtl, H., and Stemmer, C. The choreiform syndrome in children. Develop. Med. Child Neurol. 4: 119–127, 1962.

12. Childers, A. Hyper-activity in children having behavior disorders. Am. J. Orthopsychiat. 5: 227–243, 1935.

13. Minde, K., Weiss, G., and Mendelson, N. A 5-year follow-up study on 91 hyperactive school children. J. Am. Acad. Child Psychiat. 11: 595–610, 1972.

14. Weiss, G., Minde, K., Werry, J., Douglas, V., and Nemeth, E. Studies on the hyperactive child. VIII. Five-year follow-up. Arch. Gen. Psychiat. 24: 409–414, 1971.

15. Kappelman, M. Basis of learning disorders: Management implications. Child Psychiat. Hum. Develop. 5: 166–173, 1975.

16. Shrager, J., and Lindy, J. Hyperkinetic children: Early indicators of potential school failure. Comm. Ment. Health J. 6: 447–454, 1970.

17. Myklebust, H., and Boshes, B. Minimal Brain Damage in Children. United States Department of Health, Education and Welfare, Washington, D.C.: United States Government Printing Office, 1969.

18. Rutter, M., Tizard, J., and Whitmore, K. Education, Health and Behavior. New York: Wiley, 1970.

19. Eisenberg, L. Reading retardation: Psychiatric and sociologic aspects. Pediatrics 37: 352–365, 1966.

20. Coleman, J. Perceptual retardation in reading disability cases. J. Ed. Psychol. 44: 497–503, 1953.

21. Kass, C. Psycholinguistic disabilities of children with reading problems. Except. Child. 32: 533–539, 1966.

22. Stewart, M., Pitts, F., Craig, A., and Dieruf, W. The hyperactive child syndrome. Am. J. Orthopsychiat. 36: 861–867, 1966.

23. Satterfield, J., Cantwell, D., Lesser, L., and Podosin, R. Physiological Studies of the Hyperkinetic Child. Am. J. Psychiat. 128: 1418–1424, 1972.

24. Dykman, R., Peters, J., and Ackerman, P. Experimental approaches to the study of minimal brain dysfunction: A follow-up study. Ann. N.Y. Acad. Sci. 205: 93–108, 1973.

25. Conners, C., Eisenberg, C., and Sharp, I. Effects of methylphenidate (Ritalin) on paired-associate learning and Porteus maze performance in emotionally disturbed children. J. Consult. Psychol. 28: 14–22, 1964.

26. Weiss, G., and Minde, K. Follow-up studies of children who present with symptoms of hyperactivity, in C. Conners (Ed.), Clinical Use of Stimulant Drugs in Children, pp. 67–78. Amsterdam: Exerpta Medica, 1974.

27. Rutter, M., Graham, P., and Yule, W. A Neuropsychiatric Study in Childhood. Philadelphia: Lippincott, 1970.
28. Jenkins, R., and Stable, G. Special characteristics of retarded children rated as severely hyperactive. Child Psychiat. Hum. Develop. 2: 26–31, 1971.
29. Rourke, P., and Quinlan, D. Psychological characteristics of problem children at the borderline of mental retardation. J. Consult. Clin. Psychol. 40: 59–68, 1973.
30. Sprague, R., Christensen, D., and Werry, J. Experimental psychology and stimulant drugs, in C. Conners (Ed.), Clinical Use of Stimulant Drugs in Children, pp. 141–164. Amsterdam: Excerpta Medica, 1974.
31. Sarason, I. Test anxiety and intellectual performance. J. Abnorm. Soc. Psychol. 66: 73–75, 1963.
32. Bower, E. Early Identification of Emotionally Handicapped Children in School, 2nd Ed. Springfield, Ill.: Charles C Thomas, 1969.
33. Chalfant, T., and Schefelin, M. Central processing dysfunctions in children: A review of research, p. 98. National Institute of Washington, D.C.: United States Government Printing Office, 1969.
34. McCarthy, J., and Paraskevopoulos, J. Behavior patterns of learning disabled, emotionally disturbed, and average children. Except. Child. 36: 69–74, 1969.
35. White, M., and Charry, J. School Disorder, Intelligence and Social Class. New York: Columbia Teachers College Press, 1966.
36. Hinton, G., and Knight, R. Children with learning problems. Except. Child. 37: 513–519, 1971.
37. Shain, R. Neurological examination of 40 children with learning disorders. Neuropaediatrie 3: 307–317, 1970.
38. Grant, W. The physician's role in learning disabilities. Texas Med. 69: 63–66, 1973.
39. Eaves, L., Kendall, D., and Crichton, J. The early detection of minimal brain dysfunction. J. Learn. Disabil. 5: 454–462, 1972.
40. Hertzig, M., Bortner, M., and Birch, H. Neurologic findings in children educationally designated as "brain-damaged." Am. J. Orthopsychiat. 39: 437–446, 1969.
41. Denckla, M. Language disorders, in J. Downey and N. Low (Eds.), The Child with Disabling Illness, pp. 227–304. Philadelphia: Saunders, 1974.
42. Keele, D., Keele, M., Huizinga, R., Bray, N., Estes, R., and Holland, L. Role of special pediatric evaluation in the evaluation of a child with learning disabilities. J. Learn. Disabil. 8: 40–45, 1975.
43. Kenny, T., and Clemmens, R. Medical and psychological correlates in children with learning disabilities. J. Pediat. 78: 273–277, 1971.
44. York, R., Heron, J., and Wolff, S. Exclusion from school. J. Child Psychol. Psychiat. 13: 259–266, 1972.
45. Pasamanick, B., Rogers, M., and Lilienfeld, A. Pregnancy experience and the development of behavior disorder in children. Am. J. Psychiat. 112: 613–618, 1956.

46. Rapoport, J., Quinn, P., and Lamprecht, F. Minor physical anomalies and plasma dopamine beta-hydroxylase activity in hyperactive boys. Am. J. Psychiat. 131: 386–390, 1974.
47. Conners, C. Controlled trial of methylphenidate in preschool children with minimal brain dysfunction. Int. J. Ment. Health 4: 61–74, 1975.
48. Denhoff, E. The natural life history of children with minimal brain dysfunction. Ann. N.Y. Acad. Sci. 205: 188–205, 1973.
49. Rubin, R., Rosenblatt, C., and Balow, B. Psychological and educational sequelae of prematurity. Pediatrics 52: 352–63, 1973.
50. Caputo, D., and Mandell, W. Consequence of low birth weight. Develop. Psychol. 3: 363–383, 1970.
51. Bernstein, J., Page, J., and Janicki, R. Some characteristics of children with minimal brain dysfunction, in C. Conners (Ed.), Clinical Use of Stimulant Drugs in Children pp. 24–35. Amsterdam: Excerpta Medica, 1974.
52. Hardy, J. Birth weight and subsequent physical and intellectual development. New Eng. J. Med. 289: 973–974, 1973.
53. Chase, H., and Byrnes, M. Trends in "prematurity": United States, 1950–1967. Am. J. Publ. Health 60: 1967–1983, 1970.
54. Conners, C., Taylor, E., Meo, G., Kurtz, M., and Fournier, M. Magnesium pemoline and dextroamphetamine: A controlled study in children with minimal brain dysfunction. Psychopharmocologia 26: 321–336, 1972.
55. Safer, D. A familial factor in minimal brain dysfunction. Behav. Genet. 3: 175–186, 1973.
56. McKay, R. The newborn infant, in W. Nelson, V. Vaughan, and R. McKay (Eds.), Textbook of Pediatrics, 9th Ed, pp. 353–369. Philadelphia: Saunders, 1969.
57. Werry, J., Weiss, G., and Douglas, V. Studies on the hyperactive child. I. Some preliminary findings. Can. Psychiat. Assoc. J. 9: 120–130, 1964.
58. Schain, R., and Reynard, C. Observations on effects of a central stimulant drug (methylphenidate) in children with hyperactive behavior. Pediatrics 55: 709–716, 1975.
59. Ingram, T. A characteristic form of overactive behavior in brain damaged children. J. Ment. Sci. 102: 550–558, 1956.
60. Hutt, S., and Hutt, C. Hyperactivity in a group of epileptic (and some non-epileptic) brain-damaged children. Epilepsia 5: 334–351, 1964.
61. Bradley, C. Behavior disturbances in epileptic children. JAMA 146: 436–441, 1951.
62. Denhoff, E. Cerebral palsy: Medical aspects, in W. Cruickshank (Ed.), Cerebral Palsy: Its Individual and Community Problems, 2nd Ed., p. 5. Syracuse: Syracuse University Press, 1966.
63. Silver, L. Familial patterns in children with neurologically-based learning disabilities. J. Learn. Disabil. 4: 349–358, 1971.
64. Morrison, J., and Stewart, M. A family study of the hyperactive child syndrome. Biol. Psychiat. 3: 189–195, 1971.

65. Quinn, P., and Rapoport, J. Minor physical anomalies and neurologic status in hyperactive boys. Pediatrics 53: 742–777, 1974.

66. Cantwell, D. Genetics of hyperactivity. J. Child Psychol. Psychiat. 16: 181–197, 1975.

67. Tizard, B., and Rees, J. The effect of early institutional rearing on the behavior problem and affectional relationships of four-year-old children. J. Child Psychol. Psychiat. 16: 61–73, 1975.

68. Klatskin, E., McNamara, N., Shaffer, D., and Pincus, J. Minimal organicity in children of normal intelligence: Correspondence between psychological test results and neurologic findings. J. Learn. Disabil. 5: 213–218, 1972.

69. Conners, C. The syndrome of minimal brain dysfunction: Psychological aspects. Pediat. Clin. N. Am. 14: 749–766, 1967.

70. Satterfield, J., Cantwell, D., Saul, R., and Yusin, A. Intelligence, academic achievement and EEG abnormalities in hyperactive children. Am. J. Psychiat. 131: 391–395, 1974.

71. Werry, J., Weiss, G., Douglas, V., and Martin, J. Studies on the Hyperactive Child. III. The effect of chlorpromazine upon behavior and learning ability. J. Am. Acad. Child. Psychiat. 5: 292–312, 1966.

72. Capute, A., Neidermeyer, F., and Richardson, F. The electroencephalogram in children with minimal cerebral dysfunction. Pediatrics 41: 1104–1114, 1968.

73. Werry, J., Minde, K., Guzman, A., Weiss, G., Dogan, K., and Hoy, E. Studies on the hyperactive child. VII. Neurologic status compared with neurotic and normal children. Am. J. Orthopsychiat. 42: 441–451, 1972.

74. Paine, R., Werry, J., and Quay, H. A study of "minimal cerebral dysfunction." Develop. Med. Child Neurol. 10: 505–520, 1968.

75. Ingram, T. Soft signs. Develop. Med. Child Neurol. 15: 527–530, 1973.

76. Garfield, J. Motor impersistence in normal and brain-damaged children. Neurology 14: 623–630, 1964.

77. Barcai, A. Predicting the response of children with learning disabilities and behavior problems to dextroamphetamine sulfate. Pediatrics 47: 73–80, 1971.

78. Wolff, P., and Hurwitz, I. Functional implications of the minimal brain damage syndrome. Sem. Psychiat. 5: 105–115, 1973.

79. Miller, R., Palkes, H., and Stewart, M. Hyperactive children in suburban elementary schools. Child Psychiat. Hum. Develop. 4: 121–127, 1973.

80. Douglas, V. Stop, look and listen: The problem of sustained attention and impulse control in hyperactive and normal children. Can. J. Behav. Sci. 4: 259–282, 1972.

81. Stevens, D., Boydstun, J., Dykman, R., Peters, J., and Sinton, D. Presumed minimal brain dysfunction in children: Relationship to performance on selected behavioral tests. Arch. Gen. Psychiat. 16: 281–285, 1967.

82. Ackerman, P., Peters, J., and Dykman, R. Children with specific learning disabilities: WISC profiles. J. Learn. Disabil. 4: 150–166, 1971.

83. Boder, E. Developmental dyslexia: A diagnostic screening procedure based on three characteristic patterns of reading and spelling, in B. Bateman (Ed.), Learning Disorders, Vol. 4, 328–332. Seattle: Special Child Publications, 1971.

84. Rie, H. Hyperactivity in children. Am. J. Dis. Child. 129: 783–789, 1975.

85. Sprague, R., and Toppe, L. Relationship between activity level and delay of reinforcement in the retarded. J. Exp. Child Psychol. 3: 390–397, 1966.

86. Juliano, D. Conceptual tempo, activity and concept learning in hyperactive and normal children. J. Abnorm. Psychol. 83: 629–634, 1974.

87. Sykes, D., Douglas, V., and Morgenstern, G. Sustained attention in hyperactive children. J. Child Psychol. Psychiat. 14: 213–220, 1973.

88. Sykes, D., Douglas, V., Weiss, G., and Minde, K. Attention in hyperactive children and the effect of methylphenidate (Ritalin). J. Child Psychol. Psychiat. 12: 129–139, 1971.

89. Anderson, R., Halcomb, C., and Doyle, R. The measurement of attentional deficits. Except. Child 39: 534–538, 1973.

90. Lapouse, R., and Monk, M. An epidemiologic study of behavior characteristics in children. Am. J. Publ. Health 48: 1134–1144, 1958.

91. Macfarlane, J., Allen. L., and Honzik, M. A developmental study of the behavior problems of normal children between twenty-one months and fourteen years. Berkeley, Calif.: University of California Press, 1954.

92. Werry, J., and Quay, H. The prevalence of behavior symptoms in younger elementary school children. Am. J. Orthopsychiat. 41: 136–143, 1971.

93. Rutter, M., Yule, W., Berger, M., Yule, B., Morton, J., and Bagley, C. Children of West Indian immigrants. I. Rate of behavioral deviance and of psychiatric disorder. J. Child Psychol. Psychiat. 15: 241–262, 1974.

94. Schultz, E. Prevalence of behavioral symptoms in rural elementary school children. J. Abnorm. Child Psychol. 2: 17–24, 1974.

95. Shepard, M., Oppenheim, M., and Mitchell, S. Childhood Behaviour and Mental Health. New York: Grune and Stratton, 1971.

96. Werner, E., Bierman, J., Simonian, K., Connor, A., Smith, R., and Campbell, M. Reproductive and environmental casualties: A report on the 10-year follow-up of the children of the Kauai pregnancy study. Pediatrics 42: 112–127, 1968.

97. Alley, G., and Solomons, G. Minimal cerebral dysfunction as it relates to social class. J. Learn. Disabil. 4: 246–250, 1971.

98. Knobel, M., Wolman, M., and Mason, E. Hyperkinesis and organicity in children. Arch. Gen. Psychiat. 1: 310–321, 1959.

99. Marine, E., and Cohen, R. The impact of a community mental health center program on the operation of a university child guidance center. J. Am. Acad. Child Psychiat. 14: 49–65, 1975.
100. Glos, J. Minimal brain dysfunction in children (Translation). Psychol. Apatopsychol. Diet. (Czech.) 4: 335–364, 1969.
101. Kahn, D., and Gardner, G. Hyperactivity: Predominant diagnosis in child referrals. Frontiers Psychiat., 5(9): 3, 1975.
102. Hanvik, L., Nelson, S., Hanson, H., Anderson, A., Dressler, W., and Zarling, V. Diagnosis of cerebral dysfunction in child. Am. J. Dis. Child. 101: 364–375, 1961.
103. Safer, D. Factors affecting outcome in a school mental health service. Commun. Ment. Health J. 10: 24–32, 1974.
104. Cantwell, D. Psychiatric illness in a pediatric clinic. Presented at the American Psychiatric Association Meeting, Hawaii, May 1973.
105. Mendelson, W., Johnson, N., and Stewart, M. Hyperactive children as teenagers. J. Nerv. Ment. Dis. 153: 273–9, 1971.
106. Douglas, V. Differences between normal and hyperkinetic children, in C. Connors (Ed.), Clinical Use of Stimulant Drugs in Children, pp. 12–23. Amsterdam: Excerpta Medica, 1974.
107. Silver, A., and Hagin, R. Specific reading disability: Follow-up studies. Am. J. Orthopsychiat. 34: 95–102, 1964.
108. Menkes, M., Rowe, J., and Menkes, J. A twenty-five year follow-up study on the hyperkinetic child with minimal brain dysfunction. Pediatrics 39: 393–399, 1967.
109. Shelley, E., and Riester, A. Syndrome of minimal brain damage in young adults. Dis. Nerv. Syst. 33: 335–338, 1972.
110. Safer, D., Heaton, R., and Allen, R. Characteristics of multisuspended jr. high students, (Unpublished data). 1975.
111. Minde, K., Lewin, D., Weiss, G., Lavigueur, H., Douglas, V., and Sykes, E. The hyperactive child in elementary school: A 5-year, controlled, follow-up. Except. Child. 38: 215–221, 1971.
112. Laufer, M. Long-term management and some follow-up findings on the use of drugs with minimal cerebral syndromes. J. Learn. Disabil. 4: 519–522, 1971.
113. Lewis, D., Sacks, H., Bella, D., Lewis, M., and Heald, E. Introducing a child psychiatric service to a juvenile justice setting. Child Psychiat. Hum. Develop. 4: 98–114, 1973.
114. Weiss, G., Kruger, E., Danielson, U., and Elman, M. Effect of long-term treatment of hyperactive children with methylphenidate. Can. Med. Assoc. J. 112: 159–165, 1975.
115. Safer, D., and Allen, R. Factors associated with improvement in severe reading disability. Psychol. Schools 10: 110–118, 1973.
116. Kagan, J. Emergent themes in human development. Presidential Address to the Annual Meeting of the Eastern Psychological Association, New York, April 4, 1975.
117. Clements, S., and Peters, J. Minimal brain dysfunctions in children: Concepts and categories. World Med. J. 19: 54–55, 1972.
118. Dykman, R., Ackerman, P., Clements, S., and Peters, J. Specific learning disabilities: An attentional deficit syndrome, in H. Mykel-

bust (Ed.), Progress in Learning Disabilities, Vol. II, pp. 56–93. New York: Grune and Stratton, 1971.

119. Shetty, T. Alpha rhythms in the hyperkinetic child. Nature 234: 476, 1971.

120. Blakiston's Gould Medical Dictionary, 3rd Ed., p. 1515. New York: McGraw-Hill Book Company, 1972.

121. Wender, P. Minimal Brain Dysfunction in Children. New York: Wiley, 1971.

122. Huessy, H., Marshall, C., and Gendron, R. Five hundred children followed from grade 2 through grade 5 for the prevalence of behavior disorder. Acta paedopsychiat. 39: 301–309, 1973.

123. Conners, C. Rating scales for use in drug studies with children. Psychopharm. Bull. Spec. Issue (Pharmacotherapy of Children) 24–84, 1973.

124. Laufer, M., and Denhoff, E. Hyperkinetic behavior syndrome in children. J. Pediat. 50: 463–474, 1957.

125. Cohen, N., Weiss, G., and Minde, K. Cognitive styles in adolescents previously diagnosed as hyperactive. J. Child Psychol. Psychiat. 13: 203–209, 1972.

126. Carter, J., and Diaz, A. Effects of visual and auditory background on reading test performance. Except. Child. 38: 43–50, 1971.

127. Worland, J., North-Jones, M., and Stern. J. Performance and activity of hyperactive boys and normal boys as a function of distraction and reward. J. Abnorm. Child Psychol. 1: 363–377, 1973.

128. Cruse, D. The effects of distraction upon performance of brain-injured and familial retarded children, in E. Trapp and P. Himelstein (Eds.), Readings on the Exceptional Child, pp. 490–492. New York: Appleton-Century-Crofts, 1962.

129. Campbell, S., Douglas, V., and Morgenstern. G. Cognitive styles in hyperactive children and the effect of methylphenidate. J. Child Psychol. Psychiat. 12: 55–67, 1971.

130. Shores, R., and Haubrich, P. Effect of cubicles in educating emotionally disturbed children. Except. Child. 36: 21–24, 1969.

131. Gardner, W., Cromwell, R., and Roshee, J. Studies in activity level. II. Effects of distal visual stimulation in organics, familials, hyperactives, and hypoactives. Am. J. Ment. Defic. 63: 1028–1033, 1959.

132. Ambrosino, S., and Del Fonte, T. A psychoeducational study of the hyperkinetic syndrome. Psychosomatics 14: 207–213, 1973.

133. Wender, P. Minimal brain dysfunction in children. Pediat. Clin. N. Am. 20: 187–202, 1973.

134. Miller, C., Clements, S., Hardy, M., Hsia, D., Knott, L., Mark, H., Rabe, E., and Work, H. Minimal Brain Dysfunction–National Project on Learning Disabilities in Children, in N. Haring (Ed.), Minimal Brain Dysfunction in Children: Educational, Medical and Health Related Services, Public Health Service Publication No. 2015, Washington, D.C.: United States Department of Health, Education and Welfare, United States Government Printing Office, 1969.

135. Butter, H., and La Pierre, Y. The effect of methylphenidate on sensory perception and integration in hyperactive children. Int. Pharmacopsychiat. 9: 235–244, 1974.
136. Wikler, A., Dixon, J., and Parker, J. Brain function in problem children and controls: Psychometric, neurological, and electroencephalographic comparisons. Am. J. Psychiat. 127: 634–645, 1970.
137. Werry, J. Developmental hyperactivity. Pediat. Clin. N. Am. 15: 581–599, 1968.
138. Campbell, S. Cognitive styles and behavior problems of clinic boys: A comparison of epileptic, hyperactive, learning disabled, and normal groups. J. Abnorm. Child Psychol. 2: 307–312, 1974.
139. Kaufman, N., and Kaufman, A. Comparison of normal and minimally brain dysfunctioned children on the McCarthy Scales of Children's Abilities. J. Clin. Psychol. 30: 69–72, 1974.
140. Gittelman-Klein, R., and Klein, D. Methylphenidate effects in learning disability in children. Presented at the Annual Meeting of the American Psychiatric Association, Honolulu, Hawaii, May 1973.
141. Haring, N., and Bateman, B. Introduction, in N. Haring (Ed.), Minimal Brain Dysfunction in Children: Educational, Medical and Health Related Services, Public Health Service Publication No. 2015, pp. 1–4. Washington, D.C.: United States Department of Health, Education and Welfare, United States Government Printing Office, 1969.
142. Valett, R. Programming Learning Disabilities. Fearon Publishers, Palo Alto, Calif., 1969.
143. Harris, A. A comparison of formulas for measuring degree of reading disability, in R. Leibert (Ed.), Diagnostic Viewpoints in Reading, pp. 113–120. Newark, Del.: International Reading Association, 1971.
144. Yule, W. Predicting reading ages on Neale's Analysis of Reading Ability. Br. J. Educ. Psychol. 37: 252–255, 1967.
145. Reed, J. Reading achievement as related to differences between WISC verbal and performance IQ's. Child Develop. 38: 836–840, 1967.
146. Jencks, C. Inequality: A reassessment of the effect of family and schooling in America. New York: Basic Books, 1972.
147. Berger, M., Yule, W., and Rutter, M. Attainment and adjustment in two geographic areas. II. The prevalence of specific reading retardation. Brit. J. Psychiat. 126: 510–519, 1975.
148. Amante, D. Visual-motor malfunction, ethnicity, and social class position. J. Spec. Ed. 9: 247–259, 1975.
149. Peters, J., Davis, J., Goolsby, C., Clements, S., and Hicks, T. Screening for MBD, Physicians Handbook. Summit, N.J.: CIBA Medical Horizons, 1973.
150. Laufer, M. Cerebral dysfunction and behavior disorder in adolescents. Am. J. Orthopsychiat. 32: 501–506, 1962.
151. Schwebel, A. Effects of impulsivity on performance of verbal tasks in middle- and lower-class children. Am. J. Orthopsychiat. 36: 13–21, 1966.

152. Mischel, W., and Gilligan, C. Relay of gratification, motivation for the prohibited gratification, and responses to temptation. J. Abnorm. Soc. Psychol. 69: 411–417, 1964.
153. Rogers, M., Lilienfeld, A., and Pasamanick, B. Prenatal and perinatal factors in the development of childhood behavior disorders. Baltimore: Johns Hopkins University Press, 1955.
154. Hallgren, B. Specific dyslexia: A clinical and genetic study. Acta Psychiat. Neurolog. Suppl. 65: 1–287, 1950.
155. Morrison, J., and Stewart, M. Bilateral inheritance as evidence for polygenicity in the hyperactive child syndrome. J. Nerv. Ment. Dis. 158: 226–228, 1974.
156. Drillien, C. The growth and development of the prematurely born infant. Baltimore: Williams & Wilkins, 1964.
157. Galante, M., Flye, M., and Stephens, L. Cumulative minor deficits: A longitudinal study of the relation of physical factors to school achievement. J. Learn. Disabil. 5: 75–80, 1972.
158. Kappelman, M., Rosenstein, A., and Ganter, R. Comparison of disadvantaged children with learning disabilities and their successful peer group. Am. J. Dis. Child. 124: 875–879, 1972.
159. Pasamanick, B., and Knoblock, H. Brain damage and reproductive casualty. Am. J. Orthopsychiat. 30: 298–305, 1960.
160. Stewart, M., Thach, B., and Freidin, M. Accidental poisoning and the hyperactive child syndrome. Dis. Nerv. Syst. 31: 403–407. 1970.
161. Kenny, T., Clemmens, R., Hudson, B., Lentz, G., Cicci, R., and Nair, P. Characteristics of children referred because of hyperactivity. J. Pediat. 79: 618–622, 1971.
162. Zrull, J., Westman, J., Arthur, B., and Rice, D. An evaluation of methodology used in the study of psychoactive drugs for children. J. Am. Acad. Child Psychiat. 5: 284–291, 1966.
163. Sleator, E., and von Neumann, A. Methylphenidate in the treatment of hyperkinetic children. Clin. Pediat. 13: 19–24, 1974.
164. Ellis, M., Witt, P., Reynolds, R., and Sprague, R. Methylphenidate and the activity of hyperactives in the informal setting. Child Develop. 45: 217–220, 1974.
165. Rapoport, J., and Benoit, M. The relation of direct home observations to the clinic evaluation of hyperactive school age boys. J. Child Psychol. Psychiat. 16: 141–147, 1975.
166. Victor, J., Halverson, C., and Buczkowski, H. Objective measures of first and second grade boys free play and teacher ratings on a behavior problem checklist. Psychol. Schools, 439–443, 1973.
167. Halverson, C., and Waldrop, M. The relations of mechanically recorded activity level to varieties of preschool play behavior. Child Develop. 44: 678–681, 1973.
168. Gesell, A., and Amatruda, C. Developmental Diagnosis: Normal and Abnormal Child Development, 3rd Ed., pp. 317–347. New York: Paul B. Hoebner, Inc., 1951.
169. Goodenough, F. Measurement of Intelligence by Drawings. New York: World Book Company, 1926.

170. Shetty, T. Photic response in hyperkinesis of childhood. Science 174: 1356–1357, 1971.
171. Milstein, V., and Small, J. Photic responses in "minimal brain dysfunction." Dis. Nerv. Syst. 35: 355–361, 1974.
172. Rosenfeld, G., and Bradley, C. Childhood behavior sequelae of asphyxia in infancy. Pediatrics 2: 74–84, 1948.
173. Hohman, L. Post-encephalitic behavior disorders in children. Bull. Johns Hopkins Hosp. 33: 372–375, 1922.
174. Thurston, D., Middlekamp, J., and Mason, E. The late effects of lead poisoning. J. Pediat. 47: 413–423, 1955.
175. Blau, A. Mental changes following head trauma in children. Arch. Neurol. Psychiat. 35: 723–769, 1936.
176. Bowlby, J., Ainsworth, M., Boston, M., and Rosenbluth, D. The effects of mother-child separation: A follow-up study. Br. J. Med. Psychol. 29: 211–247, 1956.
177. Rutter, M. Maternal deprivation reassessed. Baltimore: Penguin Books, 1972.
178. Harlow, H., and Harlow, M. The affectional systems, in A. Schrier, H. Harlow, and F. Stollnitz (Eds.), Behavior of Non-Human Primates, Vol. II, pp. 287–334. New York: Academic Press, 1965.
179. Kugel, R., and Parsons, M. Children of deprivation: Changing the course of familial retardation. Washington, D.C.: United States Department of Health, Education and Welfare, Children's Bureau, United States Government Printing Office, 1967.
180. Rutter, M. Emotional disorder and educational under achievement. Arch. Dis. Childhood. 49: 249–256, 1974.
181. Peters, J., Dykman, R., Ackerman, P., and Romine, J. The special neurological examination, in C. Conners (Ed.), Clinical Use of Stimulant Drugs in Children, pp. 53–66. Amsterdam: Excerpta Medica, 1974.
182. Schleifer, M., Weiss, G., Cohen, N., Elman, M., Cvejic, H., and Kruger, E. Hyperactivity in preschoolers and the effect of methylphenidate. Am. J. Orthopsychiat. 45: 38–50, 1975.
183. Chess, S. Diagnosis and treatment of the hyperactive child. N.Y. State J. Med. 60: 2379–2385, 1960.
184. Conrad, W., and Insel, J. Anticipating the response to amphetamine therapy in the treatment of hyperkinetic children. Pediatrics 40: 96–98, 1967.
185. Epstein, L., Lasagna, L., Conners, C., and Rodriquez, A. Correlation of dextroamphetamine excretion and drug response in hyperkinetic children. J. Nerv. Ment. Dis. 146: 136–146, 1968.
186. Shaffer, D., McNamara, N., and Pincus, J. Controlled observations on patterns of activity, attention and impulsivity in brain-damaged and psychiatrically disturbed boys. Psychol. Med. 4: 4–18, 1974.
187. Coleman, M. Serotonin and central nervous system syndromes of childhood: A review. J. Aut. Childhood Schizophren. 3: 27–35, 1973.
188. Campbell, M., Friedman, E., DeVito, E., Greenspan, L., and Collins, P. Blood serotonin in psychotic and brain damaged children. J. Aut. Childhood Schizophren. 4: 33–41, 1974.

189. Rapoport, J., Quinn, P., Scribanu, N., and Murphy, D. Platelet serotonin of hyperactive school age boys. Br. J. Psychiat. 125: 138–140, 1974.
190. Baloh, R., Sturm, R., Green, B., and Gleser, G. Neuropsychological effects of chronic asymptomatic lead absorption. Arch. Neurol. 32: 326–330, 1975.
191. David, O., Clark, J., and Voeller, K. Lead and hyperactivity. Lancet ii: 900–903, 1972.
192. Eisenberg, L. The clinical use of stimulant drugs in children. Pediatrics 49: 709–715, 1972.
193. Walker, S. Behavior problems related to abnormal glucose metabolism. Presented at the Annual Meeting of the Society for Biological Psychiatry, Boston, 1974.
194. Webb, T., and Oski, F. Behavioral status of young adolescents with iron deficiency anemia. J. Spec. Ed. 8: 153–156, 1974.
195. Cott, A. Megavitamins: The orthomolecular approach to behavioral disorders and learning disabilities. Acad. Ther. 7: 245–258, 1972.
196. Feingold, B. Why Your Child is Hyperactive. New York: Random House, 1975.
197. Connors, C., Goyette, C., and Southwick, D. Food additives and hyperkinesis: Preliminary report of a double-blind cross-over experiment (Unpublished manuscript). 1975.
198. Satterfield, J., Atoian, G., Brashears, G., Burleigh, A., and Dawson, M. Electrodermal studies in minimal brain dysfunction children, in C. Conners (Ed.), Clinical Use of Stimulant Drugs in Children, pp. 87–97. Amsterdam: Excerpta Medica, 1974.
199. Yoss, R., and Moyers, N. The pupillogram of the hyperkinetic child and the underachiever. Abstracts from the Seventh Colloquium on the Pupil, The Mayo Clinic, Rochester, Minn., 1971.
200. Warren, R., Karduck, W., Bussaratid, S., Stewart, M., and Sly, W. The hyperactive child syndrome: Normal chromosome findings. Arch. Gen. Psychiat. 24: 161–163, 1971.
201. Birch, H. Malnutrition, learning and intelligence. Am. J. Publ. Health 62: 773–784, 1972.
202. Rapoport, J., Lott, I., Alexander, D., and Abramson, A. Urinary noradrenaline and playroom behaviour in hyperactive boys. Lancet ii: 1141, 1970.
203. Snyder, S., and Meyerhoff, J. How amphetamine acts in minimal brain dysfunction. Ann. N.Y. Acad. Sci. 205: 310–320, 1973.
204. Wender, P. Minimal brain dysfunction: Some recent advances. Pediat. Ann. 2: 42–54, 1973.
205. Shetty, T. Some neurologic, electrophysiologic and biochemical correlates of the hyperkinetic syndrome. Pediat. Ann. 2: 29–40, 1973.
206. Millichap, J., and Johnson, F. Methylphenidate in hyperkinetic behavior: Relation of response to degree of activity and brain damage, in Conners, C. (Ed.), Clinical Use of Stimulant Drugs in Children, pp. 130–140. Amsterdam: Excerpta Medica, 1974.
207. Montagu, A. The Natural Superiority of Women. New York: Macmillan, 1954.

208. Rubin, R., and Balow, B. Learning and behavior disorders: A longitudinal study. Except. Child. 38: 293–299, 1971.
209. Safer, D., Heaton, R., and Allen, R. Socioeconomic factors influencing the rate of non-promotion in elementary schools (Submitted for publication). 1975.
210. Robins, L. Deviant Children Grown Up. Baltimore: Williams & Wilkins, 1966.
211. Cervantes, L. The Drop-Out: Causes and Cures. Ann Arbor: University of Michigan Press, 1965.
212. Schaie, K., and Roberts, J. School Achievement of Children by Demographic and Socioeconomic Factors, Publication No. (HSM) 72-1011. United States Department of Health, Education and Welfare, Publication National Center for Health Statistics, Rockville, Md., November, 1971.

Chapter 3   The Pharmacological Management of Hyperactivity

STIMULANT MEDICATION: THE DRUG TREATMENT OF CHOICE

General Considerations

At the heart of much of the controversy regarding hyperactivity is the increasing reliance upon medication to treat the disorder (1). This has led to some legitimate public concern about the consequences of having hundreds of thousands of school children regularly on medication. The idea of medicating children is often disturbing to parents and to do so on such a large and increasing scale is bound to produce considerable emotion in our society. Add to this the issue of whether or not these children are being medicated to reduce classroom problems for the teacher's convenience and there are the ingredients for enough contention to make a balanced presentation on the subject difficult.

The following does not provide an exhaustive review of available information, but it attempts to provide sufficient factual information to aid in the decision of whether or not to use medication and to aid in the process of choosing and scheduling medication, evaluating its efficacy, and following its continued use.

Stimulant medication is the most commonly used and single most effective treatment for HA behavior. Numerous studies demonstrate the striking and immediate effects of stimulants on hyperactive children. In fact, 1 week of a stimulant drug compared to 1 week of placebo (a

---

Figures 1 and 2 are reprinted from Conners, C. November, 1971. Recent Drug Studies with Children. 4(9): 476–481, Journal of Learning Disabilities. Copyright 1971 by Professional Press, Inc. Reprinted by special permission of Professional Press, Inc.

pharmacologically inert substance) for as few as 8–12 HA children can show a statistically significant improvement for the stimulant treatment (2–5). These and other studies (6, 7) leave no doubt that stimulants behaviorally benefit most hyperactive children, whereas identical sugar pills do not (8–14).

It is, therefore, not surprising that since the mid-1960's, there has been a great upsurge in the use of stimulant medication for hyperactive children (1). This has been generated both by the drug revolution which hit psychiatry in the mid-1950's, and by the continuing series of impressive reports on the benefits of stimulants by researchers from Johns Hopkins, Harvard, McGill, and the University of Illinois. Now, nearly 2% of all elementary school students receive medication for the treatment of hyperactivity, which means that at least 300,000–400,000 children in the United States receive prescribed stimulant drugs (1). Given the estimate that 5% of elementary school children are hyperactive, then approximately one-third of HA children in the 6–12 year age range receive such medication. In this regard, it is of note that children of the well-to-do tend to receive more stimulant medication than others, probably because they receive more and better medical care (1).

At present, two stimulants comprise nearly all the market for the pharmacological treatment of hyperactivity (1). These are Ritalin (methylphenidate), which has been used to treat HA children since 1956, and dextroamphetamine (usually sold as Dexedrine), which has been in use for these children since 1937. Benzedrine (dl-amphetamine) and Deaner (deanol) (15) are now rarely prescribed. Cylert (pemoline) (16, 17) is another stimulant; it just entered the United States market for the treatment of hyperactivity in 1975.

Indications for Treatment

The primary indication for stimulant drug treatment in children is hyperactivity. Although the data are somewhat mixed, it appears that the more hyperactive the child, the better the clinical response (3, 8, 10, 18–20). Likewise, and again the data is mixed, it appears that the more neurologically deviant the HA child (21–23), the more likely he is to benefit from the medication (a). Learning skills in nonhyperactive, learning-impaired children do not show a beneficial change after stimulant drug treatment (24).

GOVERNMENT CONTROLS ON STIMULANTS

In 1970, there was a good deal of newspaper publicity concerning the use of stimulant medication by school children in Omaha. The newspapers erroneously reported that 5–10% of school children in Omaha had been placed on stimulants and the story hit all over the country (25). Consequently, a House Subcommittee opened hearings on the matter and some further inaccurate information came forth (26). At that time (1970), there was a great concern over the misuse of amphetamines or pep pills by adolescents and young adults. Teenagers in droves were taking these "uppers" for kicks and highs. Drug abusers were mainlining methamphetamine (Methedrine), one of the amphetamines known as speed, and, as a result, they became vulnerable to vascular damage (27, 28) and death. Truck drivers were taking amphetamines, frequently Benzedrine, known as "Bennies," to keep awake. Although the drug worked and truckers could then drive through the night, it impaired their judgment (29). Untold numbers of overweight adults were taking amphetamines for appetite control, even though there was little evidence that these drugs alone resulted in any long term benefit in weight reduction (30). Athletes were taking stimulants to decrease their fatigue in tests of endurance. In 1967, 23 million prescriptions were filled for stimulants, mostly for the treatment of obesity and depression (31), and in the late 1960's approximately half of the amphetamines manufactured were hitting the black market (32, 33).

Consequently, in 1970 and 1971, the Food and Drug Administration (FDA) tightened its regulations, advising doctors that stimulants were medically indicated for only three conditions, one of which was for hyperactivity in children. Subsequently, the Bureau of Narcotics and Dangerous Drugs (BNDD) required every physician who prescribed these drugs to obtain a BNDD number (b). Prescriptions for stimulants had to include the doctor's BNDD number and Dexedrine and Ritalin could not be refilled. Also with the new regulations, prescriptions for these drugs could not be phoned in to the pharmacy. In 1974, regulations for amphetamines became tighter and in Maryland, for example, not more than a 1-month supply could be prescribed on a given prescription.

The medical community responded to the problem of stimulant drug use and misuse in their usual manner, with reports. Those in relation to stimulant drug treatment for hyperactivity in children were consistently positive. The American Medical Association Council on Drugs reported that stimulants are quite effective for hyperactive children; in fact, its 1968 report listed them as the drugs of choice (34). The 1970 American Academy of Pediatrics Council on Drugs report was also generally favorable, but more cautious (35). And in 1971, a prestigious professional panel was formed under the auspices of the Department of Health, Education and Welfare (HEW), specifically, the Office of Child Development (36). They were asked to advise the country on the stimulant drug treatment of hyperactive children. Their report was unmistakably favorable to stimulants as a major treatment for hyperactivity in children. The HEW report was circulated widely within professional circles and since its issuance, there has been less misrepresentation and distortion in the media relative to stimulants for hyperactivity (c).

RESPONSES TO STIMULANTS BY HA CHILDREN

The Clinical Response

What is the type and degree of therapeutic response HA children have to stimulant medication? When stimulants are given in an adequate dose to obviously hyperactive children, 35–50% show dramatic benefit, 30–40% show moderate benefit, and 15–20% show no benefit (6, 16, 21, 37). Those who improve show less classroom restlessness, increased attention span, increased academic work output and accuracy, and improved emotional and social behavior patterns. Those who improve, improve in nearly all measurable categories of behavior, at school and at home (9, 38). Adults find that they can better tolerate the child on medication, and can help him more. The child becomes happier, more motivated, more successful, and better accepted. He can now maintain friendships (39) and complete tasks (40). Also, parents feel pleased when neighbors and teachers stop the frequent reporting of their child's misdeeds to them.

As indicated, about 35–50% of hyperactives show a dramatic response to stimulant medication. In these dramatic cases, the school teacher reports that suddenly the child is behaving pretty much as one of the others, that he is a different child who is now able to sit still and do his work (40). The improvement in 30–40% of HA children is similar but less profound. And, as mentioned, 15–20% of HA children placed on stimulants do not appear to benefit from these drugs. Of the group who do *not* benefit from stimulants, a small percentage of the children appear to do even worse on stimulants. They become more erratic and irritable. Children who have loose (verbal) associations in speech (d) (that is, they skip from subject to subject), borderline psychotics, and psychotic children have a strong tendency to this type of adverse clinical response (12, 41, 42) and they comprise possibly one-quarter or more of the group who get worse.

The beneficial responses to stimulants are clearly the result of the drug. Although 30–50% of the children improve on identical tablets, containing only lactose or a similar substance (placebos), the response to the "sugar pill" is nearly always mild and usually temporary (8–12). In other words, the suggestive or psychological effects of giving a stimulant are minor compared with the pharmacological or chemical benefits induced by the drug.

Laboratory and Academic Measures of Response

More specific data indicating the nature of the drug effect have come from laboratory studies. On attention or vigilance tests, such as the Continuous Performance Test, HA children show notable performance improvements after stimulant drug use. Relative to placebo takers, the children taking stimulants show decreased reaction time, decreased seat movement, fewer errors, and fewer omissions (43–45).

Also in laboratory studies, HA children on stimulants frequently show improved ability on the Draw-a-Man Test, the Proteus Maze Test, motor steadiness tests, perceptual discrimination tests, and on a paired associate learning task (Figure 1) (44–48). These reflect improved visual motor skills, less impulsivity, better visual and auditory discrimination, and better short term learning skills. And about half of the studies show that some I.Q. subtests (commonly in performance areas) are significantly elevated

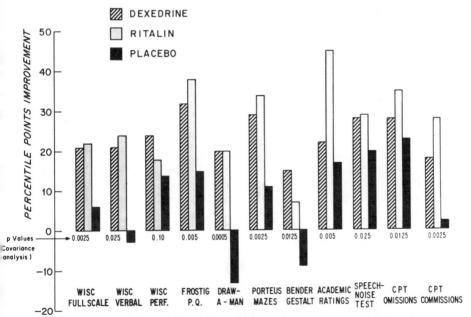

Figure 1. Psychological test changes after a 3-week test period under three treatment conditions. From Conners (38) with permission of the *Journal of Learning Disabilities.*

after stimulants compared with placebo (*49*), largely because of the ability of stimulants to improve attention and decrease impulsivity during the test. Academic achievement, likewise, can mildly improve for MBD children for a short period after stimulant treatment (*46;e*). This again appears to be largely a result of the stimulant-induced improvement in attention while the child is taking the test, rather than in any other improvement in learning ability.

Academic gains due to the *prolonged* use of stimulant drugs (alone) appear to be small, according to two 6-month drug studies (*50, 51*), and nonexistent according to a 5-year outcome study (*52*). Recent reports by Aman and Sprague (*53*) and Conners (*54*) in fact acknowledge that although stimulants benefit attention, they do not improve the retention of new information. Of note here is that any appreciable state-dependent learning does *not* occur when stimulants (*55*) are given in therapeutic ranges to HA children. (In this context, in state-dependent learning, one recalls best when under the influence of the drug if one learned that information initially when on that drug).

Other Data on Response

Parent check list accounts of the behavior of hyperactive children on stimulant drugs also give evidence of a significant response to the active drug and not to a placebo (*7*). Such parent reports of the child's response to stimulants are highly correlated to teacher reports (*56*), particularly in relation to drug-induced changes in restlessness, inattentiveness, and misconduct.

Still another correlation that provides specific evidence of stimulant drug action is the significant positive relationship between teacher ratings and laboratory measures. Those children who show the greatest improvement on laboratory measures after the administration of stimulants also generally show improved teacher ratings as a result of this medication (*3*).

INITIATION OF STIMULANT TREATMENT

Choice of a Stimulant

The choice of which stimulant to use is up to the family doctor and he is influenced in this decision, to a great extent, by his comfort with the one which is most familiar. Ritalin is now the most popular (*1*). Its clinical effect is generally equivalent to that of Dexedrine and Cylert. The major advantage of Ritalin and Cylert over Dexedrine is the fact that their appetite suppressant effects average only about one-third those of Dexedrine (*57;f*).

Dextroamphetamine (Dexedrine) has the following minor advantages over Ritalin and Cylert: it has been used for hyperactivity for 39 years rather than 20 years (Ritalin) or 1 year (Cylert); in addition to the tablet form, it comes in a liquid or elixir form (for small children), and in a long acting form, the spansule; and it is a bit less costly than Ritalin and much less costly than Cylert. Nonetheless, the effect of Dexedrine on appetite suppression can be a problem and in part for this reason, its use in HA children, relative to the use of Ritalin and Cylert, is declining.

Most HA children respond to any one of the three stimulants favorably. In about 20% of the clinical trials, however, one stimulant will work when the other does not (58).

Cylert, because it is new, will presumably be generally used as an alternative to Ritalin and Dexedrine for the next few years. It creates less appetite suppression than Dexedrine and has a longer duration than tablets of Ritalin and Dexedrine. However, unlike the other two drugs which achieve their maximum effect on the day of administration, Cylert can take up to 3 weeks to demonstrate dramatic benefits (16).

Dose and Dose Schedule

Ritalin can be given in a single daily dose for school day purposes; the dose then is usually 20 mg (1 peach-colored tablet) taken in the morning before school. Alternatively, it can be given twice daily as 1 10-mg tablet (which is light green in color) before school and 1 10-mg tablet at noon. Not infrequently, when given twice daily, the strength of the morning tablet has to be increased to 20 mg to maintain effectiveness. This may occur after a few months or so. The average total daily dose of Ritalin is 20–30 mg. The company that manufactures Ritalin recommends that the drug be given before meals (because an acid pH is necessary for absorption of the drug), but taking the drug after breakfast seems not to appreciably alter the clinical response. A 10-mg tablet generally lasts 3–4 hours, whereas a 20-mg tablet has a clear clinical effect for 4–5 hours. Because of this, a 20-mg tablet of Ritalin lasts from approximately 8:30 a.m. to 1:00 or 1:30 p.m. and does suffice for school day purposes for 60–70% of children who benefit from stimulants (37, 59). For young elementary school children, the single daily dose of Ritalin can be given for a few days as one-half of a 20-mg tablet until the child gets used to the medication. Then the full tablet is usually necessary.

Dextroamphetamine is usually prescribed in a 5-mg tablet, twice daily (Dexedrine is orange and heart shaped). It is given at 8 to 8:30 a.m. and again at noon. Alternatively, a 10-mg single daily dose (2 tablets) can be given in the morning before school. When given twice daily, occasionally the strength of the morning dose has to be raised to 10 mg (or 2 tablets) for effectiveness. The spansule is best begun at a 10-mg dose. If the 15-mg spansule is the beginning dose, at least 10% of HA children will experience a prominent degree of insomnia. If the 10-mg Dexedrine spansule results in only moderate benefit, an additional 5-mg tablet in the morning can be added. For children from 3–6, one can use Dexedrine elixir (*g*). It is best to be cautious with Dexedrine for preschool children, and to start with a half-teaspoon dose in the morning and a half-teaspoon at noon. A half-teaspoon is 2.5 mg. Generally, it is best not to use an after school or late afternoon dose of a stimulant because this increases the risk of insomnia and tends to prolong appetite suppression (*60; h*).

Cylert is used in a single, morning dose of 37.5 or 75 mg.; the 37.5-mg tablet is orange colored and the 75-mg tablet is tan. It is best to start Cylert at 37.5 mg. The 75-mg dose can temporarily cause insomnia (*16*).

Because of concerns about long term side effects of stimulants, many physicians now recommend that the medication be used primarily only during school days. The academic school year comes out to about 180 days, which is approximately one-half of the calendar year. If a single daily dose of Ritalin or Cylert is prescribed only on school days, then the child receives only 180 tablets a year.

There are times in which stimulants are useful outside of school hours: on weekends and during the summer. Some parents find it necessary to give their child one-half of his usual daily school dose before church, before afternoon family visiting, and on rainy days. Furthermore, this dose can be useful for periods of summer camp, bible school, and the like. Additionally, when urgently needed to reduce marked parental aggravation or marked neighborhood hostility which the child is observed to provoke, the child can be placed on stimulants during the summer, preferably at one-half the usual school dose.

The Drug Trial: Starting Stimulant Treatment

Since stimulant medication isn't always beneficial, it should always be started as a trial. The trial of medication needn't be long. Within 1–3 weeks, one usually knows whether the medication works. The easiest way to initiate the trial is to use a single daily dose of a stimulant, only on school days. At the end of a week or so, the teacher should be asked to describe the child's behavior for that week (*i*). This can be quantified by asking her to complete a check list on the child (see Chapter IV) which would include such items as: leaves the seat unexcused, doesn't complete school work, restless, short attention span, speaks out of turn, and makes disruptive noise. This teacher report or check list can easily be communicated or conveyed to the physician through the school nurse, or, if need be, through the guidance counselor.

If the classroom report indicates that the child on medication was only somewhat or moderately better than he had been before medication, one should probably then raise the dose to 30 mg of Ritalin (1½ 20-mg tablets), or 15 mg of dextroamphetamine (3 tablets) or a 75-mg tablet of Cylert. If the drug was reportedly not beneficial at all, one should then check to see if the child took the medication. If an adult watched the child put the pill in his mouth and observed him before and during the swallow, checking his mouth, then one can feel reassured on this account. In instances where there is real doubt that the child took the pill, it is usually helpful to request then that it be administered in school. If the child took the medication and showed no benefit, then the initial dose can be doubled, to 40 mg of Ritalin, 20 mg of Dexedrine, or 75–112.5 mg of Cylert, preferably in a single daily dose before school (j).

Dose adjustments immediately and routinely follow unsatisfactory drug trials. After each dose adjustment, a teacher inquiry should be made. Here again, the report is best conveyed from a member of the school staff (preferably the school nurse) to the physician, rather than through the parent to the doctor. Generally, the drug trial can stop with 40 mg of Ritalin, 20 mg of dextroamphetamine, or 112.5 mg of Cylert, although some go higher. The company that manufactures Ritalin recommends its use in doses up to 60 mg per day.

Occasionally, one can request that the school nurse administer the pill to the child for a week or so, stop it for a week or so, and inquire if the teacher noticed an appreciable difference. Equivocal or mild drug responses to stimulants at a high dose can be viewed for practical purposes as negative responses.

PSYCHOLOGICAL CONSIDERATIONS
FOR STIMULANT TREATMENT

Counseling for Stimulant Drug Treatment

When discussing medication with the parents and the HA child, it is important to discuss the benefits and drawbacks of stimulant drug treatment, the drawbacks of no treatment, and the frequency of improvement with medication. Many parents have misconceptions about stimulants and see them as narcotics. These misconceptions need to be clarified. Parents are told that for these children stimulants are not habit forming and create no physical dependency or craving. Likewise, they are told that there is no evidence to suggest that taking medication in childhood creates a tendency for the child to make a habit of pill consumption later. Furthermore, it is important to point out that these drugs do not sedate the child or leave him "spaced out."

Both parent and child often feel reassured by the idea of a drug trial. They feel they can gain something when the physician states, "We'll try it for a short time and evaluate its effectiveness." Not infrequently, HA children, particularly of junior high school age, are hesitant to take medication because they fear it will tarnish their social image. When a child is opposed to medication the physician can simply recommend it, and suggest that a no-drug period with teacher ratings be initiated to see whether to not the child can successfully do without the medication for the next few weeks. Younger HA children, following this plan, can seldom maintain cooperative and attentive school behavior and usually agree to a trial of medication within a week or 2. Some midadolescents, however, can exert sufficient control for this period to avoid the need for medication. The no-drug trial can also be used in response to resistances to continuing the medication on the child's part during later years of treatment.

Pressures on the Physician to Prescribe

Parental pressures on the physician to prescribe can be a problem. Some parents cannot tolerate their child at all when he is restless. Some want the child "sedated" primarily for their own comfort and convenience, medicating the child at all hours. Instead of adjusting to some extent to their child's restlessness, these parents use only one response: the pill. When the neighbors complain or the sibs fight, they go for the pill. Even when their child reaches 14 and is less restless but still fidgety, they are still unwilling to cope with their child's nonmedicated temperament. Some of these parents even administer more medication to their child than is prescribed and it behooves the doctor in these instances to check on the number of pills prescribed for that child over a given time period to make sure the medication was not overadministered.

School pressure on the physician to prescribe usually occurs in association with a suspension. Infrequently, some school officials may even indicate to parents that the child will only be readmitted to school if he is on medication. Others forcefully indicate that the child *must* behave differently in school when (and if) he returns; otherwise he will be suspended quickly again and possibly expelled. This threat challenges the doctor and parents to think of a dramatic, rapid, relatively inexpensive solution. In this age of high drug use, pills come to mind quickly. This may indeed be an appropriate treatment consideration, but its implementation should follow a careful diagnostic evaluation.

SIDE EFFECTS OF STIMULANTS

Short Term

There are a number of side effects that can occur with stimulants. These are primarily temporary and minor in their effect (*61*). During the first week, and occasionally during the second, about 15% of children given stimulants evidence or complain of one of the following: headaches, moodiness, stomach aches, and increased talkativeness (Figure 2) (*16, 38*). The headache is usually frontal, transient, and mild. Moodiness consists of a tendency to cry. Stomach aches are transient and often associated with nausea (*38*). In some sensitive children, pallor (a decrease in color in the face) can occur with higher doses of stimulants (*k*). From 25 to 50% of children experience an appetite decrease initially, more so with dextro-amphetamine than with Ritalin (*38, 48, 60*). It tends to last longer in the day than the therapeutic effect of the drug. With daily use over time, it becomes less prominent (*16*). Insomnia does not generally occur with the single daily administration of a tablet or two of Ritalin or Dexedrine in the morning. If a noon dose of a stimulant or a long acting capsule (Dexedrine Spansule) or tablet (Cylert) is administered, insomnia can occur. When the stimulant is still in the child's system at bedtime, it can keep him awake, often until 11 p.m. or midnight. As with anorexia, drug-induced insomnia lasts beyond the period of obvious therapeutic effects of the tablet. When

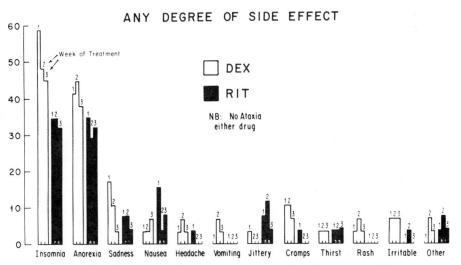

Figure 2. Side effects reported by parents for 3 weeks of treatment with two stimulants. Any degree of side effect, whether moderate or severe, is shown. DEX: Dexedrine; RIT: Ritalin. From Connors (*38*) with permission of the *Journal of Learning Disabilities*.

insomnia occurs, irritability may occur the next day, giving the appearance that day of an adverse clinical response to the stimulant drug administered. Pupillary dilatation without visual impairment occurs for some. Very rarely, a hallucinatory episode can occur with stimulants (*62, 63*). Likewise, dyskinetic episodes (such as writhing movements of the face and neck) can occur, although they also are very rare (*12, 61*).

When side effects, such as those mentioned, occur, it is usually best to temporarily decrease the dose for a few days until the child gets used to the medication. Then the dose can be raised as need be for clinical effectiveness. Side effects of stimulants are almost never enough of a problem to warrant discontinuing the medication.

Most of the temporary side effects of stimulants for children, such an insomnia and appetite suppression, are similar to those of adults. In addition, most of the beneficial effects of stimulants, such as improved attention, are also the same for children and for adults. Why then do people say that hyperactive children have a paradoxical response to stimulants? The major reason is that hyperactive children become less restless (on tasks) when on stimulants, whereas, if anything, stimulants can increase the activity level of adults (*64*). The only other major response to stimulants that differentiates HA children and adults is the development of euphoria, or feeling of well-being. About two-thirds of normally active adults or young adults become "high" on moderate to high doses of stimulants (*65, 66; l*). Hyperactive children, on the other hand, do not become high or euphoric on stimulant medication (*m*). Should hyperactive children experience a notable mood change on stimulants, it is usually a temporary phase of depressive irritability, an occasional but infrequent side effect.

Long Term Side Effects

The matter of long term side effects of stimulants has been insufficiently studied (*n*). The only long term side effect which has been reported is a minor degree of suppression of the growth rate which can occur, particularly with the long term use of dextroamphetamine (*57*). With higher doses of Ritalin, this can also be somewhat of a problem (*52, 57*). Children on Dexedrine grow (on average) at approximately 60–75% of their expected annual rate during the period they are on the medication. The suppression of weight gain is most prominent during the initial year on Dexedrine. When abruptly taken off of the drug, these children show a distinct growth rebound (*67*). As an example, children off dextroamphetamine for the summer grow at a rate 2–3 times that of their monthly on-medication rate. The ultimate degree of growth rebound after long term use of dextroamphetamine and high doses of Ritaline is substantial (*12, 67*), so that in the great majority of cases, if growth suppression occurs, it is temporary. However, whether or not the rebound suffices in all cases to recover the total growth suppressed is not known (*12, 52, 67*).

Serious side effects of stimulant drugs given to hyperactive children are reported infrequently, which suggests that they are indeed infrequent. If this is true, it can be assumed then that these drugs are quite safe for long term use in hyperactive children. We assume that this is generally true. However, long term drug studies are needed to bear this out scientifically. One reassuring fact is that these drugs do *not* cause euphoria or craving in hyperactive children (*12*). Presumably, this is why no evidence to date suggests that young adults who were hyperactive and on stimulants as children misused stimulants after their restlessness faded (*68*).

Further long term studies are needed to appraise the effect of stimulants on sleep, heart rate, behavior, and learning. Some preliminary evidence suggests that dextroamphetamine given two or three times daily decreases stage 4 sleep in HA children and that there are stages 4 and REM increases when the drug is abruptly terminated (*69; o*). There is also evidence showing that Ritalin causes a mild increase in resting heart rate during the period of drug effect (*70*). However, after 4 months of treatment with Ritalin, this appears to no longer be the case (*70*).

PROBLEMS IN MANAGING CONTINUED STIMULANT TREATMENT

Maintaining Effectiveness

To clarify the effectiveness of stimulant medication, it is necessary to compare an on-medication school report or check list with that obtained before the onset of medication use. A parent-relayed account of the child's classroom adjustment is often inadequate for this purpose because parents frequently convey a distorted version of the teacher's impressions. For accuracy, then, the doctor should get a school-conveyed teacher report and decide after that.

Should the medication, according to teacher reports, be no longer effective, there are a number of possible considerations to explore. First, it is essential to ascertain if the child took the medication. Only one-third to one-half of psychiatric outpatients take tranquilizers as prescribed (*71*) and this can be an even greater problem for children. If this is suspected, a responsible adult, such as a school nurse, must check carefully to see that the pill actually went into the child's mouth and down his throat. A second reason why the medication may no longer be effective is that the dose is now too low. In one-quarter to one-half of the cases, after an optimum dose is found initially, it is necessary, a few months or more later, to raise the dose for effectiveness (72; p). Another reason why the medication is no longer effective is that a major degree of tolerance may develop. Generally, there is only a mild degree of tolerance to the behavioral effects of stimulants in hyperactive children (12), although there is tolerance to many physiological effects of these drugs (70). However, on occasion, a prominent degree of tolerance develops to the therapeutic effects of stimulants such that a drug change is required (58, 73).

Determining Duration

Another consideration in long term stimulant medication treatment of hyperactive children is how long the child should be on medication. The continued need for medication can easily be determined by annual trials of a no-medication period (72). These drug-free periods should occur at the beginning of each school year, but they can be initiated or repeated later in the school year as need be. After the child has been in school for a week or so with no medication, the parent should check with the teacher, and request that a teacher checklist be mailed to the doctor. If, off medication, the child is again his usual restless, inattentive self, the doctor will probably renew the medication. If the drug is clinically beneficial each year, it may be necessary to continue stimulant drug use until the early teens. Usually at age 14 or 15, the medication becomes no longer necessary because of the decrease in the child's restlessness (q). However, this is not true for all hyperactive children. Some clearly benefit by the medication at ages 15 and 16. The assumption by some that after puberty the hyperactive child will no longer have a "paradoxical response" to stimulants (74) is not true. These children show the same response to stimulants in their teens as they did in their childhood and prepuberty years (20, 39, 75, 76).

Avoiding Unscheduled Changes

A problem which occurs during continued stimulant drug treatment for hyperactive children is that the parents may stop the medication without consulting the doctor, even when the medication was useful. This usually occurs at the time of refill. Reasons for it include the following: one parent is strongly against medication or fears side effects and pressures his spouse at the time of refill. (Often this is the father, since it is customarily the mother who takes the child to the doctor.) Another reason is that with no adverse or critical school reports, the parent feels that the crisis is over and the medicine can be stopped. A third and quite frequent reason for stopping is that it is too time-consuming or costly to see the doctor for a refill. If the doctor's visit costs $10–12 and the prescription costs $12.00 ($r$), this can be a burden for many families. Still another reason for a parent stopping the medication is that she believes the medication is no longer effective, even though a school report might well contradict this. If, for example, her son gets into a fight at school, she may see this as grounds for assuming that the medication is no longer beneficial and stop it, or convince the doctor to do so. A fifth reason for the abrupt cessation of medication is that the child's complaints of side effects have convinced the parent to stop the drug (s).

Providing Adequate Medical Follow-up

Because of reports of growth suppression in long term use, particularly after dextroamphetamine and higher doses of Ritalin, it is helpful to have the child's weight and height checked annually. This can be done by the school nurse and reported to the doctor. Most elementary school children gain about 5–7 pounds annually, and grow 2–2½ inches annually. If the child has not grown at his expected, premedication rate, the matter should be looked into. Pediatricians generally check this on a growth percentile chart (77).

If the child is growing substantially less than would be expected for his age and sex (relative to his predrug rate) then the doctor can consider a number of moves. If dextroamphetamine was prescribed, he could switch to Ritalin or Cylert. If he prescribed Ritalin twice daily, he could switch to once-daily dose schedule. He could also try to decrease the total dose of the stimulant. Or he could try a bedtime diet supplement.

There is another good reason to switch from one stimulant medication to another. If one stimulant does not work, it would be reasonable to try another. One would certainly want to exhaust the possibilities with stimulants first, particularly if the child upon re-evaluation still appeared clearly to fit the HA clinical picture. The reason for this is that stimulants are by far the most effective drug treatment for HA children (6, 14), and they also appear to be the safest. So why leave the known to a drug group of doubtful value?

IS STIMULANT MEDICATION TREATMENT SUFFICIENT?

The school results of stimulants are positive for hyperactive children from all socioeconomic levels; they all average an 80% improvement rate (78). However, children from poorly organized families generally start out with more problems, so that their ingrained deviant patterns tend to persist, even when the medication lessens their restlessness and inattentiveness. On the other hand, medication can benefit HA children from organized homes so that they no longer have outstanding adjustment problems. In these instances, then, stimulant medication plus some counseling can constitute a sufficient and adequate medical and psychological treatment for HA.

NONSTIMULANT MEDICATION FOR HYPERACTIVE CHILDREN

Phenothiazines

There are a number of nonstimulant medications that can be useful for the HA child. The most frequent alternatives to stimulant medication used by doctors are the most commonly used major tranquilizers, the phenothiazines. About 5–10% of HA children on drugs for their behavior receive these tranquilizers (1). The two most commonly used phenothiazine tranquilizers for children are Mellaril (thioridazine) and Thorazine (chlorpromazine). These medications have the effect of lessening restlessness and quelling anxiety. However, they do not beneficially influence attention span in MBD children (11, 43). In fact, in short term studies, there is a mild tendency for these phenothiazines to impair attention, reaction time, and motor performance (t). The dose of Mellaril and Thorazine which is commonly prescribed is 10–25 mg, two or three times a day. For quite anxious older children, the dose occasionally has to be raised to 50 mg two or three times a day.

The most common side effects of Mellaril and Thorazine in children are drowsiness and an appetite increase, leading to weight gain (79). Some other side effects have been infrequently reported with these drugs in children. A sensitivity of the skin to sunlight can occur, particularly with Thorazine (61). Uncommonly, in children prone to seizures, Thorazine can also decrease the seizure threshold. Inhibition of ejaculation in male teenagers and a temporary lowering of the white blood cell count can occur, particularly with Mellaril. Muscular spasms in the facial area (called dystonias) can occur with these drugs as can a number of other side effects (61). A full discussion of the side effects of phenothiazine tranquilizers is beyond the scope of this section. However, as with stimulants, side effects following the temporary use of these drugs at the recommended dosage are few and generally minor (61). Side effects from long term use of tranquilizers may yet become a more serious consideration, particularly if one assumes that children can have most of the same long term side effects that adults on phenothiazines can experience. In any event, there are only two comprehensive studies, as of 1975 (*52, 79*), on the long term side effects of phenothiazines in children; much more needs to be done.

The phenothiazines are useful for HA children who are psychotic, borderline psychotic, or mentally subnormal. In fact, psychotic HA children react better to major tranquilizers than to stimulants (*41*). Mentally retarded restless children may do well with either type of medication, a stimulant or a phenothiazine (*80, 81*), and a comparative trial of each may well be necessary. One measurement of drug effect to consider in the seriously retarded is stereotyped movements, e.g., bizarre posturing and repetitive movements. They have been reported to decrease after Mellaril is given (*82*). The HA child who shows *no* evidence of mental retardation or psychotic thinking will in all likelihood do best on stimulants and in all likelihood will not be appreciably benefited by phenothiazines (*6, 14*). Stimulants then, not tranquilizers, are the treatment of choice for typical HA children.

Antidepressants

In the last 3—5 years, the antidepressants have become a major drug group for the treatment of hyperactivity in children. Of these, only imipramine (Tofranil, SK-pramine, or Imavate) is officially recommended for children under age 12. Also, imipramine is the only drug of this group which has been carefully explored for the treatment of HA children (*73, 83—86*). The total recommended daily dose of imipramine for hyperactivity is 50—180 mg per day, and caution is urged for doses over 200 mg per day (*87*). A single evening dose or morning plus after school administration of the drug is generally recommended. Unlike its action on depressive symptoms (when the drug takes weeks to be clearly effective) the effect of antidepressants on hyperactivity becomes apparent on the day it is ingested.

The major side effects of imipramine in children and adolescents are: dry mouth, suppression of appetite, weight loss, nausea, sweating, tremor (*87*) and sleepiness (*88*). Seizures have also been reported with this drug (*89*).

Generally, the available data suggest that antidepressants are less effective than stimulants (*85, 86*) and that tolerance to the drug effect is not uncommon (*84, 86; u*).

Minor Tranquilizers and Sedatives

Minor tranquilizers and sedatives are, after phenothiazine tranquilizers, next most popular for use in HA children. Less than 5% of hyperactive children receive these (*1*). Of this group, the two most used are Benadryl (diphenhydramine) and Atarax (hydroxyzine). They are sedative type drugs with some tranquilizing effects. Benadryl is a generally safe antihistamine drug. It is occasionally effective in young hyperactive children and can be helpful, particularly for some anxious, restless, preschool children. For the young, it comes in an elixir. The most common side effect of Benadryl is drowsiness. Therefore, some physicians give it as a sedative for HA children to take at night. The usual daily dose of Benadryl for hyperactivity is 100–200 mg. For nighttime use, 50–100 mg will usually suffice.

The other drug in this category which deserves mention is Atarax. It also has antihistamine effects. Even more so than Benadryl, it has been the product of little research in children. To date, double blind research with these two drugs suggests they are not very effective for hyperactivity (*3, 60*).

Other Types of Medication

Lithium has been tried on children who did not respond favorably to stimulants; the results have been disappointing (*90, 91*). Haldol (haloperidol) is just coming into use (*92*); however, it is not yet officially recommended for children. Anticonvulsants have been tried. Of these, Dilantin (diphenylhydantoin) has been the most commonly used. Dilantin is an excellent anticonvulsant drug, but its effect on hyperactive symptoms is nil (*93–95; v*). Should the child have a seizure disorder and hyperactivity, dextroamphetamine might be particularly useful since it has been reported to have some effectiveness for some petit mal seizure disorders (*96*). Another major anticonvulsant drug, phenobarbital, tends to aggravate hyperactivity (*97*). Thus, if a hyperactive child has a grand mal or psychomotor seizure disorder, it may be preferable to use a maintenance anticonvulsant drug other than phenobarbital. In this respect, Tegretol (carbamazol) deserves consideration for psychomotor epilepsy (*98*).

Recently there has been an increased interest in psychotropic medication for mid- and late adolescents who have aggressive behavior and are impulsive. The focus has been on pharmacological treatment of their episodic dyscontrol (*99*). Many of these children, possibly one-fourth, have HA histories. Some new, preliminary drug studies with this population have been reported; they suggest that Dilantin (*99*), Serax (oxazepam) (*100*), and lithium (*101*) might help many to control the impulsive anger of these teenagers. However, further studies need to be done for this population.

NOTES

a. Recent data also suggest that HA children who are good responders to stimulants exhibit visual and auditory evoked potentials on these drugs that are significantly different from those of non-HA children (on these drugs) (*14, 22, 102*). However, some of the data are contradictory (*103*).

b. In 1975, the BNDD was subsumed under the Drug Enforcement Administration (DEA). Consequently, the BNDD number will be referred to increasingly as the Federal DEA number.

c. In 1975, the report of the Council on Child Health of the American Academy of Pediatrics (*104*) was clearly favorable to stimulants. They stressed that stimulants are very effective for HA children and that they are not a constraint on freedom. Rather, the report stated, hyperactivity and impulsivity constrain freedom.

d. Although some HA children who loosely associate in speech do worse on stimulant medication, this does not contraindicate a drug trial. It does suggest, however, that close follow-up is necessary and that the likelihood of therapeutic benefit from stimulant medication for these children is less than for other hyperactives (*12*).

e. Although long term academic gains from the use of a stimulant drug appear to be nil, Weiss et al. (*52*) found that HA children on Ritalin (methylphenidate) did better than comparison groups in their school promotion rate. Presumably, improved classroom behavior when on the drug accounted for this result.

f. Caffeine has also been prescribed for hyperactivity in children (*105*). However, recent double blind studies indicate that caffeine is no better than placebo in its effects on HA children (*5, 106–108*).

g. The administration of stimulant drugs presents more difficulties for preschool than for school age HA children because for preschoolers the diagnosis is less clear, and the treatment evaluation is more complex (*109*). Schleifer et al. (*109*) also reported that stimulant drug treatment for this population was, on average, less effective than for older HA children. Conners (*110*), however, found that stimulants were clearly useful for preschool HA children.

h. The after school dose of dextramphetamine clearly increases insomnia and anorexia for over 75% of HA children for over a month (*60*). For some children, however, a stimulant tablet taken before bedtime apparently does not interfere with sleep (*111*).

i. The reason the teacher's evaluation is listed as the exclusive outcome measure is that she is in the best position to see the behavioral effects of the drug. Furthermore, teacher ratings are more reliable indices of drug outcome than are parent ratings (*112*).

j. A placebo to compare for therapeutic efficacy would be useful (*12*), but it is rarely employed in clinical practice.

k. The pallor presumably reflects some cutaneous vasoconstriction, as would be indicated also by the fact that stimulants decrease skin temperature (*113*).

l.   It is of note that approximately one-third of adults become dysphoric or sleepy after the oral administration of amphetamines (65, 66, 114). This drowsiness is correlated with EEG changes (65).

m.   Two responses to accidental overdose of stimulants in nonhyperactive children are, interestingly enough, euphoria and hyperactivity (115); of note in this respect is one report indicating that the least restless HA children were the only ones to show hyperactivity as a drug side effect (18).

n.   Long term use of medication can be arbitrarily defined as the use of the drug for 2 or more years (57). Duration of drug use varies depending on such factors as: the age of the HA child (duration decreases with advancing age) (75), and the style and training of the doctor (child psychiatrists prescribe more) (116). In reports in the literature, stimulant drug use was utilized an average of 6 (116), 9 (117), 22 (88), and 28 months (12) in four different studies.

o.   In children, there are also studies indicating that stimulants do not alter EEG recorded sleep stages (118, 119). However, in adults, the evidence again indicates that daytime doses of stimulants alter sleep patterns, particularly REM and slow wave sleep (120).

p.   Theoretically, dose increases should be related in part to a child's size. Consequently, a dose of 20 mg of Ritalin for a 40-kg child would have to be raised to 30 mg when the child reaches 60 kg. With this logic, Sleator and Sprague (59) base their dose calculations routinely on body weight. Furthermore, they found that such a dosing arrangement resulted in fairly consistant performance data (121). Safer and Allen (75), however, found that the dose needed for classroom benefit did not significantly relate to age (which in group data is proportional to weight). Additionally, Weiss et al. (52) revealed that, if anything, the dose of Ritalin necessary for thera-peutic benefit actually decreased in the teens when weight gain is rapid. Along this line, we have found that dose corrections using body weight alone can lead to more variability than accuracy in some areas of psychopharmacological research, and that dosing in proportion to estimated blood volume yields the least variant drug-performance data (122).

q.   Many doctors with no supportive data have warned against prescribing stimulant medication for HA children when they are over 12 years of age. Millicap (123) and Werry (124) argue that giving stimulants to teenagers increases the risk of drug abuse. Chapel (125) states that stimulants are not necessary over age 12, and Huessey et al. (74) state that the drug is no longer clinically useful for the HA teenager. Only the study by Weiss et al. (52) provides any documentation for this concern: their data suggest that stimulants might suppress growth during the adolescent growth spurt.

r.   As of mid-1975, the cost of Ritalin is about $9.00 for 100 10-mg tablets and about $12.00 for 100 20-mg tablets. Cylert costs about $14.00 per 100 for the 37.5-mg tablets and $24.00 per 100 for the 75-mg tablets. The cost of Dexedrine is about $5.50 for 100 5-mg tablets. The cost of dextroamphetamine sulfate is about $4.00 per

100 tablets. The cost of other drugs mentioned is as follows: imipramine (25-mg tablets) $10.00–12.00 per 100; Mellaril (25-mg tablets) $12.00 per 100.

s. Taking medication for behavior is viewed with disfavor by many HA children, particularly those over age 12 (75). It concretizes their feeling that they are different from other children.

t. It should be stressed that it is the sedative effects of phenothiazine drugs which slow reaction time, motor responses, and attentiveness, and that a good deal of tolerance develops to these effects. Consequently, longer term studies are needed to better evaluate the effects of phenothiazine tranquilizers on learning. The two long term studies in print on the effects of phenothiazines on learning in children are unfortunately contradictory. McAndrew et al. (79) cite three cases of a learning inhibition presumably caused by phenothiazines, but Weiss et al. (52) report no long term impairment due to these drugs. For adults, the evidence suggests that one of the phenothiazines, chlorpromazine, tends to temporarily impair learning (126).

u. The similarity in the response of HA children (e.g., treatment efficacy, side effects) to both antidepressants (e.g., imipramine) and stimulant drugs suggests that these drug groups have an area of pharmacological commonality. Fawcett and Siomopoulos (127) found this to be true in their studies with adult depressives. Those who responded clinically to a stimulant (amphetamine) also responded well to a tricyclic antidepressant (imipramine).

v. The possibility of a drug interaction needs to be considered when combining stimulant drugs with antidepressive drugs. Methylphenidate (Ritalin) for instance, has been reported to retard the metabolism of imipramine (128, 129). Because of the synergistic (additive) effects of Ritalin and imipramine, these two drugs are occasionally given simultaneously in treatment (12). Drug interaction findings for the combination of Ritalin and Dilantin (diphenylhydantoin) are inconsistent (128, 130).

LITERATURE CITED

1. Krager, J., and Safer, D. Type and prevalence of medication used in the treatment of hyperactive children. New Eng. J. Med. 291: 1118–1120, 1974.

2. Yang, D., Fisch, M., and Lamm, S. Rehabilitation of learning in a hospital class using psychoactive drugs. J. Learn. Disabil. 6: 486–494, 1973.

3. Safer, D., Allen, R., Calabria, R., Rodriguez, A., and Graham, R. Laboratory correlates of methylphenidate in hyperactive children (Unpublished manuscript). 1972.

4. Arnold, L., Wender, P., McCloskey, K., and Synder, S. Levoamphetamine and dextroamphetamine: Comparative efficacy in the hyperkinetic syndrome. Arch. Gen. Psychiat. 27: 816–822, 1972.

5. Garfinkel, B., Webster, C., and Sloman, L. Methylphenidate and caffeine in the treatment of children with minimal brain dysfunction. Am. J. Psychiat. 132: 723–728, 1975.
6. Millichap, J., and Fowler, G. Treatment of "minimal brain dysfunction syndromes." Pediat. Clin. N. Am. 14: 767–777, 1967.
7. Conners, C. Symposium: Behavior modification by drugs. II. Psychological effects of stimulant drugs in children with minimal brain dysfunction. Pediatrics 49: 702–708, 1972.
8. Steinberg, G., Troshinsky, C., and Steinberg, H. Dextroamphetamine-responsive behavior disorder in school children. Am. J. Psychiat. 128: 174–179, 1971.
9. Conners, C. A teacher rating scale for use in drug studies with children. Am. J. Psychiat. 126: 884–888, 1969.
10. Satterfield, J., Cantwell, D., Saul, R., Lesser, L., and Posesin, R. Response to stimulant drug treatment in hyperactive children: Prediction from EEG and neurological findings. J. Aut. Childhood Schizopren. 3: 36–48, 1973.
11. Werry, J., Weiss, G., Douglas, V., and Martin, J. Studies on the hyperactive child. III. The effect of chlorpromazine upon behavior and learning ability. J. Am. Acad. Child Psychiat. 5: 292–312, 1966.
12. Gross, M., and Wilson, W. Minimal Brain Dysfunction. New York: Brunner/Mazel, 1974.
13. Schain, R., and Reynard, C. Observations on effects of a central stimulant drug (methylphenidate) in children with hyperactive behavior. Pediatrics 55: 709–716, 1975.
14. Saletu, B., Saletu, M., Simeon, J., Viamontes, G., and Itil, T. Comparative symptomatological and potential studies with d-amphetamine, thioridazine, and placebo in hyperkinetic children. Biol. Psychiat. 10: 253–275, 1975.
15. Conners, C. Deanol and behavior disorders in children. Psychopharm. Bull., Spec. Issue, Pharmacotherapy in Children, pp. 188–195, 1973.
16. Conners, C., Taylor, E., Meo, G., Kurtz, M., and Fournier, M. Magnesium pemoline and dextroamphetamine: A controlled study in children with minimal brain dysfunction. Psychopharmacologia 26: 321–336, 1972.
17. Page, J., Janicki, R., Bernstein, J., Curran, C., and Michelli, F. Pemoline (Cylert) in the treatment of childhood hyperkinesis. J. Learn. Disabil. 7: 498–503, 1974.
18. Millichap, J. Neuropharmacology of hyperkinetic behavior: Response of methylphenidate correlated with degree of activity and brain damage, in A. Vernadakis and N. Werner (Eds.), Drugs and the Developing Brain, pp. 475–488. New York: Plenum Press, 1974.
19. Denhoff, E. The natural history of children with minimal brain dysfunction. Pediat. Ann. 205: 158–205, 1973.
20. Maletzky, B. d-Amphetamine and delinquency: Hyperkinesis persisting? Dis. Nerv. Syst. 35: 543–547, 1974.

21. Barcai, A. Predicting the response of children with learning disabilities and behavior problems to dextroamphetamine sulfate. Pediatrics 47: 73–80, 1971.
22. Satterfield, J. EEG issues in children with minimal brain dysfunction. Sem. Psychiat. 5: 35–46, 1973.
23. Itil, T., and Simeon, J. Computerized EEG in the prediction of outcome of drug treatment in hyperactive child behavior disorders. Psychopharm. Bull. 10: 36, 1974.
24. Gittelman-Klein, R., and Klein, D. Methylphenidate effects of learning disability in children. Read at the 126th Annual Meeting of the American Psychiatric Association, Honolulu, Hawaii, May 1973.
25. Maynard, R. Omaha pupils given "Behavior" drugs. The Washington Post, June 29, 1970.
26. Gallagher, C. Hearing before a subcommittee of the Committee on Government Operations, House of Representatives, 91st Congress, Second Session, Publication No. 52-268, Washington, D.C., United States Government Printing Office, 1970.
27. Goodman, S., and Becker, D. Intracranial hemorrhage associated with amphetamine abuse. JAMA 212: 480, 1970.
28. Citron, B., Halpern, M., McCarron, M., Lundberg, G., McCormick, R., Pincus, I., Tatter, D., and Haverback, B. Necrotizing angiitis associated with drug abuse. New Eng. J. Med. 283: 1003–1011, 1970.
29. Laties, V., and Weiss, B. Performance enhancement by the amphetamines: A new appraisal, in H. Brill (Ed.), Neuropsychopharmacology, pp. 800–808. Amsterdam: Excerpta Medica, 1967.
30. Penick, S. Amphetamines in obesity. Sem. Psychiat. 1: 144–162, 1969.
31. Balter, M., and Levine, J. The nature and extent of psychotropic drug use in the United States. Psychopharm. Bull. 5: 3–13, 1969.
32. Brown, F. Hallucinogenic Drugs. Springfield, Ill.: Charles C Thomas, Publisher, 1972.
33. Ellinwood, E. The epidemiology of stimulant abuse, in E. Josephson and E. Carroll (Eds.), Drug Use: Epidemicological and Sociological Approaches, pp. 303–329. New York: John Wiley and Sons, 1974.
34. Millichap, J. Drugs in management of hyperkinetic and perceptually handicapped children. JAMA 206: 1527–1530, 1968.
35. Weiss, C., and Yaffe, S. An evaluation of the pharmacologic approaches to learning impediments. Pediatrics 46: 142–144, 1970.
36. Report of the Conference on the Use of Stimulant Drugs in the Treatment of Behaviorally Disturbed Young School Children. Psychopharm. Bull. 7: 23–29, July 1971.
37. Safer, D., and Allen, R. Single daily dose methylphenidate in hyperactive children. Dis. Nerv. Syst. 34: 325–328, 1973.
38. Conners, C. Recent drug studies with hyperkinetic children. J. Learn. Disabil. 4: 476–483, 1971.

39. Eisenberg, L., Lachman, R., Molling, P., Lockner, A., Mizelle, J., and Conners, C. A psychopharmacologic experiment in a training school for delinquent boys: Methods, problems and findings. Am. J. Orthopsychiat. 33: 431–446, 1963.
40. Bradley, C., and Bowen, M. School performance of children receiving amphetamine (benzedrine) sulfate. Am. J. Orthopsychiat. 10: 782–788, 1940.
41. Campbell, M. Biological interventions in psychoses of childhood. J. Aut. Childhood Schizophren. 3: 347–373, 1973.
42. Fish, B. The "one child, one drug" myth of stimulants in hyperkinesis. Arch. Gen. Psychiat. 25: 193–203, 1971.
43. Sprague, R., Barnes, K., and Werry, J. Methylphenidate and thioridazine: Learning, reaction time, activity and classroom behavior in disturbed children. Am. J. Orthopsychiat. 40: 615–628, 1970.
44. Sykes, D., Douglas, V., and Morgenstern. G. The effect of methylphenidate (Ritalin) on sustained attention in hyperactive children. Psychopharmacologia 25: 262–274, 1972.
45. Anderson, R., Halcomb, C., and Doyle, R. The measurement of attentional deficits. Except, Child. 39: 534–538, 1973.
46. Conners, C., Rothschild, G., Eisenberg, L., Schwartz, L., and Robinson, E. Dextroamphetamine sulfate in children with learning disorders. Arch. Gen. Psychiat. 21: 182–190, 1969.
47. Millichap, J., Aymat, F., Sturgis, L., Larsen, K., and Egan, R. Hyperkinetic behavior and learning disorders. III. Battery of neuropsychological tests in a controlled trial of methylphenidate. Am. J. Dis. Child. 116: 235–244, 1968.
48. Knights, R., and Hinton, G. The effects of methylphenidate (Ritalin) on the motor skills and behavior of children with learning problems. J. Nerv. Ment. Dis. 148: 643–653, 1969.
49. Conners, C. Pharmacotherapy of psychopathology in children, in H. Quay and J. Werry (Eds.), Psychopathological Disorders in Childhood, pp. 316–347. New York: Wiley, 1972.
50. Rie, H. Hyperactivity in children. Am. J. Dis. Child. 129: 783–789, 1975.
51. Conrad, W., Dworkin, E., Shai, A., and Tobiessen, J. Effects of amphetamine therapy and prescriptive tutoring on the behavior and achievement of lower class children. J. Learn. Disabil. 4: 509–517, 1971.
52. Weiss, G., Kruger, E., Danielson, U., and Elman, M. Effect of long-term treatment of hyperactive children with methylphenidate. Canad. Med. Assoc. J. 112: 159–165, 1975.
53. Aman, M., and Sprague, R. Effect of methylphenidate and dextroamphetamine on learning and retention, in R. Sprague, Principal Investigator, Progress Report of Grant MH 18909 from 1970–1973, March 1973.
54. Conners, C. Drug and cognitive studies in disturbed children. Psychopharm. Bull. 10: 60–61, 1974.
55. Aman, M., and Sprague, R. The state-dependent effects of methylphenidate and dextroamphetamine. J. Nerv. Ment. Dis. 158: 268–279, 1974.

56. Zrull, J., Westman, J., Arthur, B., and Rice, D. An evaluation of methodology used in the study of psychoactive drugs for children. J. Am. Acad. Child Psychiat. 5: 284–291, 1966.

57. Safer, D., and Allen, R. Factors influencing the suppressant effects of two stimulant drugs on the growth of hyperactive children. Pediatrics 51: 660–667, 1973.

58. Winsberg, B., Press, M., Bialer, I., and Kupietz, S. Dextroamphetamine and methylphenidate in the treatment of hyperactive/aggressive children. Pediatrics 53: 236–241, 1974.

59. Sleator, E., and Sprague, R. Dose effects of stimulants in hyperkinetic children (Presented at the Annual Meeting of the American College of Neuropsychopharmacology, Palm Springs, California, December 1973) Psychopharm. Bull. 10: 29–33, 1974.

60. Greenberg, C., Deem, M., and McMahon, S. Effects of Dextroamphetamine, chlorpromazine, and hydroxyzine on behavior and performance in hyperactive children. Am. J. Psychiat. 129: 532–539, 1972.

61. DiMascio, A., Soltys, J., and Shader, R. Psychotropic drug side effects in children, in R. Shader and A. DiMascio (Eds.), Psychotropic Drug Side Effects, pp. 235–260. Baltimore: Williams & Wilkins, 1970.

62. Lucas, A., and Weiss, M. Methylphenidate hallucinosis. JAMA 217: 1079–1081, 1971.

63. Greenberg, L., McMahon, S., and Deem, M. Side effects of dextroamphetamine therapy of hyperactive children. Western J. Med. 120: 105–109, 1974.

64. Janowski, D., Davis, J., and El-Yousef, M. Effects of intravenous d-amphetamine, l-amphetamine and methylphenidate in schizophrenics. Psychopharm. Bull. 10: 15–24, 1974.

65. Teece, J., and Cole, J. Effects of amphetamine on electrocortical potential and behavior. Presented at the Annual Meeting of the American Psychiatric Association, Dallas, Texas, May 3, 1972.

66. Lasagna, L., Von Felsinger, J., and Beecher, H. Drug-induced mood changes in man: Observations on healthy subjects, chronically ill patients and "post addicts." JAMA 157: 1006–1020, 1955.

67. Safer, D., Allen, R., and Barr, E. Growth rebound after termination of stimulant drugs. J. Pediat. 86: 113–116, 1975.

68. Laufer, M. Long-term management and some follow-up findings on the use of drugs with minimal cerebral syndromes. J. Learn. Disabil. 4: 519–522, 1971.

69. Allen, R., and Safer, D. Sleep changes following stimulants in children (In preparation). 1975.

70. Safer, D., and Allen, R. Side effects from long-term use of stimulants in children. Int. J. Ment. Health 4: 105–118, 1975.

71. Blackwell, B. Drug therapy: Patient compliance. New Eng. J. Med. 289: 249–252, 1973.

72. Sleator, E., Von Neumann, A., and Sprague, R. Hyperactive children: A continuous long-term placebo-controlled follow-up. JAMA 229: 316–317, 1974.

73. Gross, M. Imipramine in the treatment of minimal brain dysfunction in children. Psychosomatics 14: 283—285, 1973.
74. Huessy, H., Marshall, C., and Gendron, R. Five hundred children followed from grade 2 through grade 5 for the prevalence of behavior disorder. Acta Paedopsychiat. 39: 309—309, 1973.
75. Safer, D., and Allen, R. Stimulant drug treatment of hyperactive adolescents. Dis. Nerv. Syst. 36: 454—457, 1975.
76. Korey, S. The effects of benzedrine sulfate on the behavior of psychopathic and neurotic juvenile delinquents. Psychiat. Quart. 18: 127—137, 1944.
77. Vaughan, V. Growth and development, in W. Nelson (Ed.), Textbook of Pediatrics, 9th Ed., pp. 40—41. Philadelphia: W. B. Saunders Co., 1969.
78. Hoffman, S., Engelhardt, D., Margolis, R., Polizos, P., Waizer, J., and Rosenfeld, R. Response to methylphenidate in low socioeconomic hyperactive children. Arch. Gen. Psychiat. 30: 354—359, 1974.
79. McAndrew, J., Case, Q., and Treffert, D. Effects of prolonged phenothiazine intake on psychotic and other hospitalized children. J. Aut. Childhood Schizophren. 2: 75—91, 1972.
80. Alexandris, A., and Lundell, F. Effect of thioridazine, amphetamine and placebo on the hyperkinetic syndrome and cognitive area in mentally deficient children. Can. Med. Assoc. J. 98: 92—96, 1968.
81. Blacklidge, V., and Ekblad, R. The effectiveness of methylphenidate hydrochloride (Ritalin) on learning and behavior in public school educable mentally retarded children. Pediatrics 47: 923—926, 1971.
82. Davis, K., Sprague, R., and Werry, J. Stereotyped behavior and activity level in severe retardates: The effect of drugs. Am. J. Ment. Defic. 73: 721—727, 1969.
83. Huessy, H., and Wright, A. The use of imipramine in children's behavior disorders. Acta paedopsychiat. 37: 194—199, 1970.
84. Waizer, J., Hoffman, S., Polizos, P., and Engelhardt, D. Outpatient treatment of hyperactive school children with imipramine. Am. J. Psychiat. 131: 587—591, 1974.
85. Rapoport, J., Quinn, P., Bradbard, G., Riddle, D., and Brooks, E. Imipramine and methylphenidate treatments of hyperactive boys. Arch. Gen. Psychiat. 30: 789—793, 1974.
86. Quinn, P., and Rapoport, J. One-year follow-up of hyperactive boys treated with imipramine or methylphenidate. Am. J. Psychiat. 132: 241—245, 1975.
87. Saraf, K., Klein, D., Gittelman-Klein, R., and Groff, S. Imipramine side effects in children. Psychopharmacologia 37: 265—274, 1974.
88. Greenberg, L., Yellin, A., Spring, C., and Metcalf, M. Clinical effects of imipramine and methylphenidate in hyperactive children. Int. J. Ment. Health 4: 144—156, 1975.
89. Brown, D., Winsberg, B., Bialer, I., and Press, M. Imipramine therapy and seizures: Three children treated for hyperactive behavior disorders. Am. J. Psychiat. 130: 210—212, 1973.

90. Whitehead, P., and Clark, L. Effect of lithium carbonate, placebo and thioridazine on hyperactive children. Am. J. Psychiat. 127: 824–825, 1970.

91. Greenhill, L., Rieder, R., Wender, P., Buchsbaum, M., and Zahn, T. Lithium carbonate in the treatment of hyperactive children. Arch. Gen. Psychiat. 28: 636–640, 1973.

92. Werry, J., and Aman, M. Methylphenidate and haloperidol in children. Arch. Gen. Psychiat. 32: 790–795, 1975.

93. Pasamanick, B. Anticonvulsant drug therapy of behavior problem children with abnormal electroencephalograms. Arch. Neurol. Psychiat. 65: 752–766, 1951.

94. Looker, A., and Conners, C. Diphenylhydantoin in children with severe temper tantrums. Arch. Gen. Psychiat. 23: 80–89, 1970.

95. Conners, C., Kramer, R., Rothschild, G., Schwartz, L., and Stone, A. Treatment of young delinquent boys with diphenylhydantoin sodium and methylphenidate: A controlled comparison. Arch. Gen. Psychiat. 24: 156–160, 1971.

96. Livingston, S., Kajdi, L., and Bridge, E. The use of Benzedrine and Dexedrine sulfate in the treatment of epilepsy. J. Pediat. 32: 490–494, 1948.

97. Eisenberg, L. The management of the hyperkinetic child. Develop. Med. Child Neurol. 8: 593–598, 1966.

98. Boudelle, M. My study of Tegretol in the treatment of epilepsy, in C. Winc (Ed.), Tegretol in Epilepsy, pp. 80–88. Manchester, England: C. Nicholls and Company, 1972.

99. Monroe, R. Episodic Behavioral Disorders. Cambridge, Mass.: Harvard University Press, 1970.

100. Azcarate, C. Minor tranquilizers in the treatment of aggression. J. Nerv. Ment. Dis. 160: 100–107, 1975.

101. Sheard, M. Lithium in the treatment of aggression. J. Nerv. Ment. Dis. 160: 108–118, 1975.

102. Buchsbaum, M., and Wender, P. Average evoked responses in normal and minimally brain dysfunctioned children treated with amphetamine. Arch. Gen. Psychiat. 29: 764–770, 1973.

103. Weber, B., and Sulzbacher, S. Use of CNS stimulant medication in averaged electroencephalic audiometry with children with MBD. J. Learn. Disabil. 8: 300–303, 1975.

104. Medication for hyperkinetic children. Pediatrics 55: 560–562, 1975.

105. Schnackenberg, R. Caffeine as a substitute for schedule II stimulants in hyperkinetic children. Am. J. Psychiat. 130: 796–798, 1973.

106. Gross, M. Caffeine in the treatment of children with minimal brain dysfunction or hyperkinetic syndrome. Psychosomatics 16: 26–27, 1975.

107. Conners, C. A placebo-crossover study of caffeine treatment of hyperkinetic children. Int. J. Ment. Health 4: 132–143, 1975.

108. Huestis, R., Arnold, L., and Smeltzer, D. Caffeine versus methylphenidate and d-amphetamine in minimal brain dysfunction: A double-blind comparison. Am. J. Psychiat. 132: 868–870, 1975.

109. Schleifer, M., Weiss, G., Cohen, N., Elman, M., Cvejic, H., and Kruger, E. Hyperactivity in preschoolers and the effect of Methylphenidate. Am. J. Orthopsychiat. 45: 38–50, 1975.

110. Conners, C. Controlled trial of methylphenidate in preschool children with minimal brain dysfunction. Int. J. Ment. Health 4: 61–74, 1975.

111. Weiss, G., Minde, K., Douglas, V., Werry, J., and Sykes, D. Comparison of the effects of chlorpromazine, dextroamphetamine, and methylphenidate on the behavior and intellectual functioning of hyperactive children. Can. Med. Assoc. J. 104: 20–25, 1971.

112. Conners, C. Rating scales to use in drug studies in children. Psychopharm. Bull. Spec. Issue (Pharmacotherapy of Children) 24–84, 1973.

113. Zahn, T., Abate, F., Little, B., and Wender, P. Minimal brain dysfunction, stimulant drugs and autonomic nervous system activity. Arch. Gen. Psychiat. 32: 381–387, 1975.

114. Hill, D. Amphetamine in psychopathic states. Br. J. Addict. 44: 50–54, 1947.

115. Kalant, O. The Amphetamines: Toxicity and Addiction. Springfield, Ill.: Charles C Thomas, Publisher, 1966.

116. Greenberg, L., and Lipman, R. Pharmacotherapy of hyperactive children: Current practices. Clin. Proc. Child. Hosp. D. C., 27: 101–105, 1971.

117. Stephen, K., Sprague, R., and Werry, J. Drug treatment of hyperactive children in Chicago; in R. Sprague (Principal Investigator), Detailed Progress Report of Grant MH18909, 1970–73, pp. 1–13. Urbana, Ill.: Children's Research Center, March 1973.

118. Haig, J., Schroeder, C., and Schroeder, S. Effects of methylphenidate on hyperactive children's sleep. Psychopharmacologia 37: 185–188, 1974.

119. Feinbeig, I., Hibi, S., Braun, M., Cavness, C., Westerman, G., and Small, A. Sleep amphetamine effects in MBDS and normal subjects. Arch. Gen. Psychiat. 31: 723–731, 1974.

120. Kay, D. Sleep and some psychoactive drugs. Psychosomatics 14: 108–118, 1973.

121. Sprague, R., and Sleator, E. What is the proper dose of stimulant drugs in children. Int. J. Ment. Health 4: 75–104, 1975.

122. Allen, R., and Safer, D. Psychoactive drugs: Dose calculations. Read at the Fifth World Congress of Psychiatry, Mexico City, Mexico, 1971.

123. Millichap, J. Drugs in the management of minimal brain dysfunction. Ann. N.Y. Acad. Sci. 205: 321–334, 1973.

124. Werry, J. Treatment, in J. Menkes and R. Schain (Eds.), Learning Disorders in Children, pp. 68–69. Columbus, Ohio: Ross Laboratories, 1971.

125. Chapel, J. The hyperactive child. Missouri Med. 70: 768–774, 1973.

126. Hartlage, L. Effects of chlorpromazine on learning. Psychol. Bull. 64: 235–245, 1965.

127. Fawcett, J., and Siomopoulos, V. Dextroamphetamine response as a possible predictor of improvement with tricyclic therapy in depression. Arch. Gen. Psychiat. 25: 247–255, 1971.
128. Fann, W. Some clinically important interactions of psychotropic drugs. Southern Med. J. 66: 661–665, 1973.
129. Perel, J., Black, N., Wharton, R., and Malitz, S. Inhibition of imipramine metabolism by methylphenidate. Fed. Proc. 28: 418, 1969.
130. Kupferberg, H., Jeffery, W., and Hunninghake, D. Effects of methylphenidate on plasma anticonvulsant levels. Clin. Pharmacol. Ther. 13: 201–204, 1972.

Chapter 4   Clinical
Forms and
Evaluative Tests

There are forms that allow systematic access to valuable information and save time in the evaluation of hyperactivity in children. Also, there are standardized tests that can provide quick, reliable, and useful measures of the academic level of children. The use of such forms and tests will be discussed and examples presented.

CLASSROOM TEACHERS' BEHAVIOR CHECK LIST

A number of classroom teachers' behavior check lists (BCL) have been helpful in the identification of HA children (*1–4*). These check lists all cover essentially the same territory, but differ in length, specificity, and research support (*5, 6*). Most are a few pages in length. The most widely used and researched form is the 96-item check list devised by Conners (*1*).

The BCL presented in Chart 1 is an abbreviated form designed to fit on one 8½ X 11 inch page. Its brevity is an important asset because resistance to forms increases in proportion to their length. The initial few items on the BCL were adapted from the ratings of Werry and Quay (*7*); the rest were adapted from the work of Conners (*1*). The BCL allows 4 degrees of deviance (a little bit, moderately, quite a bit, and extremely). All the items are written as negative attributes except item III-4, "overly anxious to please."

On the BCL on Chart 1, there are a number of items characteristically checked as "moderately" to "extremely" in degree for the HA child not on medication. Those items fall into clusters (*1*) the major three of which are: 1) the hyperactive dimension (items I-1, I-2, I-4, and I-10) the inattention dimension (items I-5, I-6, and I-12), and 3) the aggression dimension (items I-7, II-6, and III-1). The hyperactivity items must be

Chart 1. Classroom teacher's behavior check list

Name of student ——————————— Date ———
Grade and/or subject ——————————————
Teacher's name ——————————————————

How many hours per day do you see this student? ————————
How many months have you had this child in your class? ————

I. Classroom behavior	Not at all	A little bit	Moder-ately	Quite a bit	Extre-mely
1. Makes disruptive noise (tapping, humming, etc.)					
2. Leaves seat (unexcused)					
3. Speaks out of turn					
4. Disturbs others (e.g., provokes others nearby)					
5. Does not attend to classroom instruction					
6. Does not complete expected classroom work					
7. Gets into fights					
8. Sad or sullen					
9. Nervous or tense					
10. Restless or overactive					
11. Overly sensitive (easily hurt)					
12. Has short span of attention					
13. Becomes easily frustrated					
14. Has temper outbursts					
II. Group participation					
1. Isolates himself from other children					
2. Is unaccepted by the group					
3. Gets pushed around					
4. Inconsiderate and selfish with other children					
5. Difficulties with the opposite sex					
6. Influences others to misbehave					
III. Response to authority					
1. Openly defiant					
2. Passively uncooperative					
3. Demands teacher's attention					
4. Overly anxious to please					

continued

Chart 1—*Continued*

IV. **Other Behavior**—Circle appropriate ones. Circle twice if prominent.
cries   fearful   lazy   wetting   tics   sloppy   steals   tattles
perfectionistic   suspicious   lies   bizarre   poor coordination
submissive   bullies   destructive   attendance problem

V. **Teacher's estimate of student achievement**

      A. Arithmetic (grade level) ―――――――――

      B. Reading (grade level) ―――――――――

VI. **Additional teacher's comments:**

―――――――――――――――――――――――――――

―――――――――――――――――――――――――――

checked at least "moderately" in degree for the diagnosis to be actively considered. The aggression category items are variably present so that their absence does not rule out the diagnosis.

The BCL can be scored for purposes of a treatment evaluation. For this, the items most diagnostic of HA (items I-1, I-2, I-4, I-5, I-6, I-7, I-10, I-12, III-6, and III-1) can be scored as 1 for "moderate," 2 for "quite a bit," 3 for "extremely," and totalled. The percentage of improvement can be obtained by the following formula:

$$\% \text{ improvement} = \frac{(\text{pretreatment BCL score}) - (\text{on treatment BCL score})}{(\text{pretreatment BCL score})} \times 100$$

Placebo responses can and do range up to 50% improvement. The vast majority of BCL treatment responses over 50% improvement, however, reflect a good drug response. Responses over 80% can be called dramatic responses; they are almost never attained with placebo, and are not commonly obtained with drugs other than stimulants.

Presented in Chart 2 is a short form version of Conners' 96-item BCL. It is a 10-item BCL listing only those items customarily sensitive to stimulant medication. It makes a quick assessment of the effect of medication possible. Its lack of depth, however, is a major drawback. An example of this limitation would be an HA child who improves appreciably in his behavioral responses with medication, but not in his impaired social skills. With the short form, the therapist would remain ignorant of the child's persistent social ineptitude in the classroom.

Teachers' behavior checklists have a satisfactory reliability; their inter-rater agreement averages $r = 0.7-0.8$ (5, 6). Additional support for teacher ratings of hyperactivity is their good correlation (0.6) to the measurement of hyperactivity by mechanical devices (8, 9). Furthermore, check list ratings on the BCL (e.g., that compiled by Conners) separate regular classroom students clearly from deviant populations (10, 11).

In elementary school, the major BCL rating should be obtained from the classroom teacher who oversees the child most of the day. In the secondary grades (seventh and up), checklists from two to three of the major subject teachers will usually suffice. The inter-rater agreement between a teacher and her aide is of course greater than between teachers who each have the child for only one 50-min period daily (a). Thus, in the secondary grades (where children have up to seven teachers), teacher inter-rater agreement in respect to hyperactivity lessens. Other factors that account for variability in teacher recordings of hyperactivity are: 1) the child tends to be less attentive to subject matter he finds more difficult

Chart 2. Abbreviated teacher questionnaire[a]

Patient name —————————————————

Teacher's observations
   Information obtained —————————— by ————————————
                        Month   Day   Year

Observation	Degree of activity			
	Not at all	Just a little	Pretty much	Very much
1. Restless or overactive				
2. Excitable, impulsive				
3. Disturbs other children				
4. Fails to finish things he starts, short attention span				
5. Constantly fidgeting				
6. Inattentive, easily distracted				
7. Demands must be met immediately; easily frustrated				
8. Cries often and easily				
9. Mood changes quickly and drastically				
10. Temper outbursts, explosive and unpredictable behavior				

Other observations of teacher (use reverse side if more space is required)

—————————————————————————————

—————————————————————————————

—————————————————————————————

[a]From Conners (6) with permission.

(e.g., he might attend less to language arts than to math); 2) the HA student may behave more poorly in class A than in class B because the teacher in class A has less classroom control; 3) eighth and ninth grade teachers show more variability in their reporting of hyperactivity because this symptom notably decreases around age 15 to 16 (*12*). (More intense phenomena are naturally more reliably rated.)

PARENT RATING SCALES

Parent rating scales of their child's behavior are used less frequently to identify and quantify hyperactivity than are teacher ratings. There are two good reasons for this: 1) parental ratings are less reliable ($r = 0.6–0.7$) than teacher ratings (*6*); 2) HA children are usually less hyperactive at home than they are at school. Parent ratings are still useful, however, particularly when they support teacher measures. Generally, the agreement between the parent and the teacher ratings of hyperactivity is good (*13, 14*).

The parent rating scale of hyperactivity in widest use is the Werry-Weiss-Peters scale (*15*), Chart 3. The scale is mainly of value in evaluating treatment efficacy. It must be borne in mind, however, that this measure only evaluates one dimension, hyperactivity.

Broader parent rating scales are quite useful in screening for a behavioral and emotional disturbance. One is presented in Chart 4. It was adapted from the longer form of Conners (*6*). It contains four major hyperactive-inattentive items (can't sit still or fidgets, constantly changing activity, won't match TV for long, fails to finish things he starts) and numerous aggressive items (e.g., fights, loses temper easily, etc.). Hyperactive children also score high on the "talks excessively" and "excitable-impulsive" items. Thus, items 1, 3, 4, 8, 12, 16, 21, and 22 of Chart 4 are most commonly checked as "moderately" to "very much" in degree for hyperactivity.

When school reports of HA are positive for 2 or 3 years consecutively, but parent reports of the child's home behavior are negative, it may indicate that a parent is denying the problem. ("I don't have problems; the school does.") (*b*). In many such cases, when that parent's spouse is interviewed individually, he will provide the expected background history. Thus, a negative parent report should by no means rule out the diagnosis of HA.

THE PARENT INFORMATION FORMS

Most child mental health clinics use application forms. These should include: 1) a child and family information section (see Chart 5); 2) a

Chart 3. Werry-Weiss-Peters activity scale[a]

	No	Some	Much
During meals			
Up and down at table	—	—	—
Interrupts without regard	—	—	—
Wriggling	—	—	—
Fiddles with things	—	—	—
Talks excessively	—	—	—
Television			
Gets up and down during program	—	—	—
Wriggles	—	—	—
Manipulates objects or body	—	—	—
Talks incessantly	—	—	—
Interrupts	—	—	—
Doing homework			
Gets up and down	—	—	—
Wriggles	—	—	—
Manipulates objects or body	—	—	—
Talks incessantly	—	—	—
Requires adult supervision or attendance	—	—	—
Play			
Inability for quiet play	—	—	—
Constantly changing activity	—	—	—
Seeks parental attention	—	—	—
Talks excessively	—	—	—
Disrupts other's play	—	—	—
Sleep			
Difficulty settling down for sleep	—	—	—
Inadequate amount of sleep	—	—	—
Restless during sleep	—	—	—
Behavior away from home (except at school)			
Restlessness during travel	—	—	—
Restlessness during shopping (includes touching everything)	—	—	—
Restlessness during church/movies	—	—	—
Restlessness while visiting friends, relatives, etc.	—	—	—
School behavior			
Up and down	—	—	—
Fidgets, wriggles, touches	—	—	—
Interrupts teacher or other children excessively	—	—	—
Constantly seeks teacher's attention	—	—	—
Subtotal score	X 0	X 1	X 2

[a]From Werry (15) with permission of *Pediatric Clinics of North America*.

Chart 4. Parent checklist of the child's behavior[a]

Name of child _____

Date _____ _____

	Not at all	Some-times	Moder-ately	Quite a bit	Very much
1. Can't sit still or fidgets					
2. Talks back to adults					
3. Won't watch TV for long					
4. Loses temper easily					
5. Bullies others					
6. Refuses to obey parent rules at home					
7. Feelings easily hurt					
8. Fights					
9. Wets the bed					
10. Fearful (e.g., of the dark)					
11. Seeks help for things he can do alone (e.g., tying shoes)					
12. Talks excessively					
13. Lacks close friends					
14. Unaffectionate					
15. Lies					
16. Fails to finish things he starts					
17. Steals					
18. Fails to return home on time					
19. Cries easily					
20. Lets himself get pushed around in play					
21. Excitable, impulsive					
22. Constantly changing activity					
23. Destructive to property					
24. Demanding					

Also, please circle appropriate behaviors (circle twice if prominent): Tics, nightmares, fire setting, soiling, trouble with the police, excessive worrying, cruelty to animals, suicide threats, overeating, sexual difficulties, truancy, afraid of going to school, pouting and sulking, daydreaming, running away from home, trouble sleeping, sadness, clumsiness, speech problems.

[a]Adapted from Conners (6).

Chart 5. Child and family information form

Child's name ——————————— Birth date ————— Age ———
Address (street) ————————————————————————
Town and zip code ——————————————————————
                                        Length of residence
Place of birth ———————————————— at present address ———
Home phone ——————— Any other phone to reach you ———
School ——————————————————— Grade ——————
Present family information (current family responsible for child)
Father's name ——————————— Age ——— Education ———
Mother's name ——————————— Age ——— Education ———
Is father employed? ——— What type of work? ——————
    Where? ——————————————— How long? ———
Is mother employed? ——— What type of work: ——————
    Where? ——————— Full time? ——— How long? ———
Is either parent a step or adoptive parent? ——————
Are the natural parents still married? —— Separated? —— Divorced? ——
Circle the name of your religion:
            Catholic   Protestant   Jewish   Other   None
List all children in family (living or deceased)

| | | School grade or |
Name	Age	vocation

Others in home (age and relationship)

parental permission form (to authorize the request for previous relevant school, medical, and social work reports); 3) a release-of-information form; 4) a background information section (see Chart 6); 5) a developmental and medical history section (see Chart 7); 6) a parent check list (see Chart 4). The last three aspects of the application material are particularly pertinent for HA. The parent check list has already been discussed.

It is important to obtain background treatment information from the parents (Chart 6), and based on this, to request reports from previous institutions and therapists. This is most helpful if obtained before the child and parents are interviewed.

The Developmental and Medical History Section (Chart 7) can save a few minutes of questions that result in "No" answers. It also guarantees a degree of completeness in the information gathering. Of course, "Yes" answers need further exploration by the clinician.

SCHOOL INFORMATION FORM

A school information form is designed to obtain pertinent behavioral and academic data from the child's school folder. What is available will vary from school system to school system (and to a lesser extent from school to school). The form in Chart 8 covers the basic school data which is needed and is generally available.

Some children have a large school folder with reports that are very useful clinically. Examples of such material are: psychological reports, medical reports, special education reports, school social worker or pupil personnel worker reports, school team reports, past teacher comments, old report cards, group I.Q. and achievement results, etc. These should be seen by, or reviewed for, the clinician if the child's school difficulties led to the mental health referral.

As a rule, most child guidance clinics do not coordinate their services with school personnel even though most clinic referrals emanate from the school (*16, 17*). An exchange of correspondence with the sharing of information and/or recommendations is a modest first step to bridge this gap. Also, the clinician should meet with the school personnel who initiated the referral and their mutual therapeutic and educational services should be interlaced. This procedure is an example of program collaboration.

SIMPLE ACHIEVEMENT TESTS

It is useful to have an achievement assessment for every child referred because of school problems inasmuch as most also have learning delays (*18*).

Chart 6. Background information section

1. What are your child's major problems?

2. Have you had any help with the behavior or developmental problems of your child from a social agency, a clinic, a private doctor or a psychologist. If so, please write below the name of the doctor and/or the agency and the name of the person who provided the assistance.

3. Has your child now or in the past been on medication for an extended period of time? Please be specific as to the name, the dose, the duration of treatment, etc.

4. Who is your child's doctor? ——————————————————————
   When did he last examine your child? ——————————————————
5. Has your child been hospitalized at any time? If so, answer below:

   Age   Reason   Length of stay
   _____

   _____

6. Have your child's brothers and sisters had any behavior, emotional, learning or speech problems? Please specify.

   _____

   _____

7. Is there other information about your child or family you feel will be helpful to us?

Chart 7. Development and medical history section

Please check the following developmental and medical variations that apply to your child. If any do, please clarify the matter with further details in the space at the end of the form.

A. The pregnancy; did you have the following:
    1. Swelling of the fingers or high blood pressure?   Yes___ No___
    2. Vaginal bleeding in the first or last 3 months?   Yes___ No___
    3. Other complications of pregnancy?   Yes___ No___
    4. Drugs other than vitamins or iron during
       pregnancy?   Yes___ No___
    5. A pregnancy of *under* 38 weeks or *over* 42 weeks
       (term is 38–42 weeks)?   Yes___ No___
B. The delivery; did you have the following:
    1. A labor of under 2 or over 16 hours?   Yes___ No___
    2. Any unusual problems during the delivery?   Yes___ No___
C. The child's early hospital course
    1. Was your child's birth weight under 5½ lbs.?   Yes___ No___
    2. Did your child have trouble breathing at birth?   Yes___ No___
    3. Did your child remain more than 5 days in the
       hospital?   Yes___ No___
    4. Was the child placed in an incubator?   Yes___ No___
D. Medical problems; did your child have
    1. Early failure to gain weight or malnutrition?   Yes___ No___
    2. Seizures or convulsions?   Yes___ No___
    3. Meningitis or encephalitis?   Yes___ No___
    4. A skull fracture or unconsciousness after head
       injury?   Yes___ No___
    5. Lead poisoning?   Yes___ No___
E. Temperament in the preschool years; did your child at
    age 2–5 show the following:
    1. A short interest or attention span?   Yes___ No___
    2. Restlessness?   Yes___ No___
    3. Frequent temper outbursts?   Yes___ No___
    4. Destructiveness with toys?   Yes___ No___
F. Developmental delays; did your child first learn to
    1. Walk after 14 months?   Yes___ No___
    2. Speak single words after 14 months?   Yes___ No___
    3. Speak in sentences after his 3rd birthday?   Yes___ No___
    4. Complete his toilet training after his 3rd
       birthday?   Yes___ No___
    5. Ride a tricycle after his 3rd birthday?   Yes___ No___
G. Learning skills; how old was he when
    1. He knew his colors?   _____ years
    2. Everyone would understand his speech?   _____ years
    3. He stopped reversals (d/b) in writing?   _____ years

---

continued

Chart 7—*Continued*

---

    4. He would sit through a full half-hour of T.V. cartoons?   ————— years

    5. He could listen to a story for more than 10 minutes?   ————— years

H. Family and social history

    1. Did either parent have a childhood learning or reading difficulty?   Yes—— No——

    2. Did either parent have serious behavior difficulties in childhood?   Yes—— No——

    3. Any mental or physical illness of note in the child's family or close relatives (e.g., epilepsy, mental retardation, physical deformity, alcoholism)?   Yes—— No——

    4. Serious marital disagreements on discipline of children?   Yes—— No——

    5. Any history of parental separation or divorce?   Yes—— No——

    6. Any recently upsetting events for the child?   Yes—— No——

    7. Any major financial problems for the parents?   Yes—— No——

Additional information or details:

_____

_____

_____

_____

_____

_____

_____

_____

_____

_____

_____

Chart 8. Basic school information

Name of child _____
Birth date _____
School _____

To the School Counselor or Nurse:

School background information is quite important for our pediatric/ psychiatric evaluation of the above-named child. A parental release for this information has been signed.

Please complete this form. If additional pertinent information is present in the child's school folder (as a psychological, medical, or special education report), please photocopy them and return them with this form.

I. What have been this child's main difficulties in school?

_____

_____

_____

_____

II. Intelligence:
Individual I.Q. score: _____ Date _____ Type of test _____
Total Score _____ Verbal _____ Performance _____
Group I.Q. scores:
Date _____ Total I.Q. Score _____
Date _____ Total I.Q. Score _____

III. Achievement scores:

		Reading grade	Arithmetic grade
Date ____ Test ____		equivalent ____	equivalent ____
Date ____ Test ____		equivalent ____	equivalent ____

IV. Past school history (Please summarize notes of previous years, as, for 1968—fearful of teacher, injurious to others, short attention span):

19_____

19_____

19_____

19_____

19_____

V. School health record summary:
Note any visual, hearing, speech problems, seizure disorders, physical handicaps, etc. _____

_____

Any medical treatment _____

_____

Any record of medication _____ What and when _____

_____

Additional health comments _____

_____

continued

Chart 8—*Continued*

VI. Other information
Please note and, if necessary, comment upon the following: reversals in writing, memory or comprehension difficulties, speech difficulty, a family history of reading disability or low intelligence ____

_____
_____

Frequent absences ___ When ___ School retention ____ When ____
Note speech correction, corrective or remedial reading, special class placement. _____
Any suspensions? _____ When and for what? _____

_____

VII. Additional information and impressions:
_____
_____
_____

Date _____ _____
Name of school official completing this form

_____   _____
Title   Phone number

These learning delays are usually not apparent in conversation or verbal inquiry and, unless evaluated, could be overlooked.

Group achievement tests are frequently an unsatisfactory means of assessing the academic level of learning disabled students, although they are useful for the achieving child (c). Teacher estimates are a far better means of estimating the academic level of learning-delayed children, although they can be up to a year or 2 off. In cases of doubt, the individual test is best. Two standard, quick, individual achievement tests are the Wide Range Achievement Test (WRAT) and the Peabody Individual Achievement Test (PIAT). The WRAT (19) is the most used, but for younger and duller children, the PIAT (20) appears better. The important test sections of these tests are the reading and arithmetic parts. Each section takes up to 10 minutes. They can be administered, after a short period of instruction, by guidance counselors, nurses, nonprofessional volunteers, etc.

Word lists are an alternative, more rapid, way to estimate reading skills (21). They do not test comprehension and the clinican can be misled if the child pronounces the words but does not understand what he reads. For the clinican short of time, standard word lists and their grade level are available in Chart 9.

Arithmetic problems by grade level are available in Chart 10. It is important to be aware that most reading-impaired children are also impaired in their arithmetic skills (although usually to a lesser degree) (22).

VISUAL MOTOR TESTS

Figure 1 presents the most utilized visual-motor test, the Bender-Gestalt Test (23, 24). To obtain a general measure of visual-motor skill, it is not necessary for the hurried clinician to ask the child to duplicate every item on this test. Items A, 4, 7, and 8 are usually simplest to administer. Rough norms for the Bender-Gestalt test are shown in Figure 2.

AUDITORY MEMORY SKILLS

The simplest test of auditory memory is a test of the immediate recall of digits. Digits are read off at a rate of 1 per second and the child is asked to repeat them back (usually at a rapid rate). Thus, the evaluator says 8 . . . 3 . . . 7 . . . 9 . . . 4 and the child repeats 83794. The average adult can uaually recall 7 digits. The average 5–6-year old can recall 4, 7–9-year old 5, and 10–12-year old 6. Poor auditory memory skills commonly coexist with reading difficulty (25).

Chart 9. Standard word lists by grade level

Primer	1st grade	2nd grade	3rd grade
see	wish	town	praise
and	good	drink	several
go	name	young	journey
can	show	smile	bench
play	live	river	destroy
not	dark	lunch	excuse
dog	thank	please	measure

4th grade	5th grade	6th grade	7th grade
silent	splendid	commercial	enumerate
machine	escaped	necessity	contemptuous
succeed	merchant	spectators	condescend
surface	ambition	persuasive	industrious
wrecked	especially	responsible	assumptions
region	adventure	excitement	malignant
courage	marriage	circumstances	dominion

Chart 10. Arithmetic problems by grade level

1st grade	2nd grade

1st grade
$4 - 1 =$

$7 + 3 =$

$8 - 3 =$

2nd grade
$$35$$
$$+17$$

$$32$$
$$23$$
$$+41$$

$$13$$
$$- 5$$

3rd grade
$$35$$
$$-17$$

$$451$$
$$167$$
$$+234$$

$7 \times 2 =$

4th grade
$28 \div 4 =$

$6 \times 15 =$

$$370$$
$$- 82$$

5th grade
$$63.15$$
$$-7.52$$

$$4\overline{)132.0}$$

$$96$$
$$\times 7$$

6th grade
$5/7 - 2/7 =$

$$16\overline{)428}$$

$$8.96$$
$$\times 13$$

7th grade
$1/5 \times 20 =$

$$1/2$$
$$-1/3$$

$$37\overline{)5782}$$

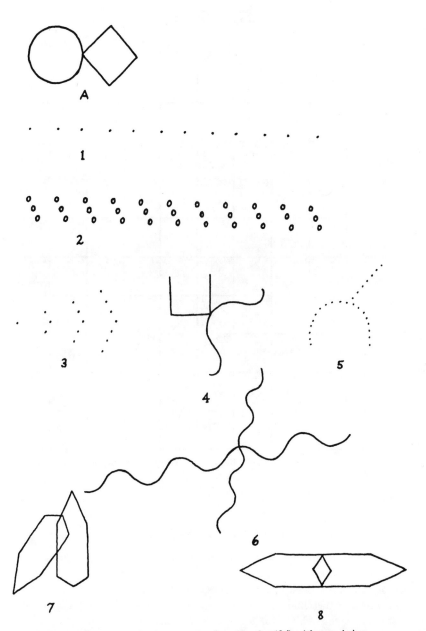

Figure 1. Bender-Gestalt visual motor test, from Bender (*24*) with permission.

TEST FIGURES

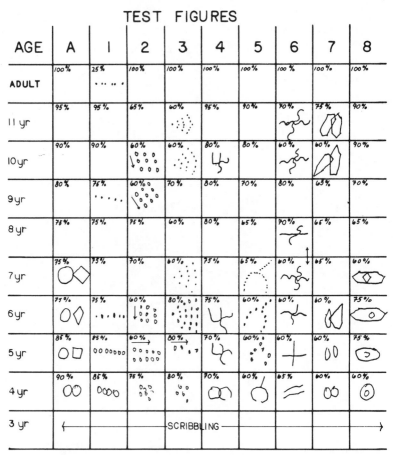

Figure 2. Maturational norms for the Bender-Gestalt visual motor test, from Bender (*24*) with permission.

DRAW-A-PERSON (HARRIS-GOODENOUGH)

The child is simply asked to draw a person. When the drawing is scored relative to age norms, it can be viewed as a simple measure of I.Q. (*26*). It can also serve as a crude index of maturity and of visual-motor skill, and it can reflect the child's sexual identification and self-concept. Further still, it can be the vehicle for a story by the child. Figure 3 presents selected drawings of HA and non-HA children.

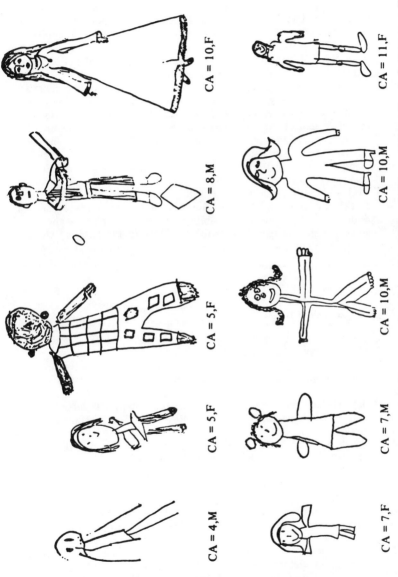

Figure 3. Examples of Draw-A-Person test. *Top row:* selected non-HA children (children of the authors); *bottom row:* HA children.

NOTES

a. Most reliable, of course, in behavior ratings are the scores of independent, trained raters who record the child's classroom behavior for
short periods at regular intervals. These ratings yield a reliability of
0.9 (7, 27).
b. It may also indicate that the child's hyperactivity is mild and is clearly
brought out only in the stress of the classroom.
c. Iowa test (ITBS) scores of students with prominent reading deficits are
usually erroneously high because these tests have a baseline that is
above the preprimer level and because the test scores are not corrected to cancel the advantages of random successful guessing. On
the fifth grade Iowa's, the baseline is the 1.1 grade level, and with
random successful guessing on this multiple choice, group-
administered achievement test, the child will score at the 3.4
grade level. On the seventh grade Iowa test, the baseline is 2.0 grade
level and with random successful guessing, the student will score
at the 4.8 grade level (28). Thus, in one seventh grade class of
450, 25 students of average ability achieved at or below the third
grade (frustration) level in reading on individual tests, (29), whereas
on the ITBS group scores, only 2 of the children scored this low.

LITERATURE CITED

1. Conners, C. A teacher rating scale for use in drug studies with
children. Am. J. Psychiat. 126: 884–888, 1969.
2. Rutter, M. A children's behavior questionnaire for completion by
teachers: preliminary findings. J. Child Psychol. Psychiat. 8: 1–11,
1967.
3. Quay, H., and Peterson, D. Manual for the Behavior Problem Checklist. Champaign, Ill.: Children's Research Center, University of
Illinois, 1967.
4. Spivack, G., and Swift, M. Devereux Elementary School Rating Scale
Manual. Devon, Pa.: The Devereux Foundation, 1967.
5. Spivack, G., and Swift, M. The classroom behavior of children: A
critical review of teacher administered rating scales. J. Spec. Ed. 7:
55–89, 1973.
6. Conners, C. Rating Scales for Use in Drug Studies with Children.
Psychopharm. Bull. Spec. Issue (Pharmacotherapy of Children)
24–84, 1973.
7. Werry, J., and Quay, H. Observing the classroom behavior of elementary school children. Except. Child. 35: 461–470, 1969.
8. Victor, J., Halverson, C., and Buczkowski, H. Objective measures
of first and second grade boys free play and teacher ratings
on a behavior problem checklist. Psychol. Schools 4: 439–443,
1973.

9. Halverson, C., and Waldrop, M. The relations of mechanically recorded activity level to varieties of preschool play behavior. Child Develop. 44: 678–681, 1973.
10. Kupietz, S., Bialer, I., and Winsberg, B. A behavior rating scale for assessing improvement in behaviorally deviant children: A preliminary investigation. Am. J. Psychiat. 128: 1432–1436, 1972.
11. Sprague, R., Christensen, D., and Werry, J. Experimental psychology and stimulant drugs, in C. Conners (Ed.), Clinical Use of Stimulant Drugs in Children, pp. 141–164. Amsterdam: Excerpta Medica, 1974.
12. Safer, D., and Allen, R. Stimulant drug treatment of hyperactive adolescents. Dis. Nerv. Syst. 36: 454–457, 1975.
13. Zrull, J., Westman, J., Arthur, B., and Rice, P. An evaluation of methodology used in the study of psychoactive drugs for children. J. Am. Acad. Child Psychiat. 5: 284–291, 1966.
14. Rapoport, J., and Benoit, M. The relation of direct home observation to a clinic evaluation of hyperactive school age boys. J. Child Psychol. Psychiat. 16: 141–147, 1975.
15. Werry, J. Developmental hyperactivity. Pediat. Clin. N. Am. 15: 581–599, 1968.
16. Berkowitz, H. A preliminary assessment of the extent of interactions between child guidance clinics and public schools, in K. O'Leary and S. O'Leary (Eds.), Classroom Management: The Successful Use of Behavior Modification, pp. 77–83. New York: Pergamon Press, 1972.
17. Loney, J., and Ordona, T. Using cerebral stimulants to treat minimal brain dysfunction. Am. J. Orthopsychiat. 45: 564–572, 1975.
18. Safer, D. Factors affecting outcome in a school mental health service. Commun. Ment. Health J. 10: 24–32, 1974.
19. Jastak, J., Bijou, S., and Jastak, S. Wide Range Achievement Test. Wilmington, Del.: Guidance Association, 1965.
20. Dunn, L., and Markwardt, F. Peabody Individual Achievement Test. Circle Pines, Minn.: American Guidance Service, 1970.
21. La Pray, M., and Ross, R. The graded word list: quick guage of reading ability. J. Reading 12: 305–307, 1969.
22. Rutter, M., and Yule, W. The concept of specific reading retardation. J. Child. Psychol. Psychiat. 16: 181–197, 1975.
23. Koppitz, E. The Bender-Gestalt Test for Young Children. New York: Grune and Stratton, 1963.
24. Bender, L. A Visual Motor Gestalt Test and Its Clinical Use: Research Monograph No. 3. New York: American Orthopsychiatric Association, 1938.
25. Rabinovitch, R. Reading problems in children: Definitions and classifications, in A. Kenny and V. Kenny (Eds.), Dyslexia: Diagnosis and Treatment of Reading Disorders, pp. 1–10. St. Louis: C. V. Mosby, 1968.
26. Harris, D. Children's Drawings as Measures of Intellectual Maturity: A Revision and Extention of the Goodenough Draw-A-Man Test. New York: Harcourt, Brace and World, 1963.

27. Burns, E., and Lehman, L. An evaluation of summated ratings and pair comparison measures of hyperkinesis. J. Learn. Disabil. 7: 504–507, 1974.

28. Hieronymus, A., and Lindquist, E. Teachers Guide for the Administration, Interpretation and Use of the Iowa Test of Basic Skills: Administrative Guide, Forms 5 and 6. Boston: Houghton-Mifflin Co., 1971.

29. Young, P. and Safer, D. Unpublished data, 1974.

Chapter 5   Home Management of Hyperactivity
Counseling the Parents

PSYCHOTHERAPEUTIC CONSIDERATIONS

The three most frequent formal psychotherapeutic considerations for HA children are: family counseling, individual psychotherapy, and behavioral therapy. Each has a different emphasis relative to the HA child. Parent or family counseling focuses on improving the home environment of the HA child; it has no direct effect on the child's hyperactivity. Individual psychotherapy, although not beneficial for the hyperactive symptom (*1; a*), may help with secondary or associated emotional difficulties these children are prone to experience. The third counseling consideration, behavioral therapy, can be of value for the hyperactivity and for structuring the school and home environments of the child.

This chapter will focus on professional counseling of the parents. Individual psychotherapy is touched on elsewhere (*b*). Behavioral therapy is discussed in a subsequent chapter.

DISCIPLINE: NONPHYSICAL PUNISHMENTS

Home management is stressed with the parents so that they can more adequately structure their environment and be more successful in child rearing. Discipline is an important component of this management. Because discipline is best arranged implemented systematically, the discussion on it will be by steps.

1. First, parental expectations for the child should be clear to him. They should be as explicit as possible, even to the point of being written

out. When the child violates a rule of the home, he should already have had at least a general idea of the consequences of his act. For example, the child knows he can't play ball in the dining area. If he does, he will be sent outside or to his room, or the ball will be confiscated for a short period.

2. The first parental response when a rule violation occurs should be to "stop and think." Was the infraction minor and ignorable, or did the child break a recognized rule of the home (or its equivalent)? If the child muttered unhappily as he went to do a chore, but did the chore, the grumbling can be ignored (c). Was the act primarily the result of the child's boredom or restlessness, or was it spiteful? If it was minor and attributable largely to restlessness, the child can be directed to a new activity and not disciplined. However, if the child had a significant temper outburst, destroyed property in anger, swore at his mother, stayed out beyond his curfew, or did not do his chores, then the parent should respond to the misconduct.

3. The parent's verbal response should be brief. Before taking disciplinary action, it is often helpful to remind the child once (and occasionally twice) about the consequences of continuing his behavior. When the child's behavior is not clearly covered by the usual rules of the house, a short explanation is particularly helpful and considerate. However, yelling, repeated reminders, strongly worded threats, condemnations, moral lectures, and arguing only serve to increase home tension and postpone effective parental action (d).

4. The parental act of discipline should be primarily behavioral. The parent should move steadily toward the child when establishing penalties for an infraction of a rule.

5. The parental response should not initially be physically punitive. The parent should try to fit the penalty to the violation in an appropriate way. For example, if the child stayed out past his curfew, his overtime should be doubled and the total time taken off the next night out. (Weekend and weekday overtime restrictions can be managed separately.)

6. For intrusive infractions, the child should be separated from the area. That is, if the child obstructs, persistently interrupts, rudely demands, or has a temper outburst, he should be placed elsewhere (e.g., his room). By sending the child away from the area where he is obstructive, the parent is responding to the child's behavioral statement, "I'll do here what I choose" and saying "No" in a clear behavioral response.

7. For violations of responsibilities (or chores), the child should lose (perhaps related) home privileges proportionately. (Examples will be presented later in this chapter.)

8. The parent should institute short, time-limited discipline. For intrusive infractions, the parent should place the child in a chair, his bedroom, or outside the front door for 5 minutes or so. For the child over 12, sending him outside is usually most feasible. At night, the bedroom area is uaually better, except when the child damages property there. For preschool hyperactives, a short period of enforced chair-sitting is usually effective.

9. A useful means of insuring an end point in discipline (for the child and parents alike) is to use a stove or cooking timer. (If this is not available, a clock will suffice). The timer should be set for the duration of the discipline. When the stove timer bell rings at 5 minutes, the discipline is over.

10. If the child doesn't get to his disciplinary area or leaves before the time is up, the parent has to physically enforce his mandate. To encourage the child to move in the proper direction or stay where he is told, a squeeze over the collar bone (using the thumb and the index finger) or one swat of the palm across the child's buttocks is usually necessary.

11. It is not useful to extend the duration of penalty if the child repeatedly defies a short one imposed, or if the penalty doesn't appear to be achieving its effect. Prolonged penalties are difficult to enforce, provoke increased retaliatory feelings in the child, and are not likely to be more effective than short ones.

PHYSICAL PUNISHMENT

Flexible parents soon find out, by a trial and error process, that a primary dependence on physical punishment is seldom effective with hyperactive children who misbehave (e). They soon find out that nonphysical penalties are more useful for hyperactive children. Further disadvantages of a heavy reliance on physical punishment for the HA child are: it often engenders a great deal of anxiety; it usually produces more retaliatory feelings than avoidance behavior or a reappraisal of misconduct; and it provides adult training for the child in physical assault, which the child can carry over to his peers.

In addition, some parents who use physical punishment as their sole means of behavioral management delay its implementation so long that they are unable to respond moderately to the child when they act. Some act too vigorously and then withdraw, overcome with guilt and fear, conveying helpless frustration. Others simply freeze up and withdraw at that point, fearing the use of excessive force. In either event, the ultimate parental message the child receives in these situations is a functionally permissive one. (A similar result occurs when one parent's punishment is followed by the other parent's attempt to compensate by permissiveness.)

Nevertheless, punishment still has its place for children and for HA children in particular. When the child is physically challenging (e.g., violating disciplinary restriction, shoving a parent), the parent has little recourse than to demonstrate that he can physically enforce the rules. To convey this to an elementary school youngster, a belt is seldom necessary; simple physical contact (such as a squeeze) will usually suffice. If the parent is not physically stronger than his physically defiant teenager and is hit or pushed by his offspring when enforcing a rule, a physical response by the spouse or a call to the Department of Juvenile Services may be helpful to communicate to the child that the parent (with other adult assistance) will ultimately control the situation.

THE LIMITATIONS OF DISCIPLINE

There is no discipline program that impressively alters the general behavior pattern characteristic of the vast majority of HA children. Whereas the use of extreme and prolonged home discipline will coerce some children to conform quietly, it will not do so for those who are hyperactive (*f*). Discipline will not lessen the HA child's general level of restlessness, nor will it notably alter his frustration tolerance or immaturity.

The systematic home policy of explicit rules and short discipline described in this section is advocated because it is simpler, more enforceable, and results in less parental frustration than prolonged and punitive policies. Implementing the disciplinary program defined here will also decrease home tensions and it can lessen marital disharmony over child rearing.

HOME RESPONSIBILITIES

The specification by parents of their children's chores and responsibilities, with a timed deadline, is helpful so that the children know (at least a minimum of) what is expected of them during the week. By behaviorally defining their expectations for their children, parents in effect make explicit the important rules of the home. In the process, minor items are ignored, thus centering the focus on these major rules and on their enforcement.

If the child doesn't clean the dishes by, for example, 7 p.m., he can lose ½ hour of prime television time, such as from 8:30 to 9:00 p.m. If the child doesn't clean up his bedroom by, for example, 7 p.m., all the misplaced items in his room can then be placed haphazardly in a cardboard box, which can then be deposited in the laundry room. Or, until the child cleans his room, he can be prevented from sitting down to eat breakfast (assuming he likes breakfast) or from going out to play (on nonschool days). Or, for every ½ hour the child overstays his night time curfew, he loses 1 hour of play time after supper the next night (double time for overtime). Essentially, privileges are appropriately tied to responsibilities to behaviorally convey the principle of the work ethic and to more judiciously enforce the child's responsibilities. Using a set time as an end point and focusing on major necessary responsibilities makes enforcement easier and more definable.

If the child doesn't do his chores on time (a gentle reminder or two is all right here), the enforcement proceeds without much note. The parent does the chore and the child loses the privilege. Such quiet enforcement puts the parent in the position of a responsible authority and helps to abort the frequent problem of increasingly angry, repetitive, functionally permissive, parental reminders.

SUPERVISION

Often, it is necessary to support parents to lessen their social restrictions on the HA child. Many parents develop a sensitivity to frequent complaints by neighbors and the school relative to their child's misconduct. As a result of numerous complaints, they often try to restrain their child in the home for long periods of time. For example, based on a bad school report, some parents insist that the child not be allowed out into the neighborhood to play for a 2-week period. Now, it is true that hyperactive children cause more trouble than others their age; consequently more parental supervision is indeed frequently necessary, as when reports indicate that the child threw stones at neighbors or bullied preschool children. However, the simplistic process of prolonged restriction to the home has gross limitations. Social restriction impedes the child's development of group skills which are largely developed in play; it increases the likelihood of retaliatory feelings on the part of the child, which can lead to home misconduct; prolonged restriction is difficult to enforce; and it is often inappropriate and injudicious.

Thus, the parents have to provide an adequate degree of supervision over their mischievious child, and yet not feed a disciplinary pattern utilizing lengthy restrictions which can easily be self-perpetuating. Generally, parents should allow their children to play outside regularly during the afterschool period. If the neighbors find the hyperactive child's play too rough, they should keep their child from him. If the hyperactive child needs parental restriction because of an act of gross neighborhood misconduct that the parent verifies (such as unprovoked assault or extortion) the social restriction, when used, should be temporary (i.e., a matter of hours generally, or a day or 2 for older children).

ANTICIPATION

Parents are advised to tolerate more than the average degree of restlessness in their HA child, and to channel activity whenever possible. Practical parents learn to anticipate routine restlessness, rather than attempting to stifle it once it blossoms, a less sophisticated approach. For example, a writing tablet can be taken in the car for long trips, or coloring books can be taken along during family visiting and trips to the restaurant. For rainy days, indoor play items that involve a restless child productively include a tape recorder, phonograph records, balloons, dolls, mechanical cars, plastic clay, magazines, and card games. In good weather, outdoor activities such as bicycle riding and roller skating can be encouraged as soon as restlessness becomes apparent.

PARENTAL SUPPORT

The counseling effort with the parents aims to aid them in supporting the child's areas of strength, so that he can taste some success. For the poorly coordinated child, possibilities include such gross motor activities as swimming, bicycle riding, skiing, line play football, and roller skating, areas in which even children with poor fine motor coordination can excel. With this focus, certain sports that require good manual dexterity, such as basketball and baseball, can be de-emphasized. For children with mechanical aptitudes, this area can be supported. For older children with academic failures, a newspaper route, babysitting, or other part-time jobs can be encouraged to give them status. Such work puts to constructive use the latent compulsive traits that many of these children have.

In some areas where the child's skills are weak, it is helpful to plan a remedial program with the parents and the school. If the child's social areas are weak, one can recommend a day camp, group counseling, recreational activities, scouts, church clubs, and the like. If academic areas are weak, it may be helpful to recommend tutoring or school-based remedial assistance.

PARENT-SCHOOL BOUNDARIES

Punishing or restricting the child because of bad school reports is usually an unsuccessful, frustrating effort. It leads to a cyclic pattern all too well known, which consists of a school complaint, parental anger, restriction of the child or physical punishment of him, and an angry or negativisitic response by the child. This is followed by renewed parental anger and further attempts at restriction or punishment. The parent is best kept off the treadmill by simply not turning negative school reports into home problems (or at most using mild penalities *if* they work) (*h*).

Parents can, however, independently support their HA child's educational development at home, and they can support good school efforts by the use of home rewards. At home, parents of learning-impaired children can be successful teachers and tutors. This does, however, require more than the usual degree of flexibility and patience. Repeatedly pushing flash cards at, or forcing homework on, a resistant, academically frustrated child are not methods which are likely to succeed. Likewise, reminding the child that he mastered a skill previously, when he now cannot understand it, is deflating for the child's ego (even though it is tempting for the frustrated adult to point out).

Of all the educational items teachable at home, the simplest and most profound a parent can teach is the joy of learning. It is taught mainly by example and by positive involvement. In cases of delayed acquisition of reading skills, the parent can read to the child daily for 5—15 minutes. In time, very slowly, the child will want to verbalize words or short sentences from daily stories, a procedure which is best when not forced. Games, such as Junior Scrabble, map puzzles, Quizmo, and Monopoly, and mathematically involved card games such as Casino, can also aid in learning. Sometimes, for young children, homework too can be made into a game.

In general, parents can make more educational mileage at home by playing the right kind of games with their child and by reading to and with him than by pressuring him, regardless of how angry the teacher becomes when the child's homework is not completed or returned.

Parent support of the child's school effort through home rewards for good school behavior is discussed in more detail in the behavior therapy chapters.

PARENT-SCHOOL DETENTE

Frequently, it is useful for the therapists to try to encourage efforts by the school and the parents to be less critical of each other. Parents whose children are criticized at school, and whose child rearing is therefore held suspect, frequently feel free to express criticism of the school, thereby setting up a back-and-forth pattern of unpleasant, ill-founded charges. The parents, for all their displaced anger toward the school, still feel guilty about their home management. In response to school pressure, they often punish their child, touching off anger in all directions. The school should be cautioned to stop frequent "what Johnny did wrong" letters to the parents and, as indicated, the parents can be advised not to respond with burdensome penalties after negative school reports.

PARENTAL HARMONY

A lack of harmony in child rearing frequently becomes an issue in the counseling of parents of HA children. A fair amount of this is stirred up by the addition of a restless, usually impulsive child into a household. Such a child can create enough havoc to nudge one parent into an extreme position relative to the youngster's behavior. This in turn customarily leads to polarization of policy by the marital pair and further disrupts home management. For example, the father mandates that his son be kept in from play but is not around to enforce it, setting up a half-hearted restriction policy by his wife. Or the father identifies with his restless, rebellious, underachieving son and justifies the boy's misconduct, thus edging his spouse to become the only parent to set limits and support community authorities. Or the mother responds with overprotectiveness to her son's immaturity and anxiety, leading the father to believe that what his son needs primarily is a firm hand.

Such parent responses are not uncommon in child rearing, but they are typically present and exaggerated when the child has a behavioral disorder. In parent counseling of these cases, better parental harmony can be achieved when both parents can be induced to shift ground and adopt some behavioral features of a common child rearing attitude. This can be done sympathetically. For example, in discussing overprotectiveness, the therapist can emphasize that the HA child needs closer parental dependency ties throughout his youth because of his immaturity and his academic and social failures. In fact, support from both parents is needed to protect the child from hurt. It should not, however, negate the need for the child to be responsible for what he can do. After all, he will become 18 in as many years as any other child his age.

BLAME

It is useful to clarify the intertwined biological and emotional aspects of the problem, particularly for distraught parents. Parents are reassured to know that the immaturity, much of the behavioral difficulty, and the restlessness of HA are biologically based and rooted in temperament. Such awareness can lessen the sense of guilt most parents of HA children feel.

However, they should also know that some parents are clearly more skillful than others in managing irritable and temperamental children (2), and that the long term behavioral outcome appears to depend moderately on this (3).

DIRECTIVE COUNSELING

If the therapist has the experience and confidence to believe that he knows more about the home management of HA children than do the parents he sees, he can choose to be directive in counseling. He can set behavioral goals in treatment and can make them vital elements in the treatment contract. Such goal setting can be evolved and observed within the framework of brief therapy. Parental agreement to goals can generally be reached by the end of the second or third professional hour. At the end of the third week of treatment, this directive therapy can be terminated if parents are not cooperating (i).

Directive counseling, like psychotherapy in general, has a variable impact. About 80% of parents are receptive to the medical aspects of counseling. About 50–70% of the parents incorporate at least a few of the disciplinary recommendations. (Parents utilize such behavioral recommendations as short discipline and decreased punitiveness far better than they utilize lessened restriction and decreased yelling.) Structured home responsibilities seem to be picked up by one-third of the parents, and about 20–40% of the parents actually make efforts to become more harmonious in child rearing.

Thus, the results of counseling the parents are far more variable than the results of stimulant medication on the child. There are, in fact, numerous cases where the counseling has had only a minimal impact. In cases where the medication is useful but the counseling never gets off the ground, it is best not to discontinue the prescription of medication, because half a loaf is better than none.

ADDITIONAL AVENUES FOR PARENTS

Along with the counseling, some parents of HA children can be advised to read on the subject of HA. An excellent book to suggest is *Raising a Hyperactive Child* by Stewart and Olds (4). A few concerned parents may be interested enough to participate in a chapter of a national organization dealing with community issues pertinent to HA children. The Association for Children with Learning Disabilities (ACLD) can be recommended for this (see Chapter 9, Note *i*). Other parents may want specific training in home behavior management. If so, they can be directed to professionally led parent workshops which use books by such authors as Wesley Becker and Gerald Patterson (see Chapter 8).

NOTES

a. The view that individual psychotherapy is not a major treatment modality for the HA child is shared by Stewart and Olds (*4*) and by Wender (*5*). Even though these authors disagree strongly on the role of stimulant medication in the treatment regimen, they do agree that individual psychotherapy has little value in treating the major features of the HA clinical picture.

b. The typical HA child gets into trouble so often that he develops the self-concept of "being bad." Likewise, his learning difficulty leads to a "being dumb" self-concept. Generally, he feels he is different because he "is" bad and dumb. In individual counseling, the therapist shows the child that being different cannot be equated with being inferior. Furthermore, he stresses that the child has certain areas of relative ability and achievement. For more details, see Reference 6.

c. Some patterns of minor misconduct can often be successfully ignored. For instance, if ignored, dress and bathing patterns of many HA adolescents will become more conforming; essentially, peer pressures then supplant parent direction. (Of course, frequent parent reminders can quickly reinstitute the children's passive resistance.)

   For some inappropriate behavior, defining the territory where the deviance will not be tolerated is a useful parental approach. Smoking, for example, may be declared unacceptable in the home, but not outside. Picking at acne can be declared unacceptable in the kitchen or the living room when the parents are there, but not in the bathroom or the child's bedroom. For more details, see Reference 7.

d. Since parents tend to yell excessively at HA children, it is recommended that they make a conscious effort to decrease this as soon as they become aware of it, and instead use the more cerebral and behavioral responses outlined in this chapter. Yelling is a complex and variable pattern. It can be a prelude to action or to inaction. It can vent anger and at the same time provoke guilt. In all instances, yelling increases home tension and antagonism. With increasing use, it becomes increasingly less successful in getting the child to change his behavior. As a persistent parental pattern, it is as crude and unsuccessful as the pattern of routinely swatting the HA child.

   Most parents who have been yelling for years don't change their style to any extent. However, because a few can, it is recommended that they stop yelling as soon as they hear themselves, maybe 2–10 sentences later. Then they should stop the vocal and switch to the cerebral response, followed, if need be, by active behavior.

e. There is obviously a temptation to utilize excessive degrees of physical punishment to manage HA children. This may explain in part why there is more child abuse inflicted upon these children (8).

f. Furthermore, attempts to discipline the misbehaving HA child into submission and break his will fare no better. Part of the reason for this is that the HA child's main problem is not usually the "will"; it is poor impulse control (9).

g. This type of time-oriented discipline can be applied to the enforcement of other rules, as coming in for supper at 5:30 p.m., or returning home and changing into play clothes by 3:45 p.m. If the child comes in late for supper but arrives within 1 hour after the meal began, he can eat the cold leftovers. If he arrives later, he gets no supper, although he can receive a cup of milk or the like at bedtime. Should the child arrive 1½ hours late from school, he then can lose 3 hours of outside play that evening or the next day, or be denied 1 hour of prime TV time (from 8 to 9 p.m.) that evening.

h. If the school disciplined the child for a mild infraction and, for example, made him stay in or after school for one period as a detention, there is no reason for the parent to add to this and inflict double jeopardy. However, if the child's conduct is not appropriately penalized in school, as when he is suspended, the parent can appropriately institute a penalty. One example of this is the imposition of a daytime social restriction for the child and parent-mandated academic requirements during times of suspension.

i. Directive behavioral counseling can be aided initially by using a short parent manual. The use of these instructional aids is particularly stressed by Schaefer et al. (10).

LITERATURE CITED

1. Eisenberg, L., Gilbert, A., Cytryn, L., and Molling, P. The effectiveness of psychotherapy alone and in conjunction with perphenazine or placebo in the treatment of neurotic and hyperkinetic children. Am. J. Psychiat. 117: 1088–1093, 1961.

2. Thomas, A., Chess, S., and Birch, H. Temperament and behavior disorders in children. New York: New York University Press, 1968.

3. Minde, K., Lewin, D., Weiss, G., Lavigueur, H., Douglas, V., and Sykes, E. The hyperactive child in elementary school: A 5 year, controlled, follow-up. Except. Child. 38: 215–221, 1971.

4. Stewart, M., and Olds, S. Raising a Hyperactive Child. New York: Harper and Row, 1973.

5. Wender, P. Minimal Brain Dysfunction in Children. New York: Wiley, 1971.

6. Gardner, R. The mutual storytelling technique in the treatment of psychogenic problems secondary to minimal brain dysfunction. J. Learn. Disabil. 7: 135–143, 1974.

7. Safer, D. Establishing boundary lines for families of children with behavior disorders. Psychiat. Quart. Suppl. 42: 86–97, 1968.

8. Green, A., Gaines, R., and Sandgrund, A. Child abuse: Pathological syndrome of family interaction. Am. J. Psychiat. 131: 882–886, 1975.
9. Loney, J., Comly, H., and Simon, B. Parental management, self-concept, and drug response in minimal brain dysfunction. J. Learn. Disabil. 8: 187–190, 1975.
10. Schaefer, J., Palkes, H., and Stewart, M. Group counseling for parents of hyperactive children. Child Psychiat. Hum. Dev. 5: 89–94, 1974.

Chapter 6   The Behavioral Approach to Management
General Considerations

When human management issues are raised, behavioral considerations are always important, particularly when the management concerns behaviorally expressed disorders of childhood such as HA. Many issues discussed previously in this book have behavioral dimensions which have been noted and even emphasized both for diagnosis and counseling. Why, then, separate chapters on behavioral approaches? Behavior therapy merits this consideration because of its systematic approach, the large body of scientific knowledge developed, and the data from controlled studies attesting to its impact on behavior.

In this chapter the general principles of behavioral management are introduced along with consideration of the philosophical and ethical controversy behaviorism has raised. Some readers may find this chapter too technical or theoretical for their purposes; the two subsequent chapters provide more explicit information for setting up behavioral management systems. For practical purposes, information from the section entitled "The General Schema" in this chapter and from the subsequent chapters suffice for describing how to set up a behavioral program.

DEFINITIONS

Behaviorism involves principally that part of psychological inquiry concerned with behavior itself. Thus it is assumed that behavior is, in itself, a "lawful" phenomena which can be systematically described, predicted, and eventually controlled without reference to nonbehavioral considerations. A behavior when carefully observed is found to be under predictable control of other behaviors and related stimuli without reference to hypothetical organism variables such as minimal brain dysfunction. Behaviorists generally view the controls on *behavior* (B) as being *stimuli* (S) and *consequences* (C). Ordered in time, S occurs before B; C occurs after B, and both are seen as determining B. The formal relationship between behavior, stimuli, and consequences has been a subject of considerable debate with conflicts centering on two schools of thought: one following Pavlov's early work emphasizing the S→B relationship and the other following Skinner's work emphasizing the B→C relationships. The latter emphasis on consequences has gained more general acceptance as significant for altering social behavior (*a*).

The contingent relation between behavior and consequences is specifically defined in terms of behavior change. Contingencies pairing behaviors either to positive (desired) consequences or to a reduction in expected negative aversive consequences lead to an increase in the behaviors and are called *reinforcement contingencies.* Contingencies pairing behaviors either to negative (aversive) consequences or to a reduction in expected positive (desired) consequences will lead to a decrease in the behaviors and are called *punishment contingencies* (see Table 1). This system would be tautological if not for the general postulate that a consequence observed to increase behaviors, never, or at least rarely, serves to decrease behavior regardless of the behavior with which it is paired (*1*). Similarly, a negative consequence will almost never work to increase behaviors with which it is paired (*b*).

Extinction is another behavioral contingency. For extinction, behavior is reduced by removing the reinforcing contingencies which have supported the behavior. Extinction of a behavior requires that most if not all significant reinforcing consequences maintaining the behavior are removed rather abruptly. The success of extinction depends upon both the degree to which significant consequences are withdrawn and the character of the contingent relation between B and C used before extinction. In particular, those unusual behaviors which received reinforcement every time they were done any fixed number of times, say five, extinguish more quickly than those behaviors which were maintained on a *variable rate of reward;* e.g., the reinforcement occurs after so many repeats of the behavior but the number of repeats required for reinforcement varies. Similarly, rewards may occur on a fixed or variable time schedule; that is, the reward occurs for the first behavior which occurs after a fixed time period, or the reward can be scheduled to occur for the first behavior occurring after a period of time which is varied from one time period to the next. A history of variability in reinforcement delivery increases resistance to extinction.

Table 1. Basic behavior contingencies

General category	Type	Conditions needed	Contingency	Effects	Example
Reinforcement (behavior increases)	Positive consequence (positive reinforcement)	1. Behavior (B) occurs naturally 2. Positive consequence (C+) available	B→C+	1. Behavior occurs more often with improved quality 2. Behavior character becomes increasingly specific to that rewarded	Teacher praise for completing an assignment
	Punishment reduction (negative reinforcement)	1. B occurs naturally 2. Negative consequence (C−) expected	B→reduction in C−	(Same as above)	Reduction of detention for improved class performance
Punishment (behavior decreases)	Negative consequence (aversive)	1. B occurs naturally 2. C− available	B→C−	1. B occurs less often 2. Escape and avoidance of learning situation may be sought 3. All behaviors may decrease	Spanking child who hits another child
	Reward reduction (response cost)	1. B occurs naturally 2. C+ *is expected*	B→reduction in C+	1. B occurs less often	Reducing allowance for a child who hit another child
Extinction		1. B occurs naturally and is maintained by B→C+ or B→C− reduction	B→no C	1. B occurs less often 2. B becomes more variable in character	
Response differentation (shaping)		1. Two behaviors [B_1 and B_2] occurring naturally; C+ available (or C− expected)	B_1→C+(or C−↓) B_2→no C	1. B_1 increases 2. B_2 decreases	
Discrimination		1. B occurs naturally 2. 2 Stimuli S_1 and S_2; C+ available (or C− expected)	S_1→B→C+ (or C−↓) S_2→B→no C	1. B occurs more often with S_1 and less often with S_2	

115

Table 2. Basic contingency schedules (specifies when C follows B)

Schedule basis (type)	Requirement for B to follow C	Behavior results expect (relative)	Example
I. No. of behaviors (ratio schedules)	1. Continuous: every B→C	Learning easy Extinction easy Behavior rate low	(Most purchases) Candy machines
	2. Fixed partial: every *n*th B→C (*n* = any fixed integer)	Learning hard Extinction hard Behavior rate high (variable increases these effects)	(most gambling), e.g., "one-armed bandits"
	3. Variable partial: every *n*th B→C *n* = integer which varies randomly after every C		
II. Time period control (interval schedule)	1. Fixed interval a) *t* = time period constant b) 1st B after *t*→C c) C delivery resets clock for new *t*	B rate erratic, higher around end *t* and beginning of each *t* Overall rate low Extinction easy	(Many large social rewards) school grades

2. Variable interval: a) t = time period varied from one period to another b) 1st B after each $t \rightarrow$ C c) child does not know t or that t is important d) C delivery resets clock for new t	Learning hard Extinction hard Behavior rate high Fading easy (increase t values)	(Many social rewards), e.g., teacher praise for "on task" behavior
III. Low rate of B (compound ratio-interval schedules) 1. Fixed maximum rate: fixed interval and ratio. If no more than n B's occur in t, C given at end of t ($n = 0, 1.2$) (t = any time value)	Learning easy Extinction easy Child may see t B rate somewhat erratic	(Many severe punishments) Detention if caught smoking twice in same quarter
2. Variable maximum rate: n and/or t in above are varied randomly, but if both are varied the rate n/t is considered the significant variable to be kept at around some low level	Learning hard Extinction hard Fading easy Child generally should know Rate desired, but not n or t Leads to more constant B rate	(Many social punishments) Teacher scolds a child for talking too much

These phenomena relate to more general considerations concerning partial rewards (*2; c*). Table 2 presents the basic reinforcement schedules, variable and fixed.

The therapeutic use of behavioral approaches has generally been termed "*behavior modification*" or "*behavior therapy.*" Within the framework of management of a clinically defined problem the term 'therapy' seems more appropriate than 'modification,' and also avoids some of the unfortunate mechanistic connotations of the word modification. Behavior therapy seeks either to change a specific aberrant behavior or to develop a missing desirable behavior. These therapies are generally openly manipulative, directive, and specific goal oriented (*3; d*). The types of behavior therapies include: reducing fears by fantasy in desensitization (*4*), increasing self-control by training with biofeedback of physiological states (e.g., heart rate) (*5*), and manipulating social systems by providing reinforcements for group behavior (*6*). The use of behavioral therapies has gained general acceptance. Several respected English language scientific journals (*7–10*) are dedicated solely to publishing on behavior research and behavior therapies and a task force of the American Psychiatric Association recently gave their approval to behavior therapy as a psychotherapeutic approach (*11*).

The particular type of behavior therapy most applicable to the problems of HA children involves the manipulation of the social system of reinforcers. Since this approach emphasizes the contingent relation between behaviors and consequences it is commonly referred to as contingency management. The essence of this approach consists of: the careful analysis of the relation between behaviors and reinforcers, the definition of desired behaviors, and the introduction of systematic changes in the reinforcement contingencies to establish the desired behaviors. The previously mentioned contingencies (see Table 1 and 2) are the tools used in this approach.

PHILOSOPHICAL ISSUES: SOULS, BRIBES, AND CARROUSELS

Behavior therapy has engendered a remarkable amount of negative emotional reactions. Some people are turned off by the mechanistic and manipulative climate a contingency system can create. They feel that a rigidly consistent and objective system fails to deal effectively with feelings and human nature. Allied with these people are those who feel that contingency systems fail to produce lasting changes because they address a person at his most superficial level, that of overt behavior. This general type of reaction stems first from a few who object to any control of human behavior. Since all management aims to establish control, such an objection seems unreasonable. The second source of this type of reaction is the tendency of some behaviorists to feel that they can revolutionize the world, presumably recreating it in their image. Skinner's *Walden Two* (*12*) has been a focus of debate for those who would produce the behaviorists' Utopia versus those who see no "soul" in the behaviorist world. These arguments generally credit behaviorism on one hand with too much power and on the other hand with too little respect for human complexities. In fact, behavioral therapy is very goal limited precisely because it recognizes it cannot deal with the immense complexity of human life. Contingency management systems, in particular, will always be an impoverished representation of the full range of behavior involved in living, simply because the very need to systematically specify behavior-consequence contingencies, to be at all possible, requires considerable simplification. Contingency management does not, and cannot, deal with the entire riches of human behavioral phenomena, let alone issues of the "soul." But to be decidedly limited is not to be ineffective. On the contrary, the very limitations of specificity lead to the ability to make and to continue small changes until desired limited goals are obtained. However, the process of achieving limited goals may disturb other aspects of social behavior; this relates to a second major objection to behavior therapies.

Since contingencies usually emphasize positive reinforcers, the contingency system establishes reinforcement contingencies or rewards for desired behaviors. Many people are turned off by the idea of giving rewards to "bad" children. They ask: why reward or bribe the child for doing what he "should" do?, that is, they feel being good should not require rewards. There are two responses to this issue. First, the critics imply that since rewards are not given for good behaviors, the behaviors must in themselves be intrinsically rewarding. Most people would agree that exceptionally good behavior should be rewarded, but the average "run-of-the-mill" good behavior, such as sitting still or not hollering out in class, should not need to be rewarded. Indeed, for most children, this may be the case, and there is an argument for developing social altruistic behavior which apparently does not depend upon external reinforcement (*e*). For HA children, however, simply sitting still is in itself an exceptionally good behavior. It takes effort and concentration for the HA child to merely exercise the self-control that comes easily to the non-HA child. Failing to recognize these individual differences and responding to them with appropriate rewards is, indeed, a serious problem. How unfair to heap praise on the cripple for learning to use his crutches to get about and yet

to respond to the HA child who has a good day with, at best, praise quali-
fied by "I knew there was no reason for you to be bad." Perhaps this
represents the crux of the issue; to many the HA child represents something more like malingering than a biologically based disorder.

This is not to say that giving too much reward cannot disturb the
equilibrium of behavioral control. Excessive external rewards can alter
expectancies so that the activities a child might find enjoyable for certain
internalized self-rewards or for certain vague social rewards become chores
done to earn certain specific rewards. This type of problem occurs principally when reinforcement contingencies are applied for a behavior which
is already quite common; usually in these cases the reinforcement contingencies fail to increase the frequency of the behavior. When the contingencies are removed the behavior's frequency decreases to less than that
observed before it was rewarded. This phenomena, which has been referred
to as "overjustification," (f) deserves some attention, especially since it
supports the view that behavioral criteria for contingency management
need to be individualized. Adding reinforcers for good behavior to "good"
children may be counterproductive. For HA children, however, the problem is almost always too little, not too much, reinforcement for the
commonplace good behaviors.

Another argument against giving rewards to "bad" children assumes
the use of differential contingencies for these children. The argument
centers on the effects upon other children if a select group is differentially
rewarded for good behavior rather than being punished consistently for
bad behavior. One major element of the behavior control system in our
society is based on modeling by vicarious punishment. Bandura (13)
presents a fairly comprehensive view of modeling for social learning. The
amount of learning required in socialization is far too large and varied to
be learned simply by reinforcements and punishments for specific behaviors. Obviously children also learn by observation, often copying the
behavior of models. Modeling is usually formulated in positive terms, that
is, the child copies the behavior of others who receive rewards (vicarious
learning from reinforcement). The child even copies the behavior of
socially powerful others who are not rewarded for their behavior (14, 15;
g). However, modeling can also serve to reduce occurrence of a behavior;
punishment of a model's behavior usually serves to reduce similar behavior
by the observer (h).

Our society's penal code contains a large portion of this type of
learning. It produces examples for the law-abiding demonstrating that they
are better off upholding the law. This creates almost a two-state phenomena; either you're on the social approval carrousel of law abiders or

you've fallen off. The law-abiding citizen is on the social carrousel; he receives some reinforcers for his socially approved behavior and avoids punishment that others receive for breaking the law. Thus, many argue for prison as a deterrent to theft; not that it would deter those who have already committed theft, but that it would deter those who are not thieves and might be tempted. Indeed, if our penal code were established to teach the law offender by punishment, then its high recidivism rate would indicate that it is rather ineffective. But its effectiveness in providing vicarious learning may be better since a relatively small percentage of citizens commit serious crimes. Indeed, one of the problems with the concept of nonpunitive rehabilitation of criminals is that it perniciously undermines the vicarious learning from punishment of lawbreakers.

Removing punishment and adding special rewards for the misbehaving HA child may similarly serve to reduce the social control on other children. This legitimate concern needs, however, to be balanced first by the recognition of the HA child's biological handicaps and second, by the realization that learning by vicarious punishment is probably a weak and limited method of social control not needed for most school children. Thus, if one is to apply the reasonably successful behavioral techniques to manage the HA child, it will be necessary to lose some uncertain benefits from vicarious punishment. Whether or not the gains in terms of improvements for the HA child and their consequences on other children outweigh possible negative effects with other children is an issue each parent, therapist, teacher, and guidance counselor must face with each situation.

Finally, the concept of bribes needs some clarification. The word "bribe" usually applies to a single large gift tied to an illegal or illegitimate activity. Good behavior is not illegal, nor do behavioral controls usually involve delayed presentation of a large gift (*i*). The Santa Claus promise of a large gift at Christmas for the child who has been "good all year" is vague and sounds suspicious; the reward is large and much delayed. Good behavioral therapies avoid both of these conditions and instead work within the framework of incentives, with small rewards for specific small behaviors and an emphasis upon social and naturally occurring rewards (*j*).

BIOLOGICAL-BEHAVIORAL DIALOGUE

Many of the preceding considerations regarding the use of behavioral therapy with HA children have been premised on recognition of the biological basis of HA. Recognition of the biological problems of HA also involves a realization that these problems do not impose any limits on behaviors an HA child can perform; they indicate instead that for the HA child a persistent effort is required to produce many of the desired "good" behaviors. In behavioral terms then, the reinforcement required to maintain good behaviors will need to be greater for HA children than non-HA children, an important point for parents and teachers to bear in mind in their relations with HA children. Even on their good days one should remember that these are special children who desperately need reinforcement. Their behavior should be reinforced especially when they are good and not a nuisance.

THE GENERAL SCHEMA

The application of contingency management to the hyperactive child is essentially the same as its application to any misbehaving child. A five-step program is usually followed:

1. Define explicitly the behavior to be changed. This can be either a new or rare behavior which needs to be encouraged (e.g., persistence at arithmetic problems), or an established behavior which needs to be discouraged (e.g., bothering a nearby peer).
2. Analyze the consequences reinforcing the behavior. Particular attention should be paid to the consequences which seem to be significant for keeping the behavior going. As a general rule behaviorists have noted that consequences most *frequently* and *immediately* associated with the behaviors are often the most significant for keeping the behavior going (e.g., classroom laughter which follows clowning). A careful analysis of the child's behavior also assists in the effort to find which consequences are likely to reinforce a new behavior. Two rules for uncovering reinforcers are: one, frequently obtained consequences and frequently chosen activities are usually reinforcing, and two, consequences reinforcing one behavior are likely to reinforce any other behavior (if laughter reinforces clowning, it would reinforce another behavior) (b).
3. Construct new reinforcing contingencies. The following guidelines help: a) rewards should be set up to establish or support a desired behavior or to reduce the frequency of an undesired behavior; b) the behavior to be changed needs to be defined in small units so that contingent rewards can be given or withheld frequently; c) for the rewards to be effective, they should occur frequently, and immediately after the behavior; d) the behaviors to be encouraged should be frequently rewarded in the initial phase.
4. Prime the behavior change to insure initial success: a) give careful specific instructions about the desired change; b) give rewards initially as

often as the behavior changes occur; c) for a new or rare behavior, it may be useful to "walk the child through" once or twice and, when appropriate, model the behavior for him.

5. Evaluate the effectiveness of the change. Recording the frequency of the behavior and its rewards provides a ready evaluation of the effectiveness of the program. If the behavior does not change in the planned direction, then the system should be altered.

PROBLEMS FREQUENTLY
ENCOUNTERED WITH CONTINGENCY MANAGEMENT

Several major problems can develop in contingency management. The most significant problem usually involves the lack of an adequate definition and observation of the behavior. The system on one hand must be precise and consistent and on the other hand it must be practical. A helpful guideline is to insure that the behavior can be defined so that its occurrence can be systematically recorded and appropriate reinforcement given (e.g., not misbehavior as such, but being out of the seat). Unless the behavior is reduced to a simple and reliable recording, the accuracy and effectiveness of the program cannot be checked. Recording can be intermittent, but it is necessary to determine both the efficiency of the program and whether or not rewards are being correctly given. In this regard it is usually easier to note and record the existence of a behavior than it is the absence of a behavior, so where possible the recording system should permit recording at the time a behavior occurs. Peers or the child himself can sometimes help with recording behaviors.

Unfortunately, even the simpler behavioral programs with only occasional recording of behavior can become time consuming. Assessing behavior, giving rewards, keeping occasional records, revising contingencies and rewards; all of those are an effort for a parent or a classroom teacher. Whatever system is designed must, therefore, be as simple as possible and yet be precise.

Selecting effective rewards poses still another problem for behavior modification. Rewards for desired behaviors need to be imaginative, well thought out, and varied. If one reward is used excessively, it may lose its reinforcing value; thus, ice cream is a good reward for young children but if used extensively it can easily lead to satiation (k). Many rewards also work to a limited degree in the obverse fashion; that is, receiving small amounts of a reward increases its reinforcing value. This occurs particularly for unfamiliar rewards (e.g., *a child not previously exposed to model building might develop an interest in it*), but it also occurs for many familiar rewards, particularly food items such as potato chips and peanuts. The process of giving reinforcers initially to stimulate interest in them is called reinforcement sampling (*16*) and is similar to the car sales technique of giving free rides in the new car. The type of rewards used with children have been categorized into edible, nonedible (tangible), social, activity, and token (*17*). Nonedible rewards include such things as: toys, model kits, clothes, and money. Social rewards include: attention, approval, status, and related items. Activity rewards include opportunities such as: gym, shop, or library privileges; movies; and time out of the house or out of school.

Tokens are generalized reinforcers which act like "money" in that they can be exchanged for any of a wide variety of other reinforcements. Since the selection of the reinforcer needs to be tailored to each individual child, the token approach is frequently used for programs involving more than one child. One reinforcer, the token, can be given which will serve to provide all of the variety required for the group of subjects. When token programs are developed it is important that rewards purchased by the tokens be sufficiently varied and interesting so that no child starts saving his tokens. A child with a large collection of tokens becomes, as a wealthy man does, somewhat independent of the behavioral contingencies (*18*).

The token price for rewards can, of course, be adjusted by the simple law of price and demand. Starting at about the fifth grade, children respond well to the substitution of points for tokens. Using points with older children resolves the persistent problems of lost, stolen, or bartered tokens. Older children, particularly those in the junior high and high school levels, can also enjoy the great American tradition of an auction, where rewards are offered for points. The auction has the advantage of establishing the price of an item in terms of its group demand (*l*); it has the disadvantage of being effective only when several group members desire the same relatively scarce reward. Rewards idiosyncratic to one or two group members should not be auctioned. Table 2 of Chapter 7 includes a list of rewards which have been effective in school and home programs.

When a behavior change is successfully induced but does not persist, the problem with the system can usually be attributed to inadequate rewards. When, however, a behavior change has not been successfully primed, the problems are more difficult to assess. The rewards could be ineffective, the priming could be inadequate, or the unit of behavior change could be too large. The last of these is the most common problem. When the behavior change requested is too large the therapist can plan a series of smaller units (or steps) of behavior change which will eventually lead to the desired larger behavior change. Attending to a task for 15 minutes may be too difficult for a hyperactive child initially, but by starting with 3- to 5-minute units it may be possible to gradually increase the "on task" time to 15 minutes.

GENERALIZATION AND DISCRIMINATION

Among the more common unfulfilled expectations of behavior therapies is that of generalization of the treatment effects to the natural environment. Generalization is a behavioral term for "carry-over" of characteristics of a learned behavior from one condition to another. Generalization can occur for stimuli; that is, a particular learned behavior occurs after new stimuli similar to that experienced during learning. For example, a child learns to respond well to one teacher, then begins to respond well to a second teacher. Generalization can also occur for behaviors as "response induction," that is, a new behavior develops which is similar to the behavior initially learned. A child learns to swim well and enters more into other sports. Specifying the basis for generalization has proven difficult, particularly for humans, in whom cognitive mediation appears to lead to idiosyncratic generalization obvious to the patient but often defying predictions by the therapist (*m*). Generalization is frequently hoped for in contingency management therapies; for example, it is often hoped that improved behaviors at home will lead to similar improved behaviors in school and with peers.

The opposite of generalization is discrimination; i.e., learning that specific behaviors will be reinforced only under specific circumstances. Thus good behavior may receive special reinforcement at home but not in school; the good behavior, therefore, is extinguished (not rewarded) in school and ceases, while it continues to increase at home where it is rewarded. (See Table 1 for a general example of discrimination contingencies.) The usual contingency management therapies with behavior problem children have shown more discrimination than generalization, owing at least in part to the frequency with which the behaviors developed are not rewarded outside of the treatment situation. Thus, improvements of a child's behavior at home have not generally led to improvements at school (*19*), and, presumably, the generalization works no better in reverse. Nor has improvement in one type of classroom behavior, such as sitting still, led to improvement in other behaviors, such as studying more (*20, 21*). Thus, even "common sense" dictates, such as "students in quiet classes will learn more," are not borne out for behavior generalization. These results should hardly seem surprising given the failure of the natural environment to provide reinforcers for simple, desired behaviors. For this reason it is particularly important that contingency management involve as many different social systems (stimuli) and as many significant (n) behaviors as possible. Particular consideration, therefore, needs to be given to the techniques used to increase generality and persistence of treatment effects.

PERSISTENCE OF TREATMENT BENEFITS:
GENERALIZATION (TRANSFERS) TO NEW SITUATIONS

At the heart of careful planning for behavior therapy is the issue of developing lasting treatment benefits. This requires, first, generalization of stimuli to include new situations and of behaviors to produce appropriate behavioral responses to new stimuli, and second, transfer of learned behavior from the control of the "therapeutic" contingencies to the control of those contingencies naturally occurring in the environment. These goals are extremely elusive and it is one of the historic curiosities of behavioral research that while much attention has been given to shaping of new desired behaviors, little has been given to the gradual transfer of learned behavior to natural contingencies. This imbalance results, in part, from the behaviorist's emphasis upon animal models and animal research, where, in the absence of verbal instructions, eliciting a new behavior can become a major work of art. For human behavior the technical problem is most often maintaining a new behavior which is elicited simply by verbal instructions, and the major work of art comes in arranging successful transfer of learning to nontherapy situations. Thus, the placebo effect of verbal instruction and observation of behavior may in itself suffice to produce a transitory change toward desired behaviors (*22–24; o*). Contingencies are, however, usually required to maintain the behavior, and careful planning is usually needed to insure successful generalization and transfer to the natural environment. The following major techniques have been developed to assist in this process.

Group rewards are a common procedure used to reduce both the immediacy of reward to an individual and the amount of effort needed to maintain a contingency management system. For group rewards the behavioral goal is set either for the collective group or for a percentage of individuals in the group. That is, the contingencies depend upon either the sum of each child's effort or upon the number of children in the group who individually reach some criterion level. In either case it is important to insure that every member of the group can contribute reasonably well to the goal. Large within-group disparities in contribution to target behaviors lead to group conflicts and failures (*p*). The rewards for group contingencies are almost always given equally to all group members, creating group support for task achievement (25).

Within-group interaction has also been directly manipulated. Contingencies established for rewarding peers and a misbehaving child when positive social interaction is reciprocated (e.g., giving points to children for making positive comments about each other), have been shown to facilitate transfer of learning to the natural environment (26; q). Presumably some of this effect comes from establishing a peer reward system for the behavior which effectively sets a norm for the group. Thus the rather artificial reinforcement contingencies of points and prizes are supplemented by the more subtle, natural social reinforcers which maintain normative behavior in groups. It is an interesting conjecture that encouraging within-group mutual support (either by directly rewarding it or by indirectly rewarding it through group rewards for achievement) will improve maintenance of the behaviors after formal contingencies are removed.

Peer group interaction is perhaps the best example of the general advantage of *social reinforcers*. The success of the social reinforcements of behavior raises the possibility of making durable therapeutic changes in the contingencies of the natural environment. Training parents, teachers, and peers to use more effectively the reinforcing power of their social approval and even their social recognition can lead to striking and durable changes in their use of reinforcing contingencies. Such results are harder to develop for tangible and/or consumatory rewards. The use of money, food, or even small prizes for reinforcers is usually hard to continue for any length of time.

The use of social rewards is an example of the still more general concept of using *natural rather than artificial reinforcers*. A natural reinforcer is defined as one which would occur to support the behavior in the natural environment in which the behavior would occur; an artificial reinforcer would not occur in the natural environment and has been added for therapeutic reasons. Thus, for hyperactive children, grades, teacher and parental attention and approval, peer attention, and, for many children, later play hours and allowance are natural reinforcers which could support good behavior for a prolonged period.

Creating *stimulus similarity* for learned behaviors may also facilitate generalization. Thus play acting or role playing may assist expression of behaviors when the situations acted out actually occur. Similarly, the use in training of therapies with significant stimulus cues from the natural environment (such as significant individuals or settings) may assist in generalization to a new environment where these cues are present. Encouraging behavior generalization also assists transfers to natural environments. Significant in this activity is the use of behaviors similar to those expected in the natural environment, particularly the coping behaviors required in new and varied situations a natural environment may present.

The transfer or change from one reinforcer to another, one stimulus or behavior to another, and even the discontinuing of the reinforcement contingencies altogether, can generally be done by a *"fading" procedure.* By gradual steps a particular reinforcer, stimulus, or behavior requirement is changed or discontinued. If a reinforcer has been given for a specified behavior, the reinforcer could be reduced in amount and/or the frequency of receiving the reinforcer reduced. The latter change in reinforcer schedule has the desirable characteristic of permitting variable reward schedules. Every so many times (or every so often) that the behavior occurs, the child will be rewarded. As noted earlier, these partial reinforcement schedules serve to resist extinction. By maintaining high levels of the behavior in the natural environment, they facilitate transfer. One of the important steps in contingency management is, therefore, to arrange the transfer from a continuous reward to a partial reward schedule. Among partial reinforcement schedules the variable interval schedules are usually easier to manage since a simple cooking timer can be used to signal when the behavior criterion period has lapsed (r).

One of the recent techniques for the transfer of learning which has been emphasized in behavioral work is the training of *self-control.* In essence this training involves the gradual transfer of responsibilities for point recording from the mentor to the student. After some experience in receiving points from the mentor, the student can start giving himself the points and be checked by the mentor. Eventually his judgment of his behavior will be the major determinant of the points he receives. This process trains a child to observe his behavior, record it accurately, and dispense rewards to himself for good behavior. "Back-up" rewards may either be continued or discontinued at this time.

Self-control conditions have been demonstrated to work for several weeks after contingency learning with some misbehaving children. In one study *(27)* with second graders using points and rewards for "on task" behavior, children were "on task" slightly more often when they gave themselves the points (self-control condition) than when the points were given by the teacher. Rewards and self-administered points were continued successfully for 5 weeks for this class. Another study *(28)* demonstrated that the appropriate classroom behavior tended to persist longer when the self-control procedure was introduced before removing the rewards. In that study the appropriate classroom behavior was observed for 4 weeks after rewards were terminated. The self-control classes maintained the behavior while classes not trained in self-control reverted to the old behaviors. Even for severely disruptive children, self-control training has maintained the gains of a token program for a 2-week follow-up period (*28*). Unfortunately, tests of the potential benefits of self-control procedures in classrooms are still rare, the follow-up periods are short, and not all of the data are this promising. In particular, self-control was not effective for severe behavior problem adolescents in a psychiatric hospital school (*29*). Nonetheless, it seems desirable for each child to evaluate his own behavior.

Transfer of social learning remains an elusive goal, particularly for the problem behaviors of the hyperactive child. Since controlling these problem behaviors has such an apparently high cost for the hyperactive child and requires such strong efforts, the use of self-control and fading are unlikely to be successful. In certain situations, however, they deserve consideration. The possibility exists that significant changes in the social or natural reinforcers for behaviors can occur in the child's natural environment. This process of increasing social reinforcers for HA children involves major changes in the behavior of a number of people, many of whom are involved with mostly non-HA children. The change would generally be of benefit to everyone concerned, but it would be hard to justify the amount of change required in order to help one hyperactive child. It would be even harder to elicit cooperation from a person to change his mode of giving social reinforcement when the person is well accustomed to one general pattern of social behavior. Increasing social reinforcers on a system basis, nonetheless, probably represents the best available therapeutic arrangement to produce desirable behavior change for the hyperactive child. This will, however, often need to be preceded by the priming effects of tangible and "artificial" rewards for the behavior change.

THE REINFORCING SYSTEMS

For the hyperactive child three major social units can be defined as the primary contingency systems: school, family, and peer groups. The school wields considerable influence upon any child and is particularly significant for the hyperactive child. It is largely within the academic constraints of the school that hyperactive children show the most aberrant behavior and, accordingly, this reinforcement system often becomes the major source of aversive contingencies for the hyperactive child's behavior. The school is usually the first to publicly single out the hyperactive child for his behavioral problems. In the family situation the hyperactive child's temper, low frustration tolerance, and motor activity will also lead to problems despite the greater degree of individual attention available. Even in peer groups, hyperactive children often have problems functioning and end up with frequent fights and/or social rejection. Behavioral contingencies within each of these major systems are discussed in more detail in the following two chapters; the interaction of these systems in relation to the HA child will be noted here.

Since the most frequent communications between the school and the parents are critical teacher reports and distorted reports by the child to his parents, these links often become a major issue. In the usual situation for the hyperactive child the school sends home a large number of negative comments and virtually no positive comments. Thus the family is left with the impression that the school dislikes the child and, of course, the child reciprocates this relation. The balance theory for attitudes in social psychology (*30, 31; s*) would generally predict that in this type of situation there are only two stable positions, as shown in Figure 1. Either the family supports the child and rejects the school, or it joins with the school and rejects the child. Parental attempts to support the child are interpreted by the school staff as failure to support the school; attempts to support the school are seen as rejection by the child. Since a child will usually hold more reinforcers for the parents than does the school, when the parent-school communication is unstable, the child can usually shift it to the stable position in which the family supports him against the school. When a therapist or counselor is consulted for a serious school misconduct problem, he will in most cases (*32*) be dealing with this school alienation position. The probability of this alienation increases significantly with the number of school suspensions. In his counseling he can generally support one of three stable positions (see Figure 1). First, he can support the existing alienation of the school and the family by seeking change mostly from one of these two systems and thereby implicitly labeling that system as "sick." Second, he can support improved relations between the school and family and seek the bulk of change from the child. Third, he can seek to alter the communication between the school and child as well as the school and parent, and support more mutually positive attitudes within the total system. The type of therapy approach chosen implicitly fits one of these models. Family therapy separates the school and family and defines the problem as a family matter; school-oriented consultation similarly separates school and family but defines the problem as a school matter. Individual child-therapy serves to isolate the child from the family as well as from the school and defines the problem as a matter for the

A. Conditions not in balance (unstable conditions)

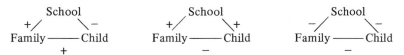

The usual initial
situation for HA
children

B. Balance positions for negative attitude between school and child

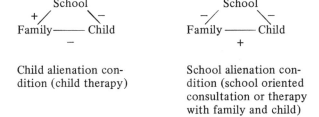

Child alienation con-   School alienation condition (child therapy)   dition (school oriented
                                consultation or therapy
                                with family and child)

C. Balance positions for positive attitude between school and child

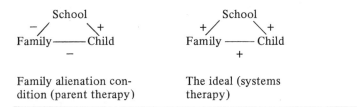

Family alienation con-   The ideal (systems
dition (parent therapy)   therapy)

Figure 1. Attitude relations in terms of a simplified balance theory

child to resolve. A combined and intergrated approach dealing with all
three areas of child, school, and family appears to hold the best hope of
changing the communication and the attitudes to become more mutually
positive. The key to creating this type of behavior change is to deal not
only with each system but also with the communication between the
systems. When the school staff changes their communication to emphasize
frequent and more positive statements about the child (given to both the
parent and the child) then they can expect reciprocity of positive acts by
the child and the family. Cohen et al. (33) showed that simply sending
home daily "success" notes for successful tasks completed served to
increase tasks the child completed in school (see Figure 2). Similarly, if a

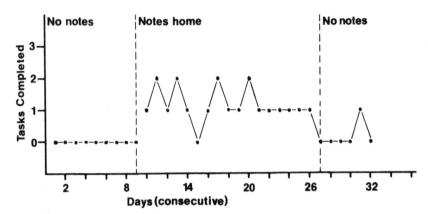

Figure 2. Example of effect of starting a simple note home indicating number of tasks completed for one student; no specific arrangements were made with the parents. (Figure taken by permission from Cohen, S. I., Keyworth, J. M., Kleiner, R. I., and Brown, W. L. Effective behavior change at the Anne Arundel Center through minimum contact interventions, in R. Ulrich, T. Stachnick, and J. Mabry (Eds.), Control of Human Behavior, Vol. III, p. 139. Scott, Foresman and Co., Glenview, Ill.)

child changes his comments to the teacher to be more appropriately positive, then the teacher will respond more positively to the child. In fact, a rather clever series of experiments (Graybard et al. (34)) showed that children can alter teacher behaviors in a direction they desire by the use of positive acts toward the teacher.

In one study(35) a teacher increased her positive communication to the children and indirectly to their families; children subsequently showed increased positive feelings about themselves and the teacher. The teacher had become a significant source of positive rewards for these children who received few such rewards. Thus, when behavioral system manipulations lead to mutually rewarding behaviors, the incidental behaviors that develop may include those of liking or affiliation. The time lag between the development of mutually rewarding behaviors and the development of the behaviors associated with liking may be long and "liking" may not occur at all if the system includes persistent aversive qualities, such as academic failure. But when the liking behaviors occur, persisting changes seem more probable.

BEHAVIOR THERAPIES COMPARED WITH OTHER THERAPIES

Comparing different psychotherapies is, of course, always difficult. However, it deserves note that behavior therapy has repeatedly been of demonstrable benefit for the classroom behaviors of misbehaving, learning-impaired children. Family counseling and individual or group psycho-therapies cannot make such a claim. Thus the evidence shows that behavior therapy is the most successful nonchemical treatment for the school problems of the hyperactive child. In some cases with only mildly disturbing school behavior problems and with well-integrated families, the child may be most easily helped by behavioral approaches to the family. In other cases where the MBD child has a major neurotic problem, regular individual counseling might be added or used to support the behavioral approach. In all psychological therapies with children—individual, family, or behavioral therapy—it is, of course, important to involve the child in the treatment effort.

Comparing behavior therapy with medication generally shows a superiority for medication in reducing misbehavior (36, 37) and a superiority for behavior therapy in increasing academic performance (38). The long term efficacy of stimulants appears to be quite limited (39, 40), but then there are also no long term data on the benefits of behavior therapy for HA children.

There is, of course, nothing incompatible between medication and contingency management. It is quite appropriate and useful to have a child on both a stimulant medication and in a contingency management program. This combination has distinct advantages. First, with medication the child can more easily attain the behavior goals for rewards. Sprague et al. (37) report that the combination of contingency management and stimulants gives somewhat superior results over either one alone (t). Second, the dose of medication could possibly be reduced with the combination of treatments, thereby reducing the risk of medication side effects. Third, adding contingency management to the use of stimulant medication provides more structure for the direction of therapy than when goals are only to reduce school complaints about the child. At this time, it indeed seems that the combination of stimulants and contingency management generally provides the best treatment plan for most MBD children.

NOTES

a. Pavlovian (classical) conditioning emphasizing the S→B relation (stimuli, bell and food→behavior, salivation) has been usefully related to a large range of learned autonomic and emotional responses. Particularly striking has been the conditioning of fear responses in children (41) and the subsequent treatment to remove fears in a child by classical conditioning (42). The Skinnerian or operant approach emphasizing the B→C relation (behavior, bar press→consequences, food available) has proven to be a practical approach for learning to solve complex problems such as those in social behavior. For example, the operant methods have been successfully applied to resocialize severely disturbed state mental patients (*16, 43, 44*) and delinquent adolescents (*45*).

Despite the antipathy that developed between the classical and Skinnerian schools of thought in psychology, most modern behavior therapies have incorporated both views. Distinctions are made between stimulus-controlled and consequence-controlled behaviors. Frequently symbolic-behavior control is added to represent the effects of the cerebral "coding" and interpretation of stimuli and consequences. Bandura (*46*) has made the rather convincing argument that no conditioning is "automatic" but rather is mediated for man by his complex neurological system; accordingly, behavior therapies must deal with cognitive expectancies and mediation.

b.   This assumption of the trans-situational nature of reinforcers serves as a good first order approximation of the nature of reinforcement. Unfortunately, there are enough exceptions to the rule to invalidate this position as a general theory. Premack (*47*) proposed an alternate theory to break the circularity in the definition of reinforcement. He suggested defining reinforcement strength by the relative probability that the behavior involved in the reinforcement would occur. Specifically he argued that for any two behaviors in a given situation, the more probable one would reinforce the less probable. Thus, food-deprived rats have a high probability of eating and a relatively low probability of seeking activity; therefore, food and eating will reinforce activity. Similarly, activity-deprived rats have a high probability of becoming active and a relatively low probability of eating; therefore, activity will reinforce eating; that is, the rats will eat more to gain access to activity. Even with electrical stimulation to the brain, the relative probability with which an animal seeks brain stimulation versus water drinking defines which will reinforce the other (*48*).

This principal has been applied to behavior therapy with contingencies making access to more probable behavior depend upon performance of less probable behavior (*49*). This permits use of reinforcers naturally occurring in the environment, provided that they occur more frequently than the behavior selected to be increased.

More recent work has raised serious questions about even the Premack question. Some reinforcers, such as drugs, appear to be situation and behavior specific; some, such as social praise, do not involve any behavior by the person in therapy; and some may involve expectancies and novelty. Both Bolles' (*50*) expectancy theory and Seligman's (*51*) behavior classifications attempt to provide new approaches to reward theories. At present, however, there is in psychology no satisfactory theoretical model describing reinforcement. Such a general theory may not even be possible.

c.   The partial reinforcement effects on extinction depend on several factors. Random variability in giving the rewards generally produces more resistance to extinction than a fixed pattern of partial reward (e.g., alternating), provided a reasonably large number of training trials are given (52). In general, resistance to extinction varies inversely with the proportion of behaviors rewarded during training (53) and directly with length of training (54). Larger reward magnitudes usually lead to *decreased* resistance to extinction after continuous reward schedules, but reward magnitude has relatively little effect on resistance to extinction after partial reward schedules (55, 56). Shifting from continuous to partial reinforcement has been shown to significantly increase resistance to extinction even if only a few trials with partial reinforcement are used (57).

d. There is often a misunderstanding of behavior therapy among clinicians not involved with behavior work. Behavior therapy has become a broad based approach to treatment united by certain methodological considerations. Yates (58) emphasizes this when he defines behavior therapy in terms of systematic use of knowledge from "experimental psychology and its closely related disciplines (philosophy and neurophysiology)." Learning theory is an important aspect of this approach, but physiology, social psychology, ethnology, perceptual theories, etc., also provide useful input for behavior therapies. This position has been forcefully argued by Lazarus (59) and exemplified by the application of cognitive dissonance research to increasing a therapist's influence with his patients (60).

The emphasis in behavior therapies is upon observable behavior change, natural histories of behavior change, and the scientific method in observing, manipulating, and evaluating behavior change, even in the clinical setting.

e. Altruistic prosocial behaviors are defined as those behaviors benefiting another, which are voluntarily engaged in and performed solely as an end in themselves, not for personal gain. These behaviors have been related to social norms and are apparently taught most effectively by modeling; that is, observation of a model actually engaging in altruistic behavior. These behaviors are not taught verbally but they have been shown to spread by example from one instance to many others (61).

f. The "overjustification" hypothesis notes essentially that if someone, for example, studies for intrinsic reward and is suddenly given extrinsic reward (e.g., money) for his studying, he will, then, begin to assume that he is studying for the extrinsic reward. When the extrinsic reward is withdrawn he will decrease his study behavior even though the addition of the extrinsic reward did not initially serve to increase the behavior (62). The loss of expected reward might be viewed as punishment. This is somewhat like the inverse "Tom Sawyer" effect. Paying to be able to whitewash a fence makes it "play"; being paid to whitewash a fence makes it "work."

g. Modeling effects can be increased by either increasing rewards given to the model while being observed or by increasing the "social power" of the model by having him dispense rewards while observed (14, 63 64). Influences on the potency of modeling appear, however, not to be general; they enhance the modeling of many but not all of the

behaviors the model performs (65). It nonetheless remains a generally significant phenomena that when a model is dispensing desired
rewards he is increasing his model strength (increased copying of his
behavior by the observers).

h. This result is, technically, cast in a comparison of reward, no-conse-
quence, or punishment for the model's behavior. The observers tend
to show the most copying of the model's behavior when the model is
rewarded and the least when the model is punished (66). These
effects are not always symmetrical since in some studies no consequence and reward have nearly equal effect (67, 68).

It is doubtful that a child with a high propensity for a behavior
such as aggression will reduce his behavior (aggressiveness) when
observing models punished for the behavior (aggression) (15). Observing models in cooperative play using mutual, cooperative solutions to problems (like those the child naturally faces) has, however,
been effective in increasing cooperativeness and decreasing aggressiveness in highly aggressive children (69).

Punishment of aggression in a model may not serve to decrease
aggressiveness in an aggressive child; however, failure to punish an
aggressive act by a model may serve to increase aggressiveness even in
aggressive children.

i. Reinforcement strength for maintaining a behavior generally decreases
with increased delay, as shown by several experimental studies (70). As
Bandura (13) notes, this relationship is probably not so important for
explicitly defined contingencies with those humans who operate
with good stimulus control and good instructional compliance. However, since the HA child operates, most likely, with poor stimulus
control and limited facility for "good behavior" responses, delay of
reinforcement will likely be a problem. The delay can, of course, be
minimized by use of tokens as secondary rewards; each token is a
reward and a certain number of tokens can be exchanged for food or
other rewards at a later time. The tokens, therefore, bridge the time
gap between behavior and primary reward. By the association between tokens and primary rewards, the tokens themselves become
rewarding, much as money is rewarding in our society.

j. The concept of social rewards is used rather loosely at times in this
chapter to include all naturally occurring rewards not given by a
strictly defined reinforcement contingency. Thus the phrase is intended to relate to informal, "natural" contingencies which can, and
often do, operate in the child's environment to support socially
desired behaviors.

k. Reward satiation is principally a problem for tangible primary rewards
such as "food." When such rewards are used it is desirable to arrange
to maximize the deprivation of the item before giving the reward;
thus, food should be given just before, or during, the regular meal
time (71). One of the reasons for developing tokens and social
rewards is to avoid the problems of satiation occurring with the
primary reward.

Note that for any reward, satiation can occur if the reward is
freely available noncontingently in the natural environment. Ayllon

and Azrin (*16*) provide an excellent series of experiments document-
ing these results with movies and soda reinforcers.

l. The use of the auction is one way to resolve the problem of savings. As
noted by Winkler (*18*), whenever a large amount of savings ac-
cumulate, performance in a token economy becomes erratic. There
are essentially four solutions proposed for the savings problem: 1)
adjust the task difficulty so that the number of points earned
balance with number spent (*18*); 2) adjust attractiveness or price of
the reinforcers by an auction or by "inflation" increasing prices (*72*);
3) require that all points earned a given day be spent within a
relatively short time, such as 2 days or a month (*73*); 4) establish a
"bank" into which large accumulations are placed to be used only
for special, large magnitude rewards offered weekly or monthly.

m. As Kanfer and Phillips (pp. 564—567 of Reference 3) point out,
behaviorists tend to use the term "generalization" a bit loosely.
Experimental psychology with infrahuman species would tend to
deal with generalization in terms of stimulus or response similarity.
Thus the pigeon trained to peck on a disc illuminated with a certain
color will peck more frequently for that color and colors close to it
in wave length than it will for colors very different from the training
color (*74*). With humans, however, verbal conditioning has shown
generalization along "semantic" dimensions (*75*), indicating that
stimuli relations are a symbolic process in man. The behaviorist
extrapolates this generalization by symbol mediation to a wide
variety of contacts. Thus a shy person can be trained to be assertive
in asking for a date with the assumption that he will also become
more assertive in other behaviors, e.g., chatting with girls (response
generalization). A patient may relate his response in a therapy
session to an event in his life and reproduce his response to this
generalized stimulus.

n. Baer and Wolf (*76*) describe what they call "entry behaviors." These
are a few key behaviors seen as establishing a small class of behaviors
which will be reinforced in the natural environment. Once the entry
behaviors have been established, the environment's "behavioral trap"
will maintain the behavior class without further therapeutic support.
Thus learning to call girls may lead to an active social life. These
entry behaviors are seen as behaviors deserving special therapeutic
consideration.

o. The frequency of occurrence of certain behaviors appears to be nearly
as much influenced by observation without "back-up" rewards as
with the back-up rewards. Smoking is one example (*77*). For many
school classes, "on task" behavior can be temporarily strongly influenced by observation alone (*22, 4*). However, for disruptive behavior
problem children such as hyperactives, the observation contingency
alone appears to be only a minor influence (*23*).

p. Large within-group disparities in task performance disturb both students and teachers. It often seems unfair to penalize a whole group
for one person's misbehavior. Harris and Sherman (*20*) describe an
extreme case of such a problem in which three students "resigned"
from the class's "good behavior" game. The teacher responded by

adding a time penalty for poor performance and these students caused their respective teams to stay late. The teacher, in this situation, created one new group to which only these three students were assigned. The new group stayed late for its first day of existence because of their noncooperation, but not after that. After 5 days, the three students were returned to their original groups without further problems.

q.   The variable interval schedule can be used in several ways. In its pure form, a reward is given for the first behavior during each period. In a compound form of variable interval and fixed ratio schedules, the reward is given after the first "n" behaviors in each period. For both of the pure and compound interval schedules it is desirable that the time condition and length of reward period be known only to the person giving the rewards. Cooking timers, if used, need to be out of sight of the child; the child should not be able to guess the period's beginning, end, or duration.

For misbehavior the inverse conditions can be taken; that is, reward can be given provided *no* misbehavior occurred in the period, or provided not more than "n" misbehaviors occurred in the period. For these conditions it is often desirable for the child to be aware of the time period.

r.   Solomon and Wahler (78) demonstrated that peers could be successfully trained to use their selective inattention to reduce classroom misbehaviors in selected problem children.

s.   The "balance theory" applies to objects and the attitudes toward these objects. Its presentation here (Figure 1) reflects the rather simple assumptions that : 1) the affective value (attitude) of bonds can be expressed by "+" or "−"; 2) all members in any given set perceive the same bonds as having the same affective value; and 3) balance occurs when objects with the same sign are linked by positive or null relations and objects of opposite signs are linked by negative or null relations.

The assumption most likely to be incorrect is that the perceptions of the attitude bonds for all members of the set are similar. For example, the school is most likely to always see the bond between the child and the family as positive, but the family or the child may not see it that way. It is interesting to note that the forced relations between a school and a negative child produces a strain on any balance model which can be relieved by appeal to concepts of "choice," view of self, and responsibility. These elements have been carefully presented elsewhere in the balance theory interpretation of cognitive dissonance (79).

LITERATURE CITED

1.   Meehl, P. E. On the circularity of the law of effect. Psychol. Bull. 47: 52–75, 1950.
2.   Robbins, D. Partial reinforcement: A selective review of the alleyway literature since 1960. Psychol. Bull. 76: 415–431, 1971.

3. Kaufer, F. H., and Phillips, J. S. Learning Foundations of Behavior Therapy, pp. 18–19. New York: Wiley and Sons, 1970.
4. Wolpe, J. The systematic desensitization treatment of neuroses. J. Nerv. Ment. Dis. 132: 189–203, 1961.
5. Wells, D. T. Large magnitude voluntary heart rate changes. Psychophysiology 10: 260–269, 1973.
6. Holmberg, A. R. Changing community attitudes and values in Peru: A case study, in R. N. Adams (Ed.), Social Change in Latin America Today, pp. 63–107. New York: Harper and Row, 1960.
7. Behavior Research and Therapy. Oxford: Pergamon Press.
8. Behavior Therapy. New York: Academic Press.
9. Journal of Applied Behavior Analysis. Lawrence, Kansas: Society for the Experimental Analysis of Behavior.
10. Journal of Behavior Therapy and Experimental Psychiatry. Oxford: Pergamon Press.
11. Birk, L., Brody, J. P., Rosenthal, A. J., Skelton, W. D. and Stevens, J. B. Behavior Therapy in Psychiatry: Report No. 5 of the American Psychiatric Association Council on Research and Development. Washington, D.C.: American Psychiatric Association, 1973.
12. Skinner, B. F. Walden Two. New York: Macmillan, 1948.
13. Bandura, A. Principals of Behavior Modification. New York: Holt, Rinehart and Winston, 1969.
14. Bandura, A., and Huston, A. C. Identification as a process of incidental learning. J. Abnorm. Soc. Psychol. 63: 311–318, 1961.
15. Bandura, A., Ross, D., and Ross, S. A. Vicarious reinforcement and imitative learning. J. Abnorm. Soc. Psychol. 67: 601–607, 1963.
16. Ayllon, T., and Azrin, N. H. The Token Economy, A Motivational System for Therapy and Rehabilitation. New York: Appleton-Century-Crofts, 1968.
17. Stainback, W. C., and Stainback, S. B. A close look at a variety of reinforcers. Train. School Bull. 69: 131–135, 1972.
18. Winkler, R. C. An experimental analysis of economic balance, savings and wages in a token economy. Behav. Ther. 4: 22–40, 1973.
19. Wahler, R. G. Setting generality: Some specific and general effects of child behavior therapy. J. Appl. Behav. Anal. 2: 239–246, 1969.
20. Harris, V. W., and Sherman, J. A. Use and analysis of the "good behavior game" to reduce disruptive classroom behavior. J. Appl. Behav. Anal. 6: 405–417, 1973.
21. McLaughlin, T. F., and Malaby, J. Intrinsic reinforcers in a classroom token economy. J. Appl. Behav. Anal. 5: 263–270, 1972.
22. Jens, K. G., and Shores, R. E. Educational materials: Behavior graphs as reinforcers for work behavior of mentally retarded adolescents. Ed. Train. Ment. Retard. 4: 21–27, 1971.
23. Long, J. D., and Williams, R. L. The comparative effectiveness of group and individually contingent free time with inner-city junior high school students. J. Appl. Behav. Anal. 6: 465–474, 1973.
24. Sulzer, B., Hunt, S., Ashby, E., Koniarski, C., and Krams, M. Increasing rate and percentage correct in reading and spelling in a fifth grade public school class of slow readers by means of a token

reward system, in E. Ramp and B. L. Hopkins (Eds.), A New
Direction for Education: Behavior Analysis 1971, pp. 5—28. Lawrence, Kan.: University of Kansas Press, 1971.

25. Hamblin, R. T., Hathaway, C., and Wordarski, J. Group contin-
gencies, peer tutoring and accelerating academic achievement, in E.
Ramp and B. L. Hopkins (Eds.), A New Direction for Education:
Behavior Analysis 1971, pp. 41—53. Lawrence, Kan.: University of
Kansas Press, 1971.

26. Patterson, G. R., and Brodsky, G. A behavior modification pro-
gramme for a child with multiple problem behaviors. J. Child
Psychol. Psychiat. 7: 277—295, 1966.

27. Glynn, E. L., Thomas, J. D., and Shee, S. M. Behavioral self-control
of on-task behavior in an elementary classroom. J. Appl. Behav.
Anal. 6: 105—113, 1973.

28. Drabman, R. S., Spitalnik, R., and O'Leary, K. D. Teaching self-control to disruptive children. J. Abnorm. Psychol. 82: 10—16, 1973.

29. Santogrossi, D. A., O'Leary, K. D., Romanczyk, R. G., and Kaufman,
K. F. Self-evaluation by adolescents in a psychiatric hospital school
token program. J. Appl. Behav. Anal. 6: 277—287, 1973.

30. Abelson, R. P., and Rosenberg, M. J. Symbolic psychologic: A model
of attitudinal cognition. Behav. Sci. 3: 1—13, 1958.

31. Rosenberg, M. J., Hovland, C. I., McGuire, W. J., Abelson, R. P., and
Brehm, J. W. Attitude Organisation and Change. New Haven,
Conn.: Yale University Press, 1960.

32. Safer, D. J. Drugs for problem school children. J. School Health 41:
491—495, 1971.

33. Cohen, S. I., Keyworth, J. M., Kleiner, R. I., and Brown, W. L.
Effective behavior change at the Anne Arundel Learning Center
through minimum contact interventions, in R. Ulrich, T. Stachnik,
and J. Mabry (Eds.), Control of Human Behavior, Vol. III: Behavior
Modification in Education, pp. 124—142. Glenview, Ill.: Scott,
Foresman and Company, 1975.

34. Graubard, P. S., Rosenberg, H., and Miller, M. B. Student applications
of behavior modification to teachers and environments or ecologi-
cal approaches to social deviancy, in R. Ulrich, T. Stachnik, and J.
Mabry (Eds.), Control of Human Behavior, Vol. III.: Behavior
Modification in Education, pp. 408—413. Glenview, Ill.: Scott,
Foresman and Company, 1973.

35. Buys, C. Effect of teacher reinforcement in elementary school pupils'
behavior and attitudes. Psychol. Schools 9: 278—288, 1972.

36. Gittelman-Klein, R., Klein, D. F., Felixbrod, J., Abikoff, H., Katz,
S., Gloisten, A., Kates, W., and Saraf, K. Methylphenidate vs.
behavior therapy in hyperkinetic children. Presented at the American Psychiatric Association Meeting, Anaheim, Calif., 1975.

37. Sprague, R. L., Christensen, D. E., and Werry, J. S. Experimental
psychology and stimulant drugs, in C. K. Conners (Ed.), Clinical
Use of Stimulant Drugs in Children, pp. 141—163, The Hague:
Excerpta Medica, 1975.

38. Ayllon, T., Layman, D., and Kandel, H. J. A behavioral-educational alternative to drug control of hyperactive children. J. Appl. Behav. Anal. 8: 137–146, 1975.
39. Minde, K., Weiss, G., and Mendelson, N. A 5-year follow-up study of 91 hyperactive school children. J. Amer. Acad. Child Psychiat. 11: 595–600, 1972.
40. Weiss, G., Kruger, E., Danielson, U., and Elman, M. The effect of long term treatment of hyperactive children with methylphenidate. Presented at American College of Neuro-psychopharmacology, Puerto Rico, 1973.
41. Watson, J. B., and Watson, R. R. Studies in infant psychology. Scient. Month. 13: 493–515, 1921.
42. Jones, M. C. A laboratory study of fear: The case of Peter. Pedagog. Sem. 31: 308–315, 1924.
43. Ayllon, T., and Azrin, N. H. Reinforcement and instructions with mental patients. J. Exp. Anal. Behav. 7: 327–331, 1964.
44. Ayllon, T., and Azrin, N. H. The measurement and reinforcement of behavior of psychotics. J. Exp. Anal. Behav. 8: 357–383, 1965.
45. Phillips, E. L. Achievement place: Token reinforcement procedures in a home-style rehabilitation setting for pre-delinquent boys. J. Appl. Behav. Anal. 1: 213–223, 1968.
46. Bandura, A. Behavior therapy and the models of man. Amer. Psychol. 29: 859–875, 1974.
47. Premack, D. Reinforcement theory, in D. Levine (Ed.), Nebraska Symposium on Motivation: 1965, pp. 123–180. Lincoln, Neb.: University of Nebraska Press, 1965.
48. Holstein, S. B., and Hundt, A. G. Reinforcement of intracranial self-stimulation by licking. Psychonom. Sci. 3: 17–18, 1965.
49. Homme, L. E. Contiguity theory and contingency management. Psychol. Rec. 16: 233–241, 1966.
50. Bolles, R. C. Reinforcement, expectancy and learning. Psychol. Rev. 79: 394–409, 1972.
51. Seligman, M. E. P. On the generality of the laws of learning. Psychol. Rev. 77: 406–418, 1970.
52. Tyler, D. W., Wortz, E. C., and Bitterman, M. E. The effect of random and alternating partial reinforcement on resistance to extinction in the rat. Am. J. Psychol. 66: 57–65, 1953.
53. Weinstock, S. Resistance to extinction of a running response following partial reinforcement under widely spaced trials. J. Comp. Physiol. Psychol. 47: 318–322, 1954.
54. Wagner, A. R. Effects of amount and percentage of reinforcement and number of acquisition trials on conditioning and extinction. J. Exp. Psychol. 62: 234–242, 1961.
55. Hulse, S. H. Amount and percentage of reinforcement and duration of goal confinement in conditioning and extinction. J. Exp. Psychol. 56: 48–57, 1958.
56. Roberts, W. A. Resistance to extinction following partial and consistent reinforcement with varying magnitudes of reward. J. Comp. Physiol. Psychol. 67: 395–400, 1969.

57. Theios, J., and McGinnis, R. W. Partial reinforcement before and after continuous reinforcement. J. Exp. Psychol. 73: 479–481, 1967.
58. Yates, A. J. Behavior Therapy. New York: Wiley and Sons, 1970.
59. Lazarus, R. S. A plea for technical and theoretical breadth. AABT Newslett. 3: 2, 1968.
60. Goldstein, A. P., Heller, K., and Sechrest, L. B. Psychotherapy and the Psychology of Behavior Change. New York: Wiley and Sons, 1956.
61. Krebs, D. L. Altruism—An examination of the concept and a review of the literature. Psychol. Bull. 73: 258–302, 1970.
62. Lepper, M. R., Greene, D., and Nisbett, R. E. Undermining children's intrinsic interest with extrinsic rewards. J. Personal. Soc. Psychol. 28: 129–137, 1973.
63. Grusec, J. E. Some antecedents of self-criticism. J. Personal. Soc. Psychol. 4: 244–252, 1966.
64. Mischel, W., and Grusec, J. Determinants of the rehearsal and transmission of neutral and aversive behaviors. J. Personal. Soc. Psychol. 3: 197–205, 1966.
65. Bandura, A., Grusec, J. E., and Menlove, F. L. Some social determinants of self-monitoring reinforcement systems. J. Personal. Soc. Psychol. 5: 449–455, 1967.
66. Liebert, R. M., Sobol, M. P., and Copemann, C. D. Effects of vicarious consequences and race of model upon imitative performance by black children. Develop. Psychol. 6: 453–456, 1972.
67. Bandura, A. Influence of models' reinforcement contingencies on the acquisition of imitative responses. J. Personal. Soc. Psychol. 1: 589–595, 1965.
68. Garrett, C. S., and Cunningham, D. J. Effects of vicarious consequences and model and experimenter sex on imitative behavior in first-grade children. J. Educ. Psychol. 66: 940–947, 1974.
69. Chittenden, G. E. An experimental study in measuring and modifying assertive behavior in young children. Monogr. Soc. Res. Child Develop. 7 (1, 31): 1942.
70. Renner, K. E. Delay of reinforcement: A historical review. Psychol. Bull. 61: 341–361, 1964.
71. Lovaas, O. I., Berberich, J. P., Perloff, B. F., and Schaefter, B. Acquisition of imitative speech by schizophrenic children. Science 151: 707, 1966.
72. Heaton, R. C., Safer, D. J., and Allen, R. P. A motivational environment for behaviorally deviant junior high school students (In preparation). 1975.
73. Atthowe, J. M., Jr., and Krasner, L. "Preliminary report on the application of contingent reinforcement procedures (token economy) on a "chronic" psychiatric ward. J. Abnorm. Psychol. 73: 37–43, 1968.
74. Guttman, N., and Kalish, H. I. Discriminability and stimulus generalization. J. Exp. Psychol. 51: 79–88, 1956.

75. Lacey, J. I., Smith, R. L., and Green. A. Use of conditioned autonomic responses in the study of anxiety. Psychosom. Med. 17: 208–217, 1955.
76. Baer, D. M., and Wolf, M. M. The entry into natural communities of reinforcement. Paper presented at American Psychological Association, Washington, D. C., 1967.
77. Sachs, L. B., and Bean, H. Comparison of smoking treatments. Behav. Ther. 1: 465–472, 1970.
78. Solomon, R. W., and Wahler, R. G. Peer reinforcement control of classroom problem behavior. J. Appl. Behav. Anal. 6: 49–56, 1973.
79. Insko, C. A., Worchel, S., Folger, R., and Kutkus, A. A balance theory interpretation of dissonance. Psychol. Rev. 82: 169–183, 1975.

Chapter 7 _____ Behavior Management in the Classroom

As previously noted, the classroom situation peculiarly elicits the major features of the HA disorder. An HA child who is mildly disturbing at home can become a severe problem at school: disturbing others, calling out, not raising his hand or staying in his seat, not listening to instruction, and not completing his work (*a*). The situation is disturbing and frustrating to both the HA child and the teacher. For the child, his HA pattern first becomes an obvious problem for life-adjustment in the classroom. Here he faces failure, punishment, and behavior demands for attention and motor inhibition unparalleled elsewhere in his life. The school experience can create a climate so that he is identified as sick (*b*).

For the teacher the problem is equally severe, as teachers know all too well. A class of 30 students will include on average 1 or 2 HA children. Most teachers, therefore, will face the problems of classroom management of HA children. In many areas of our country, classroom disturbances are already a serious issue without adding the problems of HA children. In urban areas teachers may spend as much as 80% of their day trying to keep class order (*1*). Maintaining discipline becomes particularly difficult in proportion to the number of HA children in the class (*c*). Any one HA child can consume an inordinate amount of the teacher's time without any obvious, positive result. Behavior observations of one special classroom showed that a small group of deviant, overactive children took the lion's share of the teacher's time (*2, 3*). The teacher's frustration with these children may lead to negative and aversive communication patterns often expressed almost unconsciously. The teacher, naturally enough, may experience a conflict between his accountability for teaching and his not wanting the child in the class. The situation is complicated by the justified concern for other students whose learning environment is disrupted by the

HA student. Referral to the principal's office becomes a common resolution of this conflict, particularly for older HA children.

Thus, improved classroom management of the HA child serves to benefit both the HA child and the teacher. With improved management the HA child can learn more, enjoy a more pleasant school experience, and can even require less medication. The teacher is able to devote energies and attention more constructively to the whole class.

The behavioral methods described in this chapter involve changes by the teachers to improve their classroom management. Earlier sections of this chapter deal with the basic steps in establishing contingency management systems: i.e., defining the behavior, observing the existing behavioral contingencies, establishing new contingencies, evaluating success, and fading.

The last section of this chapter focuses on the problem of reinforcing teacher behavior. Even dedicated teachers need reinforcement, particularly when instituting a major change in their classroom procedures.

DEFINE THE CLASSROOM
BEHAVIOR PROBLEMS OF THE HA CHILD

In the classroom the HA child customarily presents both poor learning and disruptive behavior. Since the "bad" behavior causes the most trouble, it is tempting to emphasize correction of this behavior with the assumption that this will also lead to improved learning. Unfortunately, this appears to be incorrect. One behavior study (4) looked at contingency efforts on noisy and disruptive behavior in two special classrooms for 1 academic year. Rewards were given, contingent on quiet, nondisruptive behavior. The noisy behaviors decreased by 80% with the contingencies. Learning as reflected by correct assignment completion was, however, essentially unaffected by the rewards. Even increasing time students spend on academic tasks does not necessarily lead to improved academic performance (4, 5). Rewarding good behavior increases good behavior but not learning. To assume that the quieter class learns more is an educational myth. Students engaged in learning tend not to be disruptive in class (6), but students who are not disruptive are not necessarily engaged in learning. In fact, the reverse approach may be better. Academic learning behaviors are probably incompatible with classroom misbehavior. Thus if the academic performance is directly rewarded, misbehavior should decrease. Ayllon and Roberts (6) demonstrated the effectiveness of this approach in a classroom. Ayllon et al. (7) further applied this to three HA children (ages 8–10) in one small class; rewarding academic success drastically reduced the children's HA symptoms without any apparent need for contingencies directly applied to the child's misbehavior. Although this worked satisfactorily in the few cases tried, it seems unlikely that it will work in all cases, particularly for children receiving group instruction. Thus, a behavioral program should probably address directly both the child's disruptive classroom behavior and his poor learning. Failing to deal with disruptive behavior will lead to school problems and unhappy teachers; failing to deal with learning will lead to continued poor achievement by the child. The emphasis, however, should be on learning first and behavior second.

Both good behavior and good learning need to be defined more precisely for each individual setting. Good behavior will usually be defined by nondisruptive behaviors such as: in class on time, in seat, no loud disruptive noises, no shouting out for the teacher's attention, and leaving at the end of the class period. The behaviors for improved learning include: being in class prepared to learn (paper, pencil, books), listening' and following instructions on task (working on assignments), correct solution to work problems and task completion (satisfactory accomplishment as determined by the teacher). Note that the behaviors are defined explicitly as those involved with learning or good social behavior. The behaviors are not defined in terms of theoretical basic items such as attentiveness, anxiety, fearfulness. It is important to avoid the use of poorly defined "psychological" states, and instead work directly with observable, specific behaviors.

ANALYZE EXISTING CONTINGENCIES

For the school child three separate areas of contingencies need to be looked at: the school system, the family, and the peer group. In the school, good *behavior* is rewarded by teacher praise, which is usually given verbally; bad behavior is punished by teacher comments, detention, non-promotion, trips to the principal's office, suspension, and critical letters home to parents. Good *learning* is rewarded by teacher's praise, positive comments on assignment sheets, and by grades; poor learning is punished by low grades, teacher comments, and nonpromotion. This represents an essentially lean set of contingencies for behavioral control. Nonetheless, the positive incentives in the system along with avoidance of punishments work well for about 70% of the children. They are, understandably, very ineffective for the misbehaving HA child. Since he seldom persists in academic tasks, those incentives requiring consistent success are unattainable. Even when he does some academic work, it is usually too little to merit a reward, particularly when rewards are based on the grading system.

Similarly, when the HA child does have a short period of decrease in disturbing behavior, it is more likely to be ignored than to be praised. In the extreme situation it has been found that the HA children's disruptive behavior apparently is reinforced by teacher attention to it (2; d). Indeed, the HA child's restlessness and misconduct may be his major claim to teacher attention. Perhaps being scolded is preferred to being either ignored or quietly rejected for academic incompetence (8).

As unbelievable as it may seem, data clearly indicate that scolding a frequently misbehaving child is closer in its behavioral effect to praising him than to punishing him. Many HA children apparently consider attention in any form rewarding. A study by O'Leary and colleagues (9) suggests that, in part, the dimension of significance is the public nature of the teacher's scolding. Personalized soft reprimands decreased disruptive behavior of misbehaving school children, whereas loud, public reprimands increased disruptive behavior. Even for soft reprimands, however, the more severely misbehaving children (two out of six evaluated) failed to respond. One nonresponder, who was apparently HA, showed high rates of disruptive behavior with soft reprimands. Perhaps some HA children find any teacher attention reinforcing, even though the teacher may intend it to be punishing. A somewhat alarming conclusion, since it indicates that for many HA children common sense notions of social punishment do not apply. There is considerable variation among teachers in the amount of attention given (usually as social punishment) to nonstudy and disruptive behavior. Classroom observations have found some teachers give 10%, whereas others given more than 80%, of their attention to students who show nonstudy or disruptive behaviors (10, 11). In effect, some teachers are frequently, unwittingly rewarding the HA child for his misbehavior, thereby complicating his learning difficulties. To correct this situation, teachers must practice ignoring minor disruptive behaviors and, instead, must emphasize cooperative student behavior. This emphasis is for many people neither natural nor easy, and, therefore, challenges the teacher's professional skills.

Offical school responses to poor achievement and misconduct by HA children often include nonpromotion and suspension. These severe punishing contingencies as a general rule are most effective when they are rarely used. Repeated use of nonpromotion leads to intense frustration on the part of the child; in response, the child will often show an increase in truancy and is likely to eventually drop out of school. Repeated use of suspension customarily leads to intensified bitterness and resentment on the part of both the parents and the child. The parents become increasingly critical of the school and do not productively respond to the school administrator's criticism of their child. This further encourages their child's school misconduct. Suspension, then, rewards the teachers by temporarily ridding them of their problem children, and rewards the misbehaving child with time off from school. In this case it is time off for bad behavior. Thus, like the teacher reprimand, official school punishment becomes rewarding for the misbehaving and underachieving HA child.

The family supports academic success by rewards given for grades, and by parental attention and praise given for academic activities such as doing homework. The family can also communicate the concept that learning is fun. Bad behavior in school and poor learning are often punished at home after the school has sent home a critical report on the child. For the nonachieving and misbehaving HA child, negative school reports become frequent. As the reports become the focus of parental action, with their implicit emphasis upon negative discipline, the parent is, unfortunately, in a position of responding only to bad information and is unable to support positive changes. This focus can easily reinforce the child's noncooperative attitude.

The role of the peer group in supporting school behavior is poorly understood largely because it has received relatively little formal attention. There seems little doubt, however, that peers hold important and significant rewards for children, particularly since class reprimands are clearly counterproductive. It is not clear, however, how peer rewards relate to school behavior. Solomon and Wahler (12) showed that the misbehaving children in a class received nearly all the peer attention while they were misbehaving. That study went on to demonstrate that the misbehaving children were much better behaved after their peers had learned to ignore their misbehavior. It seems likely, therefore, that manipulation of peer rewards can be a potent therapeutic tool when it can be accomplished.

CONSTRUCT NEW CONTINGENCIES

Three types of approaches will be presented. The first of these is the approach most likely to be practical for the average teacher, the establishment of contingencies for *one problem HA child* in the class. This approach can be readily generalized to a small group of HA children in the class. Second, as a simpler approach, *group rewards* can be given for individual or group behavior. Third, as the most thorough approach, "token economies" can be established for the *entire classroom,* thereby setting up reinforcement contingencies for each student in the class. The last two approaches will involve non-HA children in the class, but they certainly assist HA children. For convenience, each of these approaches is presented in abbreviated outline form in Table 1.

Individual Approaches
Increasing Desirable Behavior

What the Teacher Can Do in the Classroom   Several levels of reinforcement can be used by the teacher depending upon need and available resources. The simplest, and occasionally successful, first approach, involves the use of the few *social rewards* the teacher has available to dispense with some relatively high frequency, namely, attention and physical proximity. A simple way to dispense these rewards is to use a wristwatch alarm or a simple cooking timer. Set the timer for a particular time period and

Table 1. Types of classroom behavioral approaches

Individual contingencies	
Classroom	Teacher social rewards: attention, physical proximity, praise.
	Back-up rewards from class: edible, non-edible, privileges
	Point systems: using individual record with emphasis on successful academic work to earn points.
Contract	May involve teacher, counselor, child's home
Punishment	Overcorrection (making up loss, plus extra work)
	Response cost (loss of expected positive event)
	Time out (removed from school class)
Time-limited extinction	As a response to the direct challenge
Group contingencies	
Type 1	The behavior of one individual (or small group of individuals) earns points (rewards) for the entire class (individual contingency with group reward).
Type 2	Group behavior must reach goal for group reward (group contingency with group reward). Note: each individual may separately earn points for the group.
Type 3	Competition between groups with reward given to best group and/or to all groups who make a set goal ("good behavior game")

when the alarm goes off note whether or not the student has exhibited the desired behavior during the specified time period (e.g., "on task" for *all* or *nearly all* the time period, or listening and not calling out during the time period). If the student meets the behavior criteria, the teacher can verbally praise him, look at him, and/or move toward him, occasionally touching him with a pat on the back. The contact and comments should always be warm, positive, smiling, and reflect implicitly the teacher's thoughts of "good boy" (*11, 13–16*). The time interval should be varied (*e*).

These approaches work with many children including mildly HA children. For the severely misbehaving MBD child, social rewards and knowledge of results will, however, often fail to suffice to produce good behavior and learning. This is particularly the case for acquisition of new skills such as reading (*17*). *Back-up* reinforcements are, therefore, usually given in the form of immediate tangible reinforcers such as: M & M's, candies, popcorn, peanuts, crackerjacks, etc. These reinforcers are generally for immediate use. *Tokens* or *points* could also be given; these are later used to purchase back-up reinforcers which include, in addition to consumables, other items such as class privileges and time off from school for good behavior. Possible reinforcers are listed in Table 2.

Delivery of rewards, particularly for points, can be determined by the timer mentioned previously; the teacher marks the point earned on a student's card on his desk if the child exhibited the desired behavior during the time period. Alternatively, the rewards can be more automated. An automatic counter can give points when remotely triggered by a radio signal from a control carried by the teacher (*18, 19*). A clock on the child's desk could also be set to run as long as he met criteria behavior, with the teacher controlling the clock remotely. The clock, of course, requires close observation by the teacher, but has the advantage of giving continuous feedback for serious problem children. Every minute of good behavior could be worth 1 point for rewards. Use of the unit-of-time concept for measurement of behavior criteria has the advantage that the behavior demands can be gradually increased until they reach the duration of one lesson or class period.

For many children, and even some HA children aged 10 and older, the point allocation can be simplified. The points can be given on a card at the end of each lesson, or every 15 minutes (*21*). When this is the case a program can be instituted with minimum problems for the teacher and students.

What the Counselor/therapist Can Do by the Contract Method   In elementary schools, the teacher can be asked to complete a progress card with 0 (poor) or 1 (good-satisfactory) ratings for each lesson, with separate ratings for learning and behavior. The points could also be given at the natural class breaks such as lunch, recess, etc. (see Chart 1). In junior and senior high schools, the child can carry a weekly progress card around with him on which each teacher can record his behavior and learning evalua-tions at the end of each class period (see Chart 2). Generally, a rating of "0" (unsatisfactory) and "1" (satisfactory) will suffice. Verbal comment or more complicated scoring tends to confuse more than help. The teachers must understand that the ratings are important and that maxi-mum ratings indicate the child is passing. Teacher initials should also be used. At least once a week the card should be verified by the guidance counselor or other school personnel to protect against forgery.

Rewards for a large number of points on student cards can be arranged in the school or at home or in both locations. The school can reward the child by letting him leave the school early, have an extra period of shop, gym, or art, have special use of the resource room or other school privileges, see a free movie, or get dance tickets. It should be noted that children who frequently cut class or are truant have indicated that time off from school is rewarding. Parents can reward the child by having the number of points on his progress card determine the amount of his weekly or daily allowance or the amount of certain home privileges (e.g., later hours outside). Particularly useful rewards for a good school week are the weekend privileges (e.g., movies, bowling, roller skating, late weekend hours).

The counselor can use a point system in a *contract* approach to obtain family or school privileges. The point system, particularly one using progress cards and teachers' signatures, provides the basic bookkeeping system for a home-school child contract. The contract is a written agree-ment, signed by involved parties, in which the child agrees to fulfill "X" responsibilities and the parent agrees to provide "Y" privileges. It is important that the child as well as the parent sign the contract.

The therapist works to pin down an explicit acceptable contract involving the child and the parents and/or the child and the school authorities. Chart 3 is a sample of actual contracts used by clinicians. Negotiating for the contract should involve the significant parties, e.g., the child and both parents. The contract should involve the child in a commit-ment to attempt to earn the rewards as well as a clear commitment from the parents that the rewards will be given *if and only if* earned. The therapist needs to insure that parents neither fail to give the reward nor give the reward when it is not earned. Sincerity and effort don't count, only the number of points on the card count for the contingent rewards. If an allowance is given as reward for school points, the child must not be able to get the money for any other reason. Similarly, if he gets his school points but misbehaves at home, the allowance arrangement should not be altered to punish the child. The contracts should be time limited with a provision to renew the contract. This avoids a commitment which later becomes difficult or unacceptable. School and home rewards can be equally effective, but the combination is the most effective. When, however, one party (school or home) is unwilling to cooperate, then the other should be used.

In instances when specific home contracts cannot be arranged daily or weekly, notes from the school should be sent home telling what percentage of the expected work the child has done or what percentage of the maximum number of points he has earned. This information should be positive in tone, e.g.,: "John *has* completed 30 out of 40 assigned tasks," rather than: "John has failed to do 10 assignments this week." If positive information flows from the school to the home, the child's family is more likely to cooperate with the school in the future and the child is more likely to give the information to his parents.

It is also important to note that the child bears the responsibility for carrying his card around for signatures and showing it to the people who will give the rewards. Neither school staff nor parents should assume the child's responsibilities. Loss of the card or failure to get signatures means loss of reward for the child.

When the teacher is not able or willing to participate in changes in her use of social and class contingencies, then the eventual success of this approach depends upon the child's behavior improving to the point that the teacher has started praising him for his good behavior and giving him slightly better grades.

One frequently encountered problem with any point system involves the child's anger, particularly when 0–1 (all-or-none) rewards are used for the entire lesson plan. When the teacher gives a 0, the child may react angrily. He may in the extreme become verbally defiant, demanding points from teachers. If he succeeds in intimidating teachers so that they award points to "avoid the hassle" when they give 0's, then the point system becomes counterproductive. It is rewarding aggressive behavior rather than scholastic behavior. The teachers must, therefore, be advised *never* to argue or even discuss the point awards; their word is final and they should walk away from any arguments, ignoring the student's protest. The teacher should neither verbally respond to demands nor order the child to stop pressuring him. He must simply turn and walk away from the angry child. The only exception to this reaction should be to positive inquiries from the child, such as: "How can I get the point?" The child should be

Table 2. Commonly used reinforcers

Edible	Nonedible	Social	Activity	Tokens (points)
Gum	Balloons	Attention	Gym time	(For general exchange)
Candy	Clothes	Public praise	Shop time	
M & M's	Scout uniform	Posting work in school or at home	Library time	
Popcorn	Shoes, etc.	Approval	Driver's license	
Cracker Jacks	Toys (dolls, cars)	Access to privilege areas (e.g., blackboard, lavatory, parent's office, den, T.V. room)	Movies	
Sodas	Sports related items		Concerts (folk, rock, ballet)	
Cakes	Baseball cards	Time off from school	Field trips	
Pies	Baseball	Hours for out-of-house	Hobbies	
Ice cream (bars, etc.)	Sports equipment	Private areas	Theater	
Hamburgers	Records	Private times	Ballet	
Nuts (peanuts)	Music equipment	T.V. privileges	Sports teams	
Raisins	Car parts (also motorcycle, etc., parts)	Program choice	Camping	
	Motorcycle, mini-bike, bicycle	Time watching	Travel	
			Day trips	
			Overnight trips	

Furnishings for
room (T.V.,
posters, black
lights, dolls)
Telephone

Dinner out
Dinner time choice
Friend's privileges
In house, at dinner,
Overnight
Bedtime
Bath choices
Parties
Time with one parent
Special work
Collecting papers
Run recorders,
Carrying messages
Telephone privilege
Hair length
Clothing choice

Chart 1. Sample daily behavior success report for elementary school level. Note that breaks are defined by changes in lessons. Times for this are only approximate.

Circle Day: M Tu W Th F

Date:——————

Student:————————————

DAILY REPORT

Points

Time (Approx.)	Beh.	Learning	Initial	Teacher (Usual)	Comments
9–10 Lesson 1				Mrs. X Mr. Y	
10–12 Lesson 2 (10–11)				Ms. Z	
Lesson 3 (11–12)					
12:30– 1:00 Lunch				Mrs. W	
1:00– Lesson 4 2:45 (1–2)				Mr. Y	
Lesson 5 (2–2:45)					
TOTAL POINTS: TOTAL ALL POINTS:				Give points for both behavior (Beh.) & Learning Score points as follows: 0 – Not appropriate 1 – Acceptable 1^+ – Very good	

Chart 2. Sample weekly behavior success report for junior high level.

Student: _____ Week of _____ to _____ 7 —
DAY   MON   TUES   WED   THURS   FRI

	B	L	Int.	B	L	Int.	B	L	Int.	B	L	Int.	B	L	Int.	Score:
Period 1																1) B:0 = poor behavior
2																1= good behavior (acceptable)
3																2) L:0= poor learning
4																(failing or way below ability)
5																1= expected or passing learning
6																behavior
7																Teacher please score 0 or 1 for each class— if assembly give both 1's
grades/ homework comments																Please place initials under initial column (Int.)
parents Int.:																Thank you
counselor Int.:																

Chart 3. Sample behavior contract.

Contract effective starting —————————— for a 4-week period and may be renewed thereafter by mutual agreement of both parties.

—————— agrees to: Mr. and Mrs. —————— agree to:

1. Carry card to earn points in school—attempt to earn all the points each day (maximum of 14)—and bring the card home to show his parents.

2. Abide by hours (for coming in) as agreed here

3. Carry out garbage each week night between 4:00 p.m. and 6:00 p.m.

4. Tidy up room before noon on Sunday

_____

Signed:

_____

Son   date

_____

Father   date

_____

Mother   date

1. Set hours (for coming in) according to number of points earned:

   10–12 pts. - 9:30 p.m.
   8–9   pts. - 9:00 p.m.
   7–8   pts. - 8:30 p.m.
   5–6   pts. - 8:00 p.m. School nights
   4   pts. - 7:00 p.m.
   0–3   pts. - 6:00 p.m.

2. *Father* will pay allowance on Friday night based on 9¢ for each point (maximum of $5.40 for all 60 points).

3. Everyday son earns more than 9 points, there will be no negative comments about clothes that evening or next day.

4. No comments about where or what son is doing out—can only ask: "Did you have a good time"—*unless* son comes in late.

5. If room tidy on Saturday—and garbage taken out without reminder each week day—add 1 hour to weekend hours—as determined by Friday's points.

similarly instructed never to argue about points, but instead to ask what he can do to earn points in the future. The therapist or counselor should probably attempt to rehearse this with the child, using role playing to provide a model of the appropriate behavior. Both the child and the teacher will need continued support to avoid challenges and arguments about points. This problem area, along with the failure of the school or home to deliver the reinforcer and occasional forgery of points, are the major problems in the contract approach.

With regard to parents fulfilling their part of a contract, the counselor or therapist needs to take preventive actions. The contract must be realistic for the parents, that is, it must be both practical and comfortable for the parents. Occasionally, parents will agree to excessive rewards, feeling sure their child will never earn them, e.g.,: "If Johnny gets superior daily grades (12 out of 14 points) 4 out of 5 days for 6 weeks, I'll buy him a mini-bike, if I can afford it then." In this situation the parent will in effect work to prevent the boy from behaving well in school so that the parents' overcommitment is never discovered. Sometimes parents will agree to actions they really don't want to allow. For example, a parent might say: "All right, if Johnny earns an "excellent mark" he can stay out 'til 1:00 a.m. Friday and Saturday nights—but he knows I won't sleep until he comes home." The counselor or therapist must seek to find reinforcers which the parents will use once they have agreed to the contract, and he must be in tune with the subtle hints parents give indicating what they can accept. Similarly, the behavior goals for the child must be both simply defined and realistic. Most HA children will overestimate the number of points they can earn, so that in establishing a criteria for reward, it's good advice to start low and gradually increase the criteria, e.g.: start at 8 out of 14 points for the first week, increase to 10 the next week, and to 12 for all subsequent weeks. Let the child know about this increase at the start.

The counselor also needs to check with the parents and the school staff regularly to support compliance with the contract. As part of this process, it is important to look for indications that the rewards are being secretly held back, or given when they are not earned. The reinforcers in the contract must be given *if* and *only if* the child meets the agreed behavior criteria. Since home factors need to be considered in the home contract the section on the home contract in Chapter 8 should be noted.

Decreasing Undesirable Behavior

Managing Classroom Misconduct In response to student misconduct, the teacher's behavior is crucial. Card and point systems with home or school reinforcers can work to encourage specific good behaviors. Since these systems rely upon the child's carrying home the information, they do *not* lend themselves to punishment contingencies. After all, why should the child carry home bad news? Thus the teacher-enforced contingencies are the only effective *direct* approach to undesirable classroom behavior.

When serious misconduct occurs in the classroom, the teacher needs some methods to produce quick changes or to remove the child from the situation. Punishment contingencies, when effective, may produce quick changes. Punishment must, however, be as sensitive and systematic as reinforcement contingencies. The days of impulsive, physical responses by teachers are over.

When a child misbehaves, the teacher's first reaction should be to pointedly ignore the bad behavior; walk away from the child and, if possible, praise another child for his good behavior (*22, 23*). If these contingencies fail to "extinguish" bad behavior to acceptable levels, then some aversive punishment contingencies can be tried. For example, for a disruptive behavior a child could be required to *overcorrect* for his misbehavior in an appropriate manner by apologies, extra clean-up, loss of playtime, or staying in his seat after the other children have gone, etc. These aversive consequences are only mildly aversive, can be applied frequently, require little effort from the teacher, and are sometimes quickly effective (*18, 24*). Unfortunately, in the secondary schools particularly, these aversive consequences might be applied too often, thereby leading to classroom avoidance responses, such as cutting class, playing sick, and truancy. In elementary school the child's avoidance response is more often a stubborn refusal to cooperate in matters such as doing assignments. To minimize these problems, the classroom teacher's repertoire of contingencies should include one or more reinforcement contingencies presented previously.

To make punishment less personal and less abrupt a warning signal approach can be used. Verbal warnings can be used (*25*), but nonverbal ones probably work better. A distinctive slip of paper, for example, can be used as the warning signal. An example of one used in a junior high school program is given in Chart 4 (*21*). The slip is given to the child as a warning that his behavior is bad. If a second warning slip is required within a fixed time, such as one class period, then the child would receive one of the punishment contingencies, e.g., 5-minute loss of play time. The warning slip has the advantage of being a nonverbal, minimum attention warning. It should be given with a minimal amount of looking at the child and there should *not* be any verbal warning accompanying the slip. The slip should be the only indication that the bad behavior is occurring. The child should be expected to correct the misbehavior within a reasonable time (e.g.,

Chart 4. Warning slip for misbehavior used in Stemmer's Run Junior High School, Baltimore County, Maryland, and modified from forms used by William Brown at Anne Arundel Learning Center, Maryland.

D/D SLIP

PLEASE CORRECT THE FOLLOWING SERIOUS DISTURBING OR DISRUPTIVE BEHAVIOR:

1. Disruptive talking ————
2. Throwing objects ————
3. Hitting or pushing ————
4. Talking disrespectfully ————
5. Noise making ————
6. Unauthorized area ————

IF YOU RECEIVE A SECOND SLIP DURING THIS CLASS PERIOD, YOU MUST REPORT TO THE OFFICE OF THE ASST. PRINCIPAL

DATE ———— STUDENT ———————— TEACHER ————————

10–30 seconds). Failure to correct the behavior within the time limit should lead to the second warning and the consequent punishment.

Another approach to punishment contingencies serves to minimize the aversive consequences by using *response-cost* contingencies. An expected positive consequence is reduced in magnitude for each episode of misbehavior (*26*). For example, five slips of paper on the child's desk could each represent 3 minutes of his 15-minute morning recess (free time). One slip could be removed for each misbehavior with a consequent loss of 3 minutes of recess. This provides for greater flexibility in punishment using mildly aversive consequences.

Finally, the "last resort" punishment consequence involves *time out* from the class (*25, 27*). This is usually arranged by sending a child out in the hall for a couple of minutes or down to a special "time-out" area. In one arrangement, a child is given a message to take to the office which simply states that the child is to be detained for 5–10 minutes before being given a reply to take back to the teacher (*28*). Time outs have the great advantage of allowing the child a chance to "cool off" and is particularly effective if the time out deprives the child of desired social awards available in the class. If, however, during the time out the child finds reinforcers such as wandering the hall, smoking in the lavatory, or socializing with other students, then time out becomes counterproductive. Time out should, in effect, be a period of isolation without food, cigarettes, toys, radio, television, or human contact.

Where a real time out can be arranged, it has been very effective (*29, 30*). Walker and colleagues (*29*) noted that even after social rewards were well established for good behaviors, the time-out procedure was needed to keep disruptive behavior at a minimum for four out of five severely misbehaving children in one class. Unfortunately, many schools have inadequate facilities to arrange for time-out areas. Some schools solve this by developing "crisis classes" or "in-school suspension" classes. Entry to these special classes is, however, usually not under teacher control nor is it for brief durations (10 minutes to 1 hour), but rather it is under administrator control (assistant principal) and only for longer periods (1–2 days). The in-school suspensions are also too often areas of social exchange, particularly if a waiting area outside a school administrator's office is used. As difficult as it may be to organize, time out is, nonetheless, important in effective management of the misbehaving HA child. Without effective time out the previously described aversive punishment contingencies become rather frequently used for the HA child.

Managing the Direct Challenges to Authority: Time-limited Extinction One form of undesirable behavior requiring special attention is the often dramatic situation posed when a child overtly challenges the teacher's authority. The child could either passively refuse to follow a teacher's directions, such as "Go back to your seat," or he could verbally defy and even threaten the teacher by saying, for example, "I am not going to pick it up" or "Give me that book" or "Give me that point." In awarding warning slips related to punishment contingencies, HA children may "blow-up" and swear, crumple up the paper, throwing it away, or say something like "Give me another slip; I don't care if you do punish me." Younger children will tend to be defiantly stubborn whereas older children, particularly impulsive HA adolescents, will be more verbally assaultive, bordering on physical threats.

These challenging behaviors should be treated as all other undesired behaviors are. For misbehaving HA children, counterthreats by the teacher are likely to maintain the behavior and escalate the conflict. Extinction is the preferred mode of response. Where possible, the challenges should be ignored. Particularly if behavioral compliance occurs, minor verbal challenges should be ignored. In cases where the challenging behaviors require action, extinction needs to be modified using a *time-limited rule* approach. A time period is established by class custom or by teacher statement and a rule presented regarding consequences. The teacher then refers the child to the rule either explicitly or implicitly by class custom. Thus when a child fails to respond to an order claiming "I never will," the teacher responds: "You know the rules: I expect that you will begin to do that within the next 30 seconds or else you will lose recess time." The teacher has stated three things that the child needs to know: the rule, a time limit, and consequences.

For younger children a visible clock is helpful for the time limit; the teacher can refer to it, e.g.: "Start picking up the papers before the big hand gets to 4. . . ." During the time period, the teacher ignores the child's behavior and gives social rewards and her physical proximity to the well behaved children. The teacher may then say, "Johnny, that's a good book you are reading," but should avoid saying, "Johnny, it's good to see you are in your seat and not out of place like others are." The latter type of comment should be avoided because it heightens the confrontation by a veiled reference to the bad child's behavior and it directs class attention to the bad child contrary to the principal of extinction (f). For very oppositional children, the time period for starting corrective action needs to be fairly long, e.g., 2–5 minutes. The time period can gradually be reduced once the child has learned to make the behavior correction within the time period. As a clinical rule of thumb, 5–10-second time periods appear to be minimum limits for time-limited extinction.

One modification to time-limited extinction for young misbehaving children is the use of "counting." The teacher says: "Get to your seat by the time I count to 8 or else you will start losing recess time." The teacher then counts *out loud, slowly,* and generally ignores the child's behavior. Toward the end of the count it is helpful if the teacher obviously prepares to implement the consequences such as moving toward the child preparing to put him in his seat. As soon as the child *starts* corrective action, the counting should be stopped. The counting approach is less desirable than "time-limited" extinction since the child receives a fair amount of attention for misbehavior. It is, however, an appropriate approach, particularly for younger children (grade 2 or less), in situations demanding quick behavior correction, or for conditions in which timing devices are not available. Counting works particularly well when coercive consequences are to be applied, e.g., making the child sit down. Counting should always be evenly paced, slow (about 1 number per second) and the count not less than 5. At first the child will tend to wait to the very last number before responding, but eventually he will start responding earlier during the count in order to stop the conditioned aversive consequence of the count itself. Essentially, the child escapes the counting by starting corrective behavior.

For both counting and time-limited extinction it is absolutely essential that the teacher institute the consequences (punishment) if the child fails to make corrections. Since, however, the child may fail to start the corrective behavior until the very end of the time period or count, it is desirable to give him the benefit of the doubt. As in baseball, the tie goes to the runner; that is, if at the very last minute the child starts the corrective action and then follows through with the correction after the time period is over, the punishment should not be given. For example, if he starts darting to his seat at the last second, he should not be punished even though he makes it to his seat shortly after the time period ends. The significant issue is starting within the time period and following through afterwards. Failure to complete the corrective behavior should, of course, lead to punishment without further recourse.

In certain cases, particularly for older children, time-limited extinction can be established as the class procedure. For example, if a teacher uses a warning slip for punishment, the rule could be established that after receiving the slip the child has 30 seconds to take corrective action. During the time period, the child's behavior and verbal comments will be ignored as much as possible, but at the end of the time period, if correction was not made, the child would be punished. In this situation the teacher never makes any verbal comments to the student or even looks at him when giving the warning slip and while waiting for the child's corrective action.

This approach works well for older children and for teachers who can be *very consistent* about the time period. The approach does not allow flexibility in the time period based on the individual cases; it does, however, maximize the extinction condition provided that peer rewards are not given for the child's behavior during the time period.

Similar techniques work for demand behavior, such as persistent demands for a book or severe threats, e.g.: "Give me that book back or I'll get even with you." The teacher can try to respond by ignoring the behavior, not even looking at the child and attending to other children. If the demands or threats persist, however, the teacher can provide one warning and give a time limit for further similar behavior. Thus, he can say, "I don't want to hear that again for the next 5 minutes, or else you have to leave the class." In this way the teacher asserts limited control which can be expanded from 5 minutes to the entire class period. Sometimes it takes a certain flexibility to define what constitutes repeating the demand. Quiet muttering under the breath and indirect references by the child should generally be ignored.

In the use of time-limited extinction it is important that the teacher maintain a low emotional profile. Her orders and instructions should be factual, direct, and not angry or stern. The verbal statements should be slow, calm, precise, and limited. Pursed lips and stern demeanor do not assist compliance; they only let the child know that the teacher is angry, critical, and possibly concerned about loss of control. The teacher's voice should reflect her confidence in keeping control. In some situations the need for this communication taxes the teacher's professional skills. The teacher may in fact feel threatened or disturbed by an HA child's aggressiveness, particularly if the child is older. When such a problem develops, the teacher should seek assistance from colleagues and administrators to correct the situation. If the situation cannot be corrected the child may have to be removed from that teacher's class. The school authorities must provide mechanisms for teachers to seek help with such problems honestly, without fear of reprisal.

Group Contingencies

Three types of group contingencies have been used successfully in the classroom. In the type 1 group contingency, one individual problem child is allowed to earn consequences (reinforcements or punishments) for the entire class (31). This is sometimes viewed as a group reward for an individual contingency rather than a group contingency. If points are used, every class member receives the points earned by the target child. This obviously creates a good environment for training peers to support the good behavior in the problem child and ignore bad behavior. Instrumenting this procedure is relatively simple since using some large display of points earned, visible to the entire class, suffices for awarding the points. For example, the teacher could have a large set of cards with numbers on them at the front of the class; points would be awarded or removed by flipping over a new card indicating the new total number of points earned (*32*). Large marks on the blackboard is an even simpler alternative. For bookkeeping ease, it is customary to require every child to use all of his points each day so that on subsequent days all children will have the same number of points. A nonacademic time period near the end of the day could be used for children to spend remaining points. This group contingency is, perhaps, the simplest effective method to provide back-up reinforcers supporting good behavior of one or two HA children in a regular class. For two target HA children, both could be allowed to earn points for the entire class. In the extreme, of course, all students could earn points for the entire group, but then the peer support for good behavior becomes less concentrated on the one or two misbehaving children. Observation also becomes more difficult.

Type 1 group contingencies can, of course, be used for punishment. But obvious problems develop when one class member's misbehavior consistently leads to group punishment. The resulting group resentment and anger at the target child contrasts with the positive, supportive peer relations produced by type 1 group reinforcement contingencies.

Type 2 group contingencies require criterion behavior from all group members in order to obtain the consequences (32). For example, all the class must be "on task" for 10 minutes without disruptive noises in order to earn 1 point for each class member. The reinforcement points can be divided the same way as with type 1 group contingencies. Similarly, the requirement that all points are spent each day can be similarly used to reduce bookkeeping demands. As an alternative, a mark can be awarded to all the group for each instance of misbehavior of any group member. If the group gets less than a minimum number of points, an extra reinforcement privilege is awarded. Unlike type 1, type 2 group contingencies often create problems for the severely misbehaving HA child. Here he becomes a source for loss of reinforcement everyone else would have earned and is, therefore, likely to become an unpopular group member (*g*).

Type 3 group contingencies involve competition between two or more groups. Each group earns points by a type 2 group contingency, or each group competes against the other on a behavior criteria with reinforcements given to the winning group or to all groups if they pass a certain minimum standard. Thus, the reward goes to the first group to finish its task or the group with the best task accomplishment (e.g., the quietest class in the lunchroom gets extra play time). This approach is frequently referred to as "the good behavior game" (5, 33; h). This group contingency works particularly well for preparatory or clean-up tasks where the natural rewards involve allowing the group to go on to the next task in the order of successful task completion. The first group ready goes first, a particularly significant reinforcement for leaving class work for play times. This procedure supports peer modeling with teacher attention focused on successful groups rather than on the slow, disordered groups. In a comparison of type 2 with type 3 contingencies, there were no significant differences found for effectiveness in controlling "on task" behavior. The choice between the two appears to be practical matter. Type 3 is harder to administer than is type 2, but type 3 does allow the use of modeling and the natural reinforcers of "being first."

In fact, all three group contingencies appear to be equally effective in most classes and each is probably as effective or slightly more effective than individual contingencies (32). One of the interesting possibilities is that type 1 group contingencies combined with group training for appropriate peer support for the target child might provide the most effective control technique for a class with only one or two misbehaving HA children. Theoretically, this could be expected, but data are not yet available to determine whether or not this is the case.

The general outcome for group and special individual contingencies for severely misbehaving children are improvement of about 20–40% in the children's behavior. Teachers should be aware that while these are significant changes, they are by no means magic transformations of the child's behavior. In an effort to create larger magnitude changes the contingency approach can be directly extended so that each class member is on an individual contingency program. A large number of significant aspects of class activities can then become part of the reinforcement opportunities creating, hopefully, larger magnitude changes in behavior. This represents the token economy approach to classroom management.

The Classroom Token Economy

Of all behavior therapy techniques the best documented procedure, showing consistent and often dramatic benefits for misbehaving children is the token economy classroom. Since an initial report by Zimmerman and Zimmerman (15), the literature is replete with successful demonstrations of technique (13, 14, 20, 21, 30, 34–44). Given adequate facilities, this is undoubtedly the best approach to behavioral control in the classroom. In essence, the procedures are simple. Each child earns tokens or points for doing specific behaviors. In the usual case the reward is a point given for "on task" behavior. Sometimes points are given on an electronic display at the student's desk remotely triggered by an inconspicuous observer on a variable observation schedule (45). Usually, however, a teacher gives points on a card on the student's desk at fixed intervals during the lesson (21) or at the end of a lesson (20). At the end of a class period or the end of the day, students may use their points to purchase rewards. Students may be permitted to save points for large rewards, but care should be taken to avoid letting any student becoming too "wealthy." If a student saves too many points, he becomes relatively independent of the point-supported contingencies, like some wealthy individuals who are independent of the usual need to work. Too much savings also indicates that the reinforcements are not valued by the student sufficiently to induce him to spend his points (46; i).

The reinforcements can be any of the items mentioned in the list of reinforcements in Table 2. A particularly useful resource is a "reinforcement area" in the classroom or elsewhere in the school, where access to activities (e.g., playing a phonograph) can be purchased for points. Often, access to the reinforcement area costs points. Sometimes, also, activities in the reinforcement area cost additional points depending on the activity.

Careful planning is needed for managing the token economy. The system set up must ensure adequate behavior definition, behavior observation, correct and complete delivery of points earned in a manner clearly understood by the student, an adequate selection of "back-up" reinforcements and adequate opportunities to spend the points and enjoy the items purchased. Reinforcement prices and point award schedules need to be balanced to avoid too much inflation or excess savings in the economy.

In starting the token economy classroom, the initial behaviors are usually simple and emphasize social behaviors, e.g., getting to class on time, bringing a pencil and notebook, sitting in seat, not calling out. As social behaviors improve the target behaviors are gradually changed to emphasize more academic behaviors such as answering a set number of questions or completing a set of problems. Since rates of progress and learning differ between children, the token system works particularly well with individualized instruction rather than group instruction. Individual task assignment can be tailored so that each student can earn about the same number of points for academic achievement and no student is faced with academic behavioral steps which are so difficult that he gives up or so trivial he doesn't try.

The minimum facilities usually required for a token economy in a regular class are: class size of about 20–30 (j); teacher training seminars during the summer; special teacher assistants available for 60–90 minutes daily to assist with paperwork; consultation "back-up" of about 30 minutes per week per teacher to evaluate the program; and reinforcement areas with reinforcements (43, 44). For elementary schools each class can be self-contained, including the reinforcement contingencies and reinforcement areas. For junior and senior high schools, coordination needs to be established with a team of teachers instructing a section of children; the reinforcement area will usually be a separate classroom area in the school which would be staffed during specific periods of the day.

To show some of the specifics of establishing classroom token economies, consider the following two examples, one for junior high and the second for an elementary class. For a junior high section of behavior problem children a good model is provided by a modification of the Anne Arundel Learning Center procedures established by Brown and Cohen (21; k). Students can be given a class folder to carry around which contains places for points and specifications of behaviors required to earn points. A set team of teachers would be trained to award the points for each class period. In a typical class eight points would be earned for behavior specified. Initially, the points would be awarded one each for 1) coming to class on time; 2) pencil and paper ready; 3) in seat on time; 4) starting task; 5–7) working on task without calling out for each of three 15-minute periods; and 8) successful task completion. When the preparatory behaviors have been well established the behaviors could be changed so that 1 point is given for each of the following: 1) in class seat with pencil and paper on time; 2) listening to initial class directions; 3) following initial class directions; 4) no calling out during initial class directions; 5–7) following class study plan without intrusive calling out for each of three 15-minute periods; 8) successfully completing class study.

The first four major subjects are arranged for the first four periods of the day. At the beginning of the fifth period, the children report to the "reinforcement room." Those students earning 30 points (all but 2 of the number of points available) receive an "excellent day" card to take home and can use these 30 points to purchase early release from school. Students with 15 or more points can enter the reinforcement room for the afternoon where they can spend remaining points (after 15 are removed) on activities such as pool, ping pong, table games, record playing, and food items. They can also earn 4 points per period in the reinforcement room. Unused points at the end of the day enter a bank account which can be spent only at weekly auctions. The items at auction are like those described in Table 2, such as: hamburger tickets, milk, chocolates, dance tickets, toy models, trinkets, chances to play pool or ping pong with the vice principal, etc. Each item should have a minimum auction price. The auction ensures that all points have "back-up" reinforcements and helps to avoid difficulties in setting economic values of the back-up reinforcements.

For children not earning 15 points in one day, make-up work to earn points is available in the afternoon. As soon as they have completed enough tasks (5-minute tasks earn 1 point) to bring their total daily earnings up to 15 points they are allowed to enter the reinforcement room.

Grades can be determined by the number of successful task completions. Since each task is designed to be completed within one class period, most students will complete nearly all of their assignments. A and B grades are, therefore, not uncommon. The week's total school performance is rated on the basis of the number of excellent days. Four out of 5 excellent days (30 points or more) and no day with less than 25 points justifies an "excellent week" letter to be taken to the family (6; 1).

Home contracts within the family can be negotiated based on excellent day cards and excellent week letters. The parents can also be requested to attend weekly conferences at school unless their child earns an excellent week.

A useful model for an elementary class token economy is provided by McLaughlin and Malaby (41). They set up a token economy for a regular fifth and sixth grade class with an emphasis upon completion of classroom assignment. Each day the teacher listed the assignments he expected to correct that day and the assignments that should be finished in time to be corrected by the next day. The assignments were to be completed during class time. "At the beginning of each class, papers were corrected. Each student graded his own paper. Corrections were made in some medium other than that used to complete the assignment. At the end of the correction period, the teacher called students one at a time to his desk and awarded points for the number of items correct in the assignment, providing it was complete, and gave bonus points for neatness." Points were removed for incomplete assignments. The points were recorded separately by both the student and the teacher. Each Monday morning the points could be exchanged for a class privilege from a "banker." There was one student serving as banker for each privilege; he kept a record of who bought the privilege which he turned in to the teacher. After following this procedure for about 4 months, a change was made so that the day on which points could be exchanged for privileges was varied and occurred without notice, but the average time between exchange days remained about the same as before. Table 3 lists the point economy controls used in this study.

Table 3. Number of points earned or lost for specific behaviors in one elementary school classroom token economy

Behaviors that earned points	Points
1) Items correct	6–12
2) Study behavior 8:50–9:15	5 per day
3) Bring food for animals	1–10
4) Bring sawdust for animals	1–10
5) Art	1–4
6) Listening points	1–2 per lesson
8) Neatness	1–2
9) Taking home assignments	5
10) Taking notes	1–3
11) Quiet in lunch line	2
12) Quiet in cafeteria	2
13) Appropriate noon hour behavior	3
Behaviors that lost points	
1) Assignments incomplete	Amount squared
2) Gum and candy	100
3) Inappropriate verbal behavior	15
4) Inappropriate motor behavior	15
5) Fighting	100
6) Cheating	100

Reproduced from McLaughlin and Malaby (41) from the *Journal of Applied Behavior Analysis,* 1972, by permission of the Society for the Experimental Analysis of Behavior, Inc.

The results reported by McLaughlin and Malaby (41) are particularly striking. Baseline task completions ranged from 40 to 100%; during the fixed exchange period (Monday mornings) task completions generally varied between 70 and 100%, and during the variable exchange periods task completions varied between 90 and 100%.

The procedures used by McLaughlin and Malaby are particularly useful since they use privileges as back-up reinforcers rather than other more expensive items (m). The procedures are essentially simple for the teacher and, according to their report, only about a ½-hour daily of teacher time weekly was required to check the system and organize forms. Another desirable feature of this system is that the initial fixed interval schedule was changed to a variable interval schedule for obtaining back-up rein-forcers. As would be expected, the variable interval produced a more consistent, high percentage of task completions than did the fixed interval schedule. Ayllon et al. (7) have found the emphasis upon academic task success to be particularly effective with selected HA children in an elementary class. Thus, for elementary schools, the approach described by McLaughlin and Malaby seems to be particularly suited to HA children.

EVALUATION AND FADING

Each of the contingencies described above provides obvious methods for evaluation. It is often desirable to have some unobtrusive observer record behaviors, but it usually suffices for the teacher to keep his own records.

The behavior programs usually try to establish a high degree of success. In most cases the records should indicate that the behavior goals for reinforcers are obtained about 90% of the time; if a lower rate of performance is obtained consideration can be given to reducing goal expectancies or taking other corrective action. For planning evaluation stages and possible corrective action, reference to the section on problems in the preceding chapter may be helpful.

Fading and self-evaluation procedures are relatively inchoate, and firm guidelines have not been established. In fact, even the change to variable schedules of reinforcement is not a common practice in classroom contingency programs. To develop a fading program, reference should be made to the previous chapter. It deserves note, however, that many teachers have opted to continue behavioral programs rather than attempt to fade the programs, particularly for those programs not involving expensive or complicated contingencies.

BEHAVIORAL CLASSROOM PROGRAMS: PRACTICALITY, COST, AND COMPARISON WITH MEDICATION

One of the major issues of concern for behavioral classroom programs is whether or not they are effective over long periods, can be managed by the average classroom teacher, and are cost-effective. Some of the programs described above can be faulted for the last two criteria. Some teachers require punishment contingencies and are unable to use positive social reinforcers effectively. Programs requiring observers, remote radiosignaled equipment for points, or expensive back-up reinforcers may not be very cost-effective. Almost all of the contingency management programs could, however, be effective over long periods, not merely effective because of novelty or placebo effects.

Concerning cost-effectiveness, Patterson et al (47) have reported that for overactive children from 3 to 10 hours of professional time were required for individual contingencies to increase attentiveness by 20%. By using nonprofessional personnel in the classroom, 7–30 hours of time sufficed for a 40–70% reduction in overactive deviant behavior. These are certainly not particularly inexpensive approaches to managing the hyperactive child. The results should, however, be compared with other approaches; e.g., 300 hours of psychiatric consultation with teachers led to no observable change in classroom behavior of children, and similar results have been reported for tutorial time and social worker consultation (48), and for individual and group counseling of children (49). Compared with medication, the behavioral approach is relatively expensive. A prescription costs less than $5.00 a month; adding $20.00 for an initial evaluation and $10.00 every 2–3 months for a renewal of the prescription yields a total cost of about $70.00 per year over 2 years. This compares with the initial cost of the 10–30 hours of time for behavioral therapy, or about $200–900 ($n$).

Perhaps the best demonstration of the continuing efficacy, general applicability, and cost-effectiveness of a behavioral system comes from the reports of Rolling et al. (43) and Thompson et al. (49) on studies in a large southern city school system. Sixteen teachers of both elementary and junior high students were trained in behavior techniques and were provided with rather minimal support to maintain a point economy in their classrooms. The only extra help given these teachers was an aide available about 90 minutes a day. The class sizes varied from 20 to 25. A 2-year evaluation of the program showed that 14 of the 16 teachers successfully introduced the behavior contingencies. The program continued to be effective in the second year without any decrease in improved classroom behavior. Overall, the program produced dramatic behavior changes, e.g.: 80% reduction in disruptive behaviors and 50% increase in on-task behavior in these regular classes with a fairly cost-effective procedure. Unfortunately, the authors fail to report outcomes for the most disruptive and overactive children in these classes. However, one can only presume from the low rates of disruptive behavior that even the misbehaving hyperactive child must have profited from these contingencies.

TREATMENT OF CHOICE: BEHAVIOR THERAPY OR STIMULANT

Aside from relative cost, the effectiveness of behavior therapy versus stimulants for HA children needs careful consideration. Three well controlled studies in the literature concern the relative effectiveness of these methods for classroom treatment of the HA child. Sprague et al. (50)

looked at the relative efficacy of behavior treatment and methylphenidate in reducing seat movements (gross body movements while seated on a stabilimetric cushion). They found methylphenidate far superior to behavior treatment, but the combination of behavior treatment with methylphenidate was slightly, but not significantly, superior to drug effects alone. Gittelman-Klein et al. (*51*) evaluated the effects of methylphenidate and behavior therapy conducted both in the child's classroom setting and his home. Their preliminary report on an 8-week period showed that for behavior ratings there was minimal gain from the behavioral treatment alone and a far greater improvement in behavior from the medication alone. Combining behavior therapy and medication gave no better results than medication alone. Unfortunately, both of these studies involved principally very extreme cases of HA children, and neither study reported on academic performance. The last study, in its preliminary form, does not provide adequate data to evaluate the adequacy of teacher training and the success of the delivery of reinforcements.

Ayllon et al. (*7*) report on behavior therapy and methylphenidate treatment for three HA children in a special elementary class of 10 children. These children met the usual HA criteria and were dramatic responders to stimulants. The behavior therapy emphasized academic performance based on earlier work (*6, 52*), indicating that rewarding school task performance sufficed to reduce classroom misconduct (*o*). Each child received stimulants for at least 12 days, no treatment for the subsequent 3 days, and behavioral treatment for the following 12 days. Methylphenidate and behavior therapy were equally effective in reducing classroom hyperactive behavior but behavior therapy was far superior in increasing academic performance. Unfortunately, longer term outcome was not presented, nor did the study include a condition combining drugs and behavior therapy. Cost estimates for training the teacher, etc., cannot easily be made from this report. Ayllon et al. (*7*), however, raise the important issue of academic performance. They show that methylphenidate appears to have no effects on the maintenance of academic performance compared with a nomedication condition. This finding has been replicated by Layman (*52*).

What conclusions can then be drawn from the somewhat conflicting results of these studies? It can, perhaps, be cautiously suggested that the following conclusions be made for treatment of HA children.

1. For control of classroom behavior, stimulants are the simplest, most effective treatment; for dramatic responders to stimulants, behavior therapy has little to add.

2. For increasing academic performance, behavior therapy is the best documented successful approach. Stimulants improve attention and completion of classroom assignments, but they do not improve the rate of learning. It is not known whether stimulants added to behavior therapy would be better for academic performance than behavior therapy alone.

3. For the more severe HA children, behavior therapy may fail to decrease HA behavior significantly in their regular school classes, but at least for some HA children within special situations and over short periods, behavior therapy can be as effective as methylphenidate in reducing classroom HA behavior.

The decision on treatment thus becomes one determined by the resources available and the needs of the HA child. If parents or the child object to medication, school behavioral approaches should be tried. Indeed, Werry and Sprague (70) argue for trying behavioral therapy before starting medication. If the child is very hyperactive, instituting medication remains the most practical move. If, on one hand, academic performance is a major problem and is as severe or more severe than the behavior problem, behavior therapy should be considered. Combining behavior therapy and medication would seem an ideal approach for many cases, as suggested both by Eysenck and Rachman (55) and Sprague and Werry (56). Trials off medication should then be given periodically to determine whether or not the medication continues to be needed in conjunction with the behavior therapy. When economic or resource issues are paramount, then medication can be tried first with monitoring of academic performance to see whether or not behavior therapy needs to be added. Decisions in this area obviously involve a close relationship between the school and treatment personnel.

REINFORCING REINFORCERS (TEACHER SUPPORT)

A major problem in establishing behavior therapies in the classroom involves maintaining the teacher's behavior change. To start the teacher's change in behavior, it is important that the administration of the school support the program and clearly indicate this to the teacher. The teacher must also be interested and should be given some special training opportunities. After the program is started the teachers will need continued administrative interest, opportunities to present the program to other teachers, and participation in continuing evaluation meetings. Changes in the children's behavior may be too slow to maintain the teacher's behavior. Contingencies that produce changes quickly in the children's behavior are likely to maintain the teacher's behavior, whereas slow changes dampen enthusiasm. The punishment contingencies, the token economy, and type 1 group contingencies are the most likely to produce behavior change quickly and, therefore, should be used by teachers who have some reservations about behavioral contingencies. Once a dramatic change has occurred teachers can also easily forget the situation before starting a behavioral program. Periodic use of short trials without contingencies or with the contingencies applied to less significant behavior will, in these situations, help the teacher appreciate changes that have developed. It may even be the case that the contingencies can be discontinued; but the more likely result is that without the contingencies class behavior tends to return to the precontingency days. In any event, to convince oneself of the changes, baseline data need to be collected before contingencies are established and periodic trials without contingencies are helpful. Reference to the baseline period and the experience of other teachers not using the behavioral approach help to maintain teacher awareness of the program's effectiveness.

Finally, for those working with teachers on behavioral approaches, occasional classroom observation is important. A positive orientation to the teacher and the resourceful use of positive reinforcers for the teacher's behavior changes are essential for a good program (57). In the end the teacher will make the program effective or ineffective depending upon the preparation and incentives provided to him. (For a further general discussion of similar problems read Atthowe's report (58).)

OBTAINING HELP IN SETTING UP
CLASSROOM BEHAVIORAL PROGRAMS

For the educator-professional interested in setting up classroom behavioral treatment there are several avenues of help available. It must be recognized that except for a relatively few people, reading alone will not provide sufficient motivation to produce behavior change. To provide the motivation to produce a behavioral program, a first level approach is a "self-help" style organization of interested teachers willing to take time to meet regularly, discuss behavioral readings, arrange for speakers, and set behavioral goals for their classes. Almost any group so organized can find in the nearby community a sympathetic school psychologist or a psychologist who will be pleased to work with them, often on a volunteer basis. The second level approach involves using a mental health professional, usually a behavioral school psychologist or guidance counselor, to assist teachers in establishing behavior programs in their class. In a third level approach, data collection, analysis, and evaluation of behavior program effectiveness can be handled formally by "in-service" training provided by the school. This would involve something like small workshops with continuing objective goals for the teachers reviewed repeatedly during the year. In an ideal situation, follow-up (refresher) behavioral training and class observation by behaviorally oriented professionals or technicians is provided within the school structure. In any event, it deserves note that many approaches fail when first tried. Those who try and fail should not give up, but should seek some help in improving techniques. When done well, the behavior approach can be effective.

NOTES

a. Since behavioral approaches emphasize current behaviors there has been relatively little work addressed specifically to the usual diagnostic categories such as hyperactivity. Most behavioral work has dealt with current behavior problems of children and not specifically with those children with developmental HA. However, the techniques developed for the misbehaving, inattentive child apply also to the HA child. This has been shown by the few behavioral studies specifically addressed to HA children (7, 19, 45, 59–62). All of these have successfully used behavioral techniques modified somewhat for the HA child. Moreover, 25% of the children in Patterson's (62) behavior study were on medication for hyperactivity before but not after behavior treatment.

In both this chapter and the subsequent one, the behavioral approaches are adapted from those which apply to the usual HA problems such as misbehavior and poor schoolwork habits (e.g., not completing assignments, not staying on task). From the behavioral viewpoint, the HA child can be viewed as any other inattentive-misbehaving child with the following significant differences: 1) The biological nature of the disorder with its slow developmental change makes good behavior and learning a matter requiring continued effort from the HA child during his elementary and often secondary school years; 2) The success from medication in reducing behavioral symptoms increases opportunity for learning from positive contingencies (55).

b. A similar situation occurs even more clearly for mental retardation. The prevalence of mild mental retardation is approximately 8 times greater in school age children than after age 19, with the greatest "incidence" in the elementary school age (6–12 years of age) (63). Thus, 70% of all individuals who are identified as retarded are of school age; approximately two-thirds of the individuals diagnosed as retarded lose this label during late adolescence or early adulthood. These differences cannot be explained in terms of developmental changes or mortality. It, therefore, seems that the school environment in one society creates a problem of retardation by its emphasis on academic and abstract performance.

c. The distribution of HA children is unlikely to be even. The proportion of HA children with low I.Q. or with special learning disabilities is much higher than average. Thus special learning disability classes or their equivalent will contain a high proportion of MBD children (64). To the extent that schools have such special class resources, teachers are less likely to see the HA child in their regular classes. Generally, however, there remain many HA children not in special classes whom the teacher will need to manage and teach.

d. This conclusion and the subsequent discussion is based upon the covariance between attention and misbehavior across days (2) and the studies showing that quiet, personal reprimands decrease misbehavior compared with loud, public reprimands (9). The actual issue of causality is inferred and not conclusively demonstrated by these studies.

e. Alternately, a ratio procedure could be used with reward given for the first good behavior noted and every second or third (or fourth) one thereafter.

f. In this situation there is a fine line between modeling and extinction. The use of rewards with well behaved children will increase the probability of other children modeling after these well behaved children. Negative references to a particular child in a class may, however, be socially rewarding to the child. Thus, rather than risk this, no reference at all should be made. As tempting as it may be, teachers should avoid telling Johnny what he's missing out on by not behaving like Jimmy. If Johnny sees Jimmy get the rewards, he'll know what he's missing.

g. An incident like this is reported by Harris and Sherman (5) with some children who announced they were quitting the game and, thereafter, caused some serious problems. Those specific problems were solved by having the children form their own special group.

h. The competition is in effect between teams with the exception that if both teams stayed within the limits set, they both could win. Thus competition makes the points valuable even when the limits have been exceeded.

i. See discussions in previous chapter, page 137.

j. If the class consists of most if not all behavior problem children, then the class size must be smaller. In secondary education (seventh grade and up), a class of all misbehaving children should be limited to about 15 with a teacher aide available during the day. This becomes an increasing problem when students have extreme degrees of behavioral deviance and academic impairment. As these problems increase, more classroom observation, stimulation and reinforcement are required.

k. The Anne Arundel Learning Center is a self-contained school for junior high school behavior problem students (65). The modification suggested in this chapter represents a similar school program established for one class for each of eighth and ninth grades within a regular school framework at Stemmer's Run Junior High, Baltimore County (21). Use of a regular class reduces the labeling and isolation problems inherent in separate facilities for "bad boys."

l. If another level of parent communication is desired, a "good week" letter can be sent if 4 out of 5 days were excellent or good days. A good day would require 25 points. When good and excellent weeks or days are both used, the discrimination has to be carefully taught to the parents.

m. Some behavioral programs use back-up reinforcers, the cost of which becomes prohibitive. For example, Wolf et al. (66) describe a program with an estimated average cost for reinforcers of $250 per student. Other alternatives to expensive reinforcers are the "intrinsic" reinforcers described by McLaughlin and Malaby (72), free time in the classroom as successfully used by Osborne (67) to reduce "out-of-seat" time, and game techniques for recess release as used by Barrish et al. (32) to reduce misbehavior. For junior high students, Heaton et al. (21) successfully used time off from school to maintain good behavior and academic achievement; the maximum time off was 3 of 7 periods a day. Tutorial behavior programs can, of course, produce success with small reinforcement costs since individual tutorial assistance provides the needed reinforcement (68, 69). However, good tutors are not always free or available.

n. The cost for behavioral programs may well continue after the initial cost. Patterson's (62) long term evaluation of home behavior therapy reported an average of 2 hours of additional professional time were required by the families during the first year after therapy termination. This adds an additional cost of about $30–60. If the failure rate is added to the cost, then the cost per successful outcome with behavioral therapy would increase by 50% (approximately two-thirds of the cases have positive outcomes), whereas the cost for chemotherapy would increase by about 33% (approximately three-fourths of the cases have positive outcomes). Of course, some behavior therapies would make use of existing facilities in such a manner that the behavior treatment adds little to the total cost-per-child and could even decrease cost-per-child in the more expensive special facilities (7).

o. The results of other behavioral studies such as those reported by Walker et al. (29) indicate that for longer term outcome in the more severe misbehavior cases, contingencies would be needed to deal directly with the misbehavior. The results from Ayllon et al. (7) are encouraging in that they suggest that, at least for some HA children, the behavioral emphasis upon academic performance suffices to control misbehavior. It deserves note that Ayllon et al. (7) used highly structured, time-limited, short academic tasks, e.g.: 10 math problems on the board to be solved in 10 minutes or 10 questions in a reading work book to be completed in 20 minutes. This type of

academic structure is probably, in itself, helpful in reducing misbehavior (Ayllon et al (52)).

LITERATURE CITED

1. Deutsch, M. Minority group and class status as related to social and
   personality factors in scholastic achievement. Sec. Appl. Anthropol.
   Monogr. 2: 1–32, 1960.
2. Anderson, D. E. Application of a behavior modification technique to
   the control of a hyperactive child. Unpublished Master's Thesis,
   University of Oregon, 1964.
3. Staats, A. W. Learning, Language and Cognition. New York: Holt,
   Rinehart and Winston, 1968.
4. Ferritor, D. E., Buckholdt, D., Hamblin, R. L., and Smith, L. The
   noneffects of contingent reinforcement for attending behavior on
   work accomplished. J. Appl. Behav. Anal. 5: 7–17, 1972.
5. Harris, V. W., and Sherman, J. A. Use and analysis of the "good
   behavior game" to reduce disruptive classroom behavior. J. Appl.
   Behav. Anal. 6: 405–417, 1973.
6. Ayllon, T., and Roberts, M. D. Eliminating discipline problems by
   strengthening academic performance. J. Appl. Behav. Anal. 7: 71–
   76, 1974.
7. Ayllon, T., Layman, D., and Kandel, H. J. A behavioral-educational
   alternative to drug control of hyperactive children. J. Appl. Behav.
   Anal. 8: 137–146, 1975.
8. Patterson, G. R. Behavioral intervention procedures in the classroom
   and in the home, in A. E. Bergin and S. L. Garfields (Eds.),
   Handbook of Psychotherapy and Behavior Change. New York:
   Wiley, 1969.
9. O'Leary, K. D., Kaufman, K. F., Kass, R. E., and Drabman, R. S. The
   effects of loud and soft reprimands on the behavior of disruptive
   students. Except. Chil. 37: 145–155, 1970.
10. Hall, R. V., Lund, D., and Jackson, D. Effects of teacher attention on
    study behavior. J. Appl. Behav. Anal. 1: 1–12, 1968.
11. Madsen, C. H., Jr., Becker, W. C., and Thomas, D. R. Rules, praise
    and ignoring: Elements of elementary classroom control. J. Appl.
    Behav. Anal. 1: 139–150, 1968.
12. Solomon, R. W., and Wahler, R. G. Peer reinforcement control of
    classroom problem behavior. J. Appl. Behav. Anal. 6: 49–56,
    1973.
13. Hewett, F. M. Educational Engineering with emotionally disturbed
    children. Except. Child. 33: 459–467, 1967.
14. Valett, R. E. A social reinforcement technique for the classroom
    management of behavior disorders. Except. Child. 33: 185–189,
    1966.
15. Zimmerman, E. H., and Zimmerman, J. The alteration of behavior in
    a special classroom situation. J. Exp. Anal. Behav. 5: 59–60, 1962.

16. Engelhardt, L., Sulzer, B., and Altekruse, M. The counselor as a consultant in eliminating out-of-seat behavior. Element. School Guid. Counsel. 5: 196–204, 1971.

17. Staats, A. W., Staats, C. K., Schutz, R. E., and Wolf, M. The conditioning of textual responses using "extrinsic" reinforcers. J. Exp. Anal. Behav. 5: 33–40, 1962.

18. Koenig, C. H. Precision teaching with emotionally disturbed pupils. Research Training Paper No. 17, 1967, Special Education Research, Children's Rehabilitation Unit, University of Kansas Medical Center.

19. Patterson, G. R., Jones, R., Whittier, J., and Wright, M. A. A behavior modification technique for the hyperactive child. Behav. Res. Ther. 2: 217–226, 1965.

20. O'Leary, K. D., and Becker, W. C. Behavior modification of an adjustment class: A token reinforcement program. Except. Child. 33: 637–642, 1967.

21. Heaton, R. C., Safer, D. J., Allen, R. P., Spinatto, N. C., and Prumo, F. M. A motivational environment for behaviorally deviant junior high school students (Submitted for publication). 1975.

22. Buys, C. Effects of teacher reinforcement on elementary school pupils behavior and attitudes. Psychol. Schools 9: 278–288, 1972.

23. Broden, M., Bruce, C., Mitchell, M. A., Carter, V., and Hall, R. V. Effects of teacher attention on attending behavior of two boys at adjacent desks. J. Appl. Behav. Anal. 3: 205–211, 1970.

24. Haughton, E. Training counsellors as advisors of precision teaching. Presented at ECE Convention, New York, April 1968.

25. Wasik, B. H., Senn, K., Welch, R. H., and Cooper, B. R. Behavior modification with culturally deprived school children: Two case studies. J. Appl. Behav. Anal. 2: 181–194, 1969.

26. Hall, R. V., Axelrod, S., Foundopoulos, M., Shellman, J., Campbell, R. A., and Cranston, S. S. The effective use of punishment to modify behavior in the classroom, in K. D. O'Leary and S. G. O'Leary (Eds.), Classroom Management: The Successful Use of Behavior Modification. New York: Pergamon Press, 1972.

27. Whelan, R. F., and Haring, N. G. Modification and maintenance of behavior through systematic application of consequences. Except. Child. 32: 281–289, 1966.

28. Long, N. J., and Newman, R. G. A differential approach to the management of surface behavior of children in school. Bull. School Ed. Indiana Univ. 37: 47–61, 1961.

29. Walker, H. M., Mattson, R. H., and Buckley, N. Special class placement as a treatment alternative in deviant behavior in children, in F. A. M. Benson (Ed.), Modifying Deviant Social Behaviors in Classroom Settings, No. 1. Eugene, Ore.: University of Oregon Press, 1969.

30. Quay, H.C., Werry, J. S., McQueen, M., and Sprague, R. L. Remediation of the conduct problem child in the special class setting. Except. Child. 32: 509–515, 1966.

31. Kubany, E. S., Block, L. E., and Sloggett, B. B. The good behavior clock: a reinforcement time out procedure for reducing disruptive classroom behavior. Presented at a Meeting of the Hawaii Psychological Association, Honolulu, Hawaii, May 1970.
32. Long, J. D., and Williams, R. L. The comparative effectiveness of group and individually contingent free time with inner-city junior high school students. J. Appl. Behav. Anal. 6: 465–474, 1973.
33. Barrish, H. H., Saunders, M., and Wolf, M. M. Good behavior game: Effects of individual contingencies for group consequences on disruptive behavior in a classroom. J. Appl. Behav. Anal. 2: 119–124, 1969.
34. Birnbrauer, J. S., Wolf, M. M., Kidder, J. D., and Tague, C. E. Classroom behavior of retarded pupils with token reinforcement. J. Exp. Child Psychol. 2: 219–235, 1965.
35. Birnbrauer, J. S., Bijou, S. W., Wolf, M. M., and Kidder, J. D. Programmed instruction in the classroom, in L. Krasner and L. P. Ullman (Eds.), Case Studies in Behavior Modification. New York: Holt, Rinehart and Winston, 1965.
36. Clark, M., Lackowicz, J., and Wolf, M. A pilot basic education program for school dropouts incorporating a token reinforcement system. Behav. Res. Ther. 6: 183–188, 1968.
37. Haring, N. G., and Kunzelman, H. The finer focus of therapeutic behavioral management, in Educational Therapy 1. Seattle, Wash.: Special Child Publications, 1966.
38. Homme, L. E., deBaca, P. C., Devine, J. V., Steinhorst, R., and Rickert, E. J. Use of Premack principle in controlling the behavior of nursery school children. J. Exp. Anal. Behav. 6: 544, 1963.
39. Kounin, J. S., Frisen, M. V., and Norton, E. A. Managing emotionally disturbed children in regular classrooms. J. Ed. Psychol. 57: 1–13, 1966.
40. McKenzie, H., Clark, M., Wolf, M. M., Kothew, R., and Benso, C. Behavior modification of children with learning disabilities using grades as tokens and allowances as back-up reinforcers. Except. Child. 34: 745–752, 1968.
41. McLaughlin, T. F., and Malaby, J. Intrinsic reinforcers in a classroom token economy. J. Appl. Behav. Anal. 5: 263–270, 1972.
42. O'Leary, K. D., Becker, W. C., Evans, M. B., and Saudargas, R. A. A token reinforcement program in a public school: A replication and systematic analysis. J. Appl. Behav. Anal. 2: 3–13, 1969.
43. Rollins, H. A., McCandless, B. R., Thompson, M., and Brassell, W. R. Project success environment: An extended application of contingency management in inner-city schools. J. Ed. Psychol. 66: 167–178, 1974.
44. Thompson, M., Brassell, W. R., Persons, S., Tucker, R., and Rollins, H. Contingency management in the schools: How often and how well does it work? Amer. Ed. Res. J. 11: 19–28, 1974.
45. Quay, H. L., Sprague, R. L., Werry, J. S., and McQueen, M. M. Conditioning visual orientation of conduct problem children in the classroom. J. Exp. Child Psychol. 5: 512–517, 1967.

46. Winkler, R. C. An experimental analysis of economic balance, savings and wages in a token economy. Behav. Ther. 4: 22–40, 1973.
47. Patterson, G. R., Shaw, D. A., and Ebner, M. J. Teachers, peers and parents as agents of change in the classroom, in F. A. M. Benson (Ed.), Modifying Deviant Social Behaviors in Various Classroom Settings. Eugene, Ore.: University of Oregon Press, 1969.
48. Minde, K. K., and Werry, J. S. The response of school children in a low socio-economic area to extensive psychiatric counseling of their teachers: a controlled evaluation. Presented at the American Psychiatric Association Metting, Boston, 1968.
49. Kranzler, G. D. Elementary school counseling: An evaluation. Presented at the American Personnel Guidance Association Meeting, Dallas, 1967.
50. Sprague, R. L., Christensen, D. E., and Werry, J. S. Experimental psychology and stimulant drugs, in C. K. Conners (Ed.), Clinical Use of Stimulant Drugs in Children, pp. 141–163. The Hague: Excerpta Medica, 1974.
51. Helman, G., Klein, R., Klein, D. F., Felixbrod, J., Abikett, H., Katz, S., Gloisten, A., Kates, W., and Saraf, K. Methylphenidate vs. behavior therapy in hyperkinetic children. Presented at the American Psychiatric Association Meeting, Anaheim, Calif., 1975.
52. Ayllon, T., Layman, D., and Burke, S. Disruptive behavior and reinforcement of academic performance. Psychol. Rec. 22: 315–323, 1972.
53. Layman, D. A behavioral investigation: The effects of medication on disruptive classroom behavior and academic performance. Unpublished doctoral dissertation, Georgia State University, 1974.
54. Werry, J. S., and Sprague, R. L. Hyperactivity, in C. G. Costello (Ed.), Symptoms of Psychopathology, pp. 397–417. New York: Wiley, 1970.
55. Eysenck, N. T., and Rachman, S. T. The application of learning theory to child psychiatry, in T. C. Howells (Ed.), Modern Perspectives in Child Psychiatry, pp. 104–169. New York: Bruner/Mazel, 1971.
56. Sprague, R. L., and Werry, J. S. Methodology of psychopharmacological studies with the retarded, in N. R. Ellis (Ed.), International Review of Research in Mental Retardation, Vol. 5, pp. 147–219. New York: Academic Press, 1971.
57. Brown, J. C., Montgomery, R., and Barclay, J. R. An example of psychologist management of teacher reinforcement procedures in the elementary classroom. Psychol. Schools 6: 336–340, 1969.
58. Atthowe, J. M. Token economies come of age. Behav. Ther. 4: 646–654, 1973.
59. Doubros, S. G., and Daniels, G. J. An experimental approach to the reduction of overactive behavior. Behav. Res. Ther. 4: 251–258, 1966.
60. Patterson, B. R. An application of conditioning techniques to the control of hyperkinetic children, in L. Ullman and L. Krasner

(Eds.), Case Studies in Behavior Modification, pp. 370–375. New York: Holt, Rinehart and Winston, 1965.

61. Phil, R. O. Conditioning procedures with hyperactive children. Neurology 17: 921–923, 196.

62. Patterson, G. R. Retraining of aggressive boys by their parents: review of recent literature and follow-up evaluation, Can. Psychiat. Assoc. J. 19: 142–158, 1974.

63. Tarjan, G., Wright, S. W., Eyman, R. K., and Keeran, C. V. Natural history of mental retardation: some aspects of epidemiology. Am. J. Ment. Defic. 77: 369–379, 1973.

64. Rogan, L., and Lukens, J. Education, administration and classroom procedure, MBD in children, in Education, Medical and Health Related Services, Public Health Service Publication No. 2015, pp. 21–30. Washington, D.C.: Department of Health, Education and Welfare, United States Government Printing Office, 1969.

65. Cohen, S. I., Keyworth, J. M., Kleiner, R. I., and Brown, W. L. Effective behavior change at the Anne Arundel Learning Center through minimum contact interventions, in R. Ulrich, T. Stachnik, and J. Mabry (Eds.), Control of Human Behavior, Vol. III: Behavior Modification in Education, pp. 124–42. Glenview, Ill: Scott, Foresman and Company, 1974.

66. Wolf, M. M., Giles, D. K., and Hall, R. V. Experiments with token reinforcement in a remedial classroom. Behav. Res. Ther. 6: 51–64, 1968.

67. Osborne, J. G. Free-time as a reinforcer in the management of classroom behavior. J. Appl. Behav. Anal. 2: 113–118, 1969.

68. Staats, A. W., Minke, K. A., Goodwin, W., and Landeen, J. Cognitive behavior modification: "motivated learning" reading treatment with sub-professional therapy technicians. Behav. Res. Ther. 5: 283–299, 1967.

69. Staats, A. W., and Butterfield, W. H. Treatment of nonreading in a culturally deprived juvenile delinquent: An application of reinforcement principles. Child Develop. 36: 925–942, 1965.

Chapter 8 ___ Behavior Management in the Home

Some home management approaches have been presented in the parental counseling section. The assumption in counseling is that a very limited amount of professional time may enable the parents to improve their home management (a). This approach has been shown to produce improved attitudes toward the children (1, 2), but significant observed changes in home behavior have been difficult to achieve without some form of direct training (3). If the home problems for the HA child are relatively minor, a change in attitudes may suffice. For those parents who want more assistance and who are both willing and able to participate, a more complete behavioral approach can be utilized. A working basis for such an approach is provided in this chapter.

At the start a certain caution is needed. There are severe problems in successfully instituting home behavior programs. Family cooperation may be elusive; observation, recording, and implementing behavior contingencies may be difficult and erratic for the average busy family (b, 4); and establishing durable changes in home behaviors often proves to be severely complicated by the interrelated reinforcement needs of a family (3).

Despite the difficulties, home management may well be the most important aspect of nonchemical management for HA. With adequate home management, the use of medication can be limited to deal with the school problems. It seems reasonable to try to avoid the use of stimulant medications for the HA child at home. Thus, stimulants should be given on school days and, principally, early in the morning. This allows for a lower daily dose and less frequent use of medication, thereby reducing risks of side effects. The stimulant effects will have generally worn off by late afternoon and will not, therefore, be noticeable at home (5, 6; c).

A second major reason for emphasis upon better home management stems from the results from follow-up evaluations of HA children. Weiss and colleagues (7) followed HA children for 5 years; they note that the most important predictors of successful long term outcome were positive home factors combined with medication treatment (d). This result suggests that therapeutic correction of home conditions might have more long term significance than therapy aimed at reducing school problems (e). The stress of the school situation, the conspicuous nature of the school problem, and the organized pressure from school officials has directed most therapeutic concern toward school behavior. Perhaps this has been a mistaken emphasis in management. The team evaluating the HA child should look carefully at the family to see whether or not home problems exist which need help.

Unfortunately, as a result of the emphasis upon school behavior and also the relative ease of conducting school studies, the body of knowledge about home behavior management is limited (3). Behavioral research focused on home management started only in the late 1950's and early 1960's. The initial emphasis was upon very specific problem behaviors (e.g., temper tantrums), which the therapist in his office trained parents to respond to appropriately (8). Not until the last decade did this behavioral training involve a wide range of behavior problems and the use of either simulated home environment or actual observation in the home. Despite the limitations of research, some general ground rules have been developed which can assist the family counselor.

DEFINING THE BEHAVIORS: OBSERVING AND RECORDING

The often vague and global complaints parents have about their HA child's behavior need to be specified in reasonably explicit behavioral terms. Since only parent observers will be used, the behaviors do not need to be defined as explicitly for home management as for school management, but they do need to be observable behaviors and not psychological constructs (e.g., nervousness). Behaviors such as "bragging," "lying about," "teasing," "bad-mouthing," are all acceptable concepts even though somewhat vaguely defined. It may be helpful to have the parent list the usual day's schedule for the child and indicate for each time period the types of problem behaviors likely to occur. The parent can then order by significance all of the problem behaviors. A few more significant problems can then be selected for attention, but the number selected should be limited depending upon the parents' ability to record and observe the behaviors.

Some therapists prefer to work on only one behavior at a time, but more commonly a small set of up to six behaviors is selected (9–11).

As an example of the types of problem behaviors, Table 1 lists the home problems frequently occurring among children who were seen in one large child guidance clinic (12). For HA children, the most common problems tend to be overactivity, fights, temper tantrums, and so on (see Table 1 of Chapter 2).

Listing desirable behaviors which the child fails to do may be somewhat harder for parents, but is nonetheless important. Emphasis here should be on items such as cooperative behaviors, sharing, politeness, chores accomplished without reminders, homework done early, clean up after play, and close compliance with the family's hours or time schedule. These behaviors may be somewhat incompatible with the problem behaviors, in which case increasing the desired behaviors would tend to decrease the problem behaviors.

Table 1. Common home behavior problems reported

 1. Destructive
 2. Hyperactive, impulsive, unpredictable
 3. Cries easily, irritable
 4. Withdrawn, shy
 5. Perfectionistic
 6. Dreamy, daydreams
 7. Passive, overly conforming, unable to fight back
 8. Difficulty with siblings
 9. Stays out late, doesn't tell where he is going
10. Immature, thumb sucking
11. Excessive fighting
12. Compulsive acts or obsessed with specific facts
13. Anxious or worries
14. Bizarre behavior
15. Psychosomatic complaints—headaches, nausea, vomiting
16. Sleep disturbances, nightmares, terrors
17. Fearful
18. Tics
19. Nervous
20. Tense, overly sensitive
21. School phobia
22. Lies
23. Steals

Most of these were included in the list of items in "Factors of a factor analysis" by Patterson (12).

Once the behaviors are defined the parent needs to record the *rate of occurrence* of the behaviors. The parent can simply record each occurrence of the particular behavior using a 1- or 2-character code and a calendar or some special sheet posted in a convenient location. One simple code would be a minus sign for each bad behavior and a plus sign for each good behavior. In addition to the number of occurrences of the behaviors, the time span of observation should be noted. Thus the parents are told that their task is to observe and record each time their child is, for example, overly aggressive: e.g., hits or verbally threatens. The parents need to write down on the calendar the time observation starts and ends, e.g., 4:00–5:00 p.m. (see Chart 1).

If the child asks what the parent is doing, an accurate and honest answer should be provided. The child can be given as much specific information as he wants. Thus the parent can say he is counting the number of times certain things are done. If appropriate or if requested by the child, more details can be provided. For example, the child can be told that the number of his aggressive acts are being counted with the aim of eventually helping him reduce the number of times he is aggressive. The parent should realize that transitory changes in a behavior's occurrence may occur when systematic observation is started (*13*). A sample behavior sheet is given in Chart 1. For common behaviors, time of observation is important so that number per minute can be obtained; for these common behaviors the observation periods need not be the entire time the child is in the house. Rather reasonable and varied time samples can be taken from a usual evening, e.g., 5-minute periods at 5:00, 6:15, 8:25. Observation of the entire time in the house is, however, the best data if it can be reasonably obtained. For less common behaviors the number per day may suffice, making the time record less important.

Training parents in observation and recording can start in the therapist's office. If the child's behavior occurs in the office, the parents could be asked to record its occurrence there. If the behavior is not occurring in the office, the therapist could carefully rehearse the instructions and even do some role playing or verbal descriptions of a concrete situation, e.g.: "Johnny does this . . . . what do you (parents) do? Right, you make a mark here, and you record here the time you started observing." (*f*).

Some children will resent having their bad behavior counted and will threaten even worse behavior if counting is continued. Parents can usually successfully counter this by telling the child that the counting is only designed to find out if he does these things as often as is claimed in the family. If he doesn't do them very much then the counting can be stopped. The therapist can encourage the parents to openly and frankly

Chart 1. Sample parent observation sheet

"+" Behaviors	"−" Behaviors
1. Saying thank you	1. Pushing or shoving
2. Helping others	2.
3.	3.

Observation:

Date	Time start	No. "+" Behaviors	No. "−" Behaviors	Time stop	Total time	No. +/Time	No. −/Time

discuss the purpose for counting, but emotional and negative comments should be minimized.

ANALYZE EXISTING CONTINGENCIES

Parents have a wide range of powerful consequences available for contingency management. Unfortunately, many parents are unaware of the contingencies with which they give consequences, and they are often unwilling to examine them. Some parents will view an analysis as threatening and "unnatural." For these parents it can be enlightening to count the child's bad behaviors and observe what happens after the child misbehaves; reading one of the parent books on behavior modification can also help since it will remove the strangeness of the procedure. The better books (*14, 15*) also provide warm and concrete examples which help reduce the mechanistic tones of behavior management.

The few well documented studies on natural contingencies operating in the homes of behavior problem children generally indicate that the child's deviant behaviors are being supported by positive social reinforcement. Ray (*16*), working with autistic children, and Patterson et al. (*17*), observing families of misbehaving children, both noted a strong relationship between social rewards and misbehaving. The rewards included positive physical contacts, approval, and attention given even for aggressive misbehavior. Patterson et al. (*17*) report the percentage of misbehaviors receiving social rewards ranged up to 40% with a median of 22% for seven families observed. Only one of the seven families showed a near zero percentage of misbehavior being rewarded. These same families generally gave only mildly aversive consequences (e.g.: scolding) for about 20% of the misbehaviors. If these samples are typical, then the large majority (six out of seven) of the families of misbehaving children reward their child's misbehavior more than they punish it. Hawkins et al. (*18*) report the same high occurrence of rewards after misbehavior for families with behavior problem children; they also report a significant correlation ($r = 0.38$) over days between the number of rewards and the number of misbehaviors. Their data suggest that the social rewards may provide some control over the misbehaviors. Uncovering family patterns which reward misbehavior often reveals why the families defensively resist analysis and change.

ESTABLISHING NEW CONTINGENCIES

Observation Contingencies: Initial Self-control

As noted earlier, the very fact that a parent is counting the occurrence of a child's behavior serves as a behavioral contingency usually viewed as mildly aversive. If a child notes the count and is allowed to see the tally he will frequently attempt to change his behavior in the manner desired by the parent. These behavior changes are customarily transitory in nature with the observation consequence quickly losing its aversive or reinforcing value. In some rare situations, however, observation suffices to produce the desired changes.

Observation may also work to make matters worse. Mildly aversive consequences can sometimes be seen by a child as a signal or stimulus for producing more misbehavior. It is almost as if seeing how bad he is rewards a child for being bad. This response happens only very rarely and extinguishes quickly. Indeed, the effects of parental observation quickly extinguishes for better or worse; when the effects appear to persist it is more likely that, in fact, other rewards are maintaining the change.

Extinction

The first and most important step in changing home contingencies for misbehaving children is to remove or minimize any existing reinforcers for bad behavior. This extinction process has two important steps. First, identify the reinforcers. Parents can assume that any attention to a child is reinforcing. Hollering, yelling, acting hurt, threatening, teasing, and even the pointed reference about the child to others may well be rewarding to the child. It can also be generally assumed that for any of the child's persistent misbehaviors, whatever action the parent has commonly taken after the misbehavior may be rewarding (*g*). Depending on the situations, either or both of seemingly opposite consequences may be rewarding. Thus, if a child wriggles a lot at dinner, either letting him stay longer at the table or letting him leave early may reward the child for his misbehavior. The more common response to his misbehavior should be generally considered the reinforcing one, although reinforcement history needs to be considered. In effect, the therapist and parents must seek to identify the rewarding parental behaviors frequently occurring in conjunction with the child's misbehavior.

The second aspect of extinction is to remove the identified reinforcers as completely as possible. For example, misbehavior should be ignored as much as possible. One can completely ignore the child when he misbehaves and look away, turn away from him, do *not* talk to him, do *not* hear his mutters or his screams, or one can leave his presence. These acts in themselves often seriously upset a child's expectations. Ignoring, for example, temper tantrums has been shown to be very effective in eliminating them (*8*). Parents even report that if they walk away from a child throwing a temper tantrum the child may suddenly stop his seemingly uncontrollable rage, follow the parent and start the temper fit all over again. So much for the concept that a child's anger is uncontrollable; when the reward suffices, even the most fierce temper will probably be controlled.

It is, nonetheless, hard to completely ignore the child. Not responding is difficult for small misbehaviors and gets harder as the magnitude of the disturbance associated with the misbehavior increases. It is, therefore, often helpful for the parent to combine extinction with a positive social reward after the child stops the misbehavior. It will be useful to ensure that the social rewards removed from the child are now given in some new context, or else the parents may see the extinction as essentially "mean." Most parents like to see themselves as warm and "human"; extinction can be seen as cold and rejecting. Thus the therapist is well advised to pair extinction with new positive contingencies.

It should also be noted that when extinction is first tried the behavior may actually increase before it decreases. The child's temper or overactivity may become more common in the face of reinforcement withdrawal since the change may seem like an increase in variability of reward. The rewards are less common, so the behavior needs to be more common to gain the rewards. This will be only a short lived phenomena, but parents need to be advised about the problem. It can perhaps be best explained as limit testing by the child; the child will seek to test the possibility of getting his old social rewards if his behavior gets worse. Parents need to be cautioned against escalation; the extinction must be maintained or the child's new, more severe misbehavior will become rewarded and matters will be worse than before. This problem represents good reason for introducing with extinction an appropriate punishment contingency for when the misbehavior cannot be ignored.

Punishment Contingencies

Warnings and time-limited extinction Parents should attempt to establish clear warning procedures with their children. One warning should suffice. If possible, the parent should state something to the effect that he is giving a warning; further misbehavior will result in a punishment. The warning should be firm, but not angry, and should be backed up with the punishment if the child repeats the misbehavior.

A time-limited extinction can also be used. Here the child is engaging in direct disobedience to an order such as "sit down" or "go to your room." The parent then issues a time-limited warning such as "if you don't go to your room within 30 seconds I'll make you go." The time limit and some aversive consequence are both specified explicitly. During the time period the child should be ignored and the parent calm and busy, perhaps even giving attention to other children. As the end of the period approaches, the parent moves toward the child to institute the aversive consequence. The instant the child starts an appropriate response the time period is ended; all that matters is that the child starts moving or acting as desired. Should he subsequently stop, then the aversive consequence should be implemented at once. Counting (e.g., "do this before I count to 10") is particularly useful for younger children to indicate the time period for compliance. This has the advantage of rewarding the child's compliance by stopping the count. Sometimes even the warning of a count will suffice to gain compliance. But only one warning should be used. Note that the parent need not holler or yell to give the time-limited orders.

Time out The single most important element of punishment contingencies is the use of "time out" (*18, 20*). As has been described for the school situation, the time out involves removing the child from nearly all social rewards. At home, sending him to his room or to a bathroom for a few minutes (e.g., 5 minutes) usually suffices. The child may find other reinforcers in his room such as books and games and may even deny he feels badly about going to his room. The situation is fine as long as there is no very highly valued reinforcer in his room such as a T.V. or stereo or food. The purpose of time out is not to be mean to a child but simply to drastically reduce the normal expected positive consequences in the usual social situation. Short, frequently used time outs are better than longer ones.

It has been shown that without time outs some children are very difficult to control (*20*). Time out, generally combined with a warning, should be considered an essential part of the program for HA children. The time out is particularly useful when combined with extinction for misbehavior. It is instituted when the child's misbehavior reaches a point it can no longer be ignored, then one warning can be given before the time out is required.

Response Cost: Fines for Misbehavior Many behaviorists expend a great deal of effort arguing for using only positive consequences and avoiding punishment. There is, however, some data which indicate that response cost punishments are approximately as effective as reinforcement contingencies (*21*). In some situations reinforcement contingencies are indistinguishable to the child from response-cost contingencies (*h*). It is, also, often easier for parents to accept and implement response-cost procedures, particularly for misbehavior involving breaking family rules.

Response cost involves the loss of an expected positive consequence, much like a fine for a baseball player involves the loss of salary. The usual "fines" imposed on children for misbehavior involve loss of items such as: evening snacks, allowance, hours outside for play, friends in the house, T.V. watching, stereo listening, bicycle riding, etc. Essentially any of the privileges can be used, but the contingency should be immediate and short-lived so that it can be applied frequently without stirring up great emotional resentment. Where possible, response-cost contingencies should be worked out in advance and known to both parents and the child.

Overcorrection: Restitution for Destructive Acts A type of punishment contingency which is particularly appropriate for destructive and aggressive acts involves correction of the wrong act plus additional similar action. For example, if a child throws his drink he could be asked to clean up an even larger area than the one he dirtied with his drink. If he hits, he could be required to apologize and kiss (for younger children) or shake hands. If he steals he could be required to pay back either double or 10% more, depending on value. This approach has been used successfully with aggressive, retarded children in an institution (*22*). Its general applicability deserves attention.

Among the more interesting potential uses of overcorrection is the principle of paying back extra, e.g., double, for the abuse of privileges. Thus if a child stays out late, he "owes" double the amount of time late to be paid back by coming in early the next night. If he fails to take out the garbage, he has to do the chore twice for his brother. If he skips or cuts class time in school he should be required to stay extra time in school classes; the extra time should be more than the amount of time out of class without permission. If he fails to clean his room on time he has to clean it twice the next week. If he takes too many candies for a snack he loses twice as many candies.

The principle of overcorrection is usually easy for a child to understand and is frequently surprisingly well accepted by the child. The child may still resent the punishment and complain; but he can usually see the direct relation between the punishment and his behavior. The source of punishment becomes somewhat less parental and more a result of his behavior which is under his control.

Aversive Contingencies: Physical Punishment or Coercion as "Back-up" Consequences Many of the punishment contingencies specified may require physical force to implement them at least initially. Ordering a child to his room may require as the back-up consequence physically leading him to his room or paddling him on the seat and directing him to his room. The use of force with HA children is generally undesirable and should be minimized. Force, where needed, should be a back-up contingency assuring compliance with other punishment. Force should generally not be used as a primary contingency for several reasons; it builds resent-ment, it does extinguish if used often (as will happen with HA children) and therefore escalation is required to maintain effectiveness, and finally, it is needed and should be reserved for a contingency of last resort. Spanking for stealing or talking back will generally not be effective with HA children. Time-out approaches would probably work better; however, a firm spank on the seat may be needed to encourage a child to obey an order to go to the time-out area.

Reinforcement Contingencies

Social Rewards Parental attention, time, praise, and interaction are rewards strongly desired by most children, and particularly by HA chil-dren. Once behavioral goals are set, positive social attention can be given contingent on accomplishing the goals. Praising or touching the child who is quietly playing or sitting still in his seat for a couple of minutes will serve to increase this type of behavior. Unfortunately, good behaviors often tend to be ignored by parents. This is particularly a problem with HA children. They frequently disturb others so much and their misbehav-ior monopolizes parental attention so much that parents are seeking opportunities to ignore them. Relief from the constant need for attention becomes a major parental goal, particularly if parents are not using extinction procedures effectively. Parents may also, justifiably, feel that they should give attention to other children or simply to themselves. Thus, when the child behaves or remains quiet (highly valued goals for HA children) the parents naturally prefer to ignore him. In effect, parental attention and social rewards have some relatively constant maximum value of natural expression. To the extent that attention is given for misbehav-ior, good behaviors will tend to be ignored.

Another complication for giving positive rewards involves determining reasonable goals for the HA child. Parents will note that they don't praise other children for sitting still a couple minutes, and thus it seems unfair to give attention to the HA child for this behavior. Understanding the problems of HA children will assist the parents in accepting the need for small goals for the HA child. If the parent and the family see HA as a developmental handicap, with which they can help the child cope, then special constructive approaches are more likely to be accepted.

For the desired, frequently occurring behaviors of the HA child the parent can use an "alarm" watch, cooking timer, egg timer, or some other type of clock to signal intervals for purposely stopping to reward the child if he is behaving well. This procedure permits the use of variable interval observation; at the end of each interval the parent starts observing the child. Social praise and physical proximity or contact is provided for the first appropriate behavior, e.g., sitting quietly for 10 or 15 seconds. Observation is then discontinued until the next interval is over. Or, alternatively, the behavior could be casually observed during the entire period and if it was good during most of the period the child rewarded at the end of the period; thus, if the child is relatively quiet during the period, he is praised. Interval lengths can be increased after success is obtained with short intervals. As an example, consider a young child (age 5) who constantly wants to monopolize the conversation with his mother. The parent can tell the child that they are playing a new game. If the child plays for 20 seconds without bugging her, she will draw pictures with him for 30 seconds. Hands on a clock can be used as the stimulus. Once the child reaches the 20-second goal for five consecutive times, the interval would be increased to 40 seconds, and so on until the child stops his monopolistic practices for 15 minutes for 1 minute of parent time. This particular type of problem can even be practiced in the counselor's office. The counselor could initially model the behavior for the parent, and then could observe the parent.

Social praise, hugs, and "special fusses" can be effective rewards for the more difficult, less common desired behaviors. These social rewards need to be larger in magnitude since the behaviors are less often. Gold stars, brief physical contact games with parents (e.g., "ring-around-the-rosy," or arm wrestling), allowing dinner or dessert choices, going for a special treat or walk, story telling, etc., can all be used effectively in these situations. The general nature of the reward is to provide a longer period of positive social interaction. The number and variety of useful social rewards of longer duration are as great as the imagination and playfulness of the patients. Curious varieties of behavioral opportunities can be effective rewards for children and they will often be able to indicate what they like to do.

Tokens and Back-up Reinforcers   For many families social rewards may be inadequate to *initiate* behavior change in their HA children. More concrete reinforcers are, therefore, usually suggested by behaviorists. These rewards can range from food and toys to special privileges (see Table 2, Chapter 7). Data available generally indicate that the back-up rewards are usually needed for misbehaving children *(23-27; i)*; the counselor should, therefore, build these into his initial program for the parents. The rewards can be linked directly with the behavior, e.g., candy for remaining quiet while Mommy is on the telephone. As with social rewards, the delivery should be first frequent and immediate; variability and reduced frequency should then be introduced followed by discontinuing the reward. Social rewards should be paired with the back-up rewards; hopefully, the social rewards will suffice to maintain the behavior change after it has been well established.

Token or point systems provide a more general approach to back-up rewards. For older children (over age 5 or 6) this approach is generally preferable. The immediate rewards are points or tokens earned for reaching behavioral goals, e.g., 1 point for every hour without a fight with siblings. The rewards are awarded by handing them to the child, placing them in a glass jar visible to the child, or by recording points on a chart or calendar clearly visible to the child. A reinforcement "menu" can then be prepared which lists for the child various things he can buy with his tokens. Prices for items can obviously vary considerably. Larger items such as bicycles, records, stereos, Lifesaver packages, or afternoon fishing trips with Dad will, of course, have relatively high prices. The price for a reward has to be set in consideration of economic values, such as: 1) how long the child is likely to be willing to save points for the item; 2) how long it will take the child to earn the needed points; 3) how much the child wants the item; 4) how soon and often the parents feel they can afford the needed time and money. The counselor should assist the parents in *conservatively* appraising these issues.

The token system has a great advantage in terms of simple record keeping. The number of tokens provides an immediate assessment of how successful the child has been in obtaining behavioral goals. The usual procedure is to measure this as a percentage of the maximum number of tokens the child could have earned. If the parent is already recording the behaviors, the points or tokens can be essentially incorporated in the record-keeping procedure.

Parental resistance to back-up reinforcement needs to be considered in counseling. It will be helpful if the parents see these techniques as a method of breaking the current vicious cycle whereby the child's misbehavior monopolizes their time and attention. In the long run, loosely defined contingencies and social rewards will be more significant than the usual back-up rewards, but for the immediate and even intermediate term the material rewards and well defined contingencies are more effective. Explicit contingencies are particularly important at the time when systems of behaviors are expected to be changed, such as teaching the HA child that he will earn parental attention through quiet, constructive play, not through misbehavior. As an extreme example, the use of potato chips with soda can be a powerful incentive for potty training as shown by Fox and Azran (28), but in high school these children obviously do not require such reinforcements. Tokens, points, and back-up rewards are the tools for speeding behavior change but not, in general, for long term behavior maintenance. Obviously, judgment is required for deciding when to decrease and discontinue the back-up rewards.

The structured use of back-up reinforcers has as a "spin-off" the advantage of strengthening the value of the parents as models for the child. Children tend to choose as models those people who are seen as controlling the dispensing of significant rewards (29, 30). For younger children, parents naturally fill this role; for older children parents need not lose out completely. By giving nonsocial, back-up reinforcers, the parent is also increasing the value of his social reinforcers (24–27).

The Home Contract

A useful adjunct for any of the behavioral contingencies discussed above is a formal statement of agreement between parent and child regarding behaviors and consequences. Reinforcement contingencies can even be listed (Chart 3, Chapter 7). This is particularly desirable for older children (e.g., age 11 and older). The contract approach has been discussed in some detail in the classroom management section and similar considerations apply here. In negotiating the contract, particular attention should be paid to ensuring that all parties participate, that time limits are set for renegotiating the contract, and that the agreement is reasonable for all concerned.

With home contracts the therapist has a unique opportunity to use the contract for altering the structure of social contacts. Many older children desire and can use more privacy. For example, parental enquiries, room searches, pestering, and suspicious parental demands to know "what he's doing," "where he's going," are ineffective aversive experiences for older children. Parents not "bugging" their older children can be a reward for compliance with hours, good school reports, or not being nasty when home. Access to a certain degree of privacy within the house can often be a reinforcement for a wide range of socially desired behavior outside of the private area. Noisy hours can be exchanged for quiet and/or study hours.

One of the more interesting uses of the contract is to give one of the parents a larger or different role in his child's life than was the case before starting the home contract. Remote fathers who have served primarily to punish may, for example, be used as reinforcers for baseball games or trips. The contract could specify that an allowance or extra free time could be given only by the father, who then becomes a source of positive rewards for the child. Similar considerations apply for the mother who is always scolding the restless HA child while the father comes home and finds the same child enjoyable for play and "rough-housing." Mother's time in play activity could be one of the reinforcers for the child.

Whenever changes are made in the relative balance of parental control of rewards and punishment, the counselor should look at the effects on the relation between the parents. If the father starts rewarding his son more, he will receive more rewards from his son and the mother relatively fewer. This presents grounds for conflicts which may undermine the behavioral approach. The counselor can note the significant rewards for the parents and encourage development of these rewards. Particular emphasis should be given to mutual rewards between the parents.

Modeling

Parents, siblings, and other family members provide primary models for a child's behavior. A child observes their behavior and spends a lot of time imitating the behaviors seen. This learning by observation has a pervasive influence. It can be used constructively by parental attention to good behaviors of siblings; it can also be enhanced by having parents consistently dispense positive rewards (29). Parents can also appeal verbally to mythical heroes, sports figures, musicians, or others as models of the desired good behavior. For example, Santa Claus and Superman don't tap at the dinner table. Modeling can also be used in a "copy game" approach with parents promoting a stereotype of good behavior for the children to copy, such as sitting very still for 10 or 20 seconds. In these situations the emphasis is upon easily accessible demands, the goal is to communicate what is valued and that some level of valued behavior can be accomplished even by the most HA child.

Counselors are usually aware that modeling suggests the limitations of behavioral goals. If the parents do not model the behavior, the child may well *not* know how or want to perform the "desired" behavior. Home study, politeness, attitude for authorities, and respect for adults are behaviors which children often learn by observation of parents (j).

Response Satiation

One behavioral technique which can be applied to certain specific misbehavior involves an aversive-like repetition of the misbehavior under parental supervision. In theory, if a behavior has a low level of occurrence, and is maintained by its "novelty" value, or its expression of negativism, frequently repeating the behavior should lead to extinction of the reward value. In the extreme situation, frequently repeating the behavior actually becomes mildly aversive (k). For example, if the child persistently, but episodically, plays with matches he could be required to sit down and light 30 or 50 matches in a row. To prevent the return of this "match play," the child could later be allowed to light candles in the evening provided he has not been caught playing with matches that week. Response satiation can bring an immediate drop in the misbehavior. Since this may not last, a response situation (such as lighting candles for match play), is provided to maintain the extinction of the inappropriate response. Response satiation should obviously be avoided with common misbehaviors.

Training Parents in Behavior Management

Several steps have been developed for training parents in behavioral management. The procedures discussed here are based in part on the procedures described by Patterson (*3*). First, some didactic experience such as reading a book is useful for introducing the concepts, providing "social status" to support the change and improving communication between counselors and patients. A few good parent handbooks are available such as: *Living with Children* by Patterson and Guillian (*14*), *Parents are Teachers* by Becker (*15*), and *Families* by Patterson (*31*).

Patterson notes that reading a book usually does not suffice to produce changes in the behaviors of the parent seeking help (*3*); his data, however, indicate that reading a book, combined with some observation training, yielded about 50% of the total therapeutic gains (*9*). As a second step, the parents should be guided through the behavior process. Sequential training will be needed in four consecutive areas: 1) observing and recording behaviors, 2) establishing reinforcement contingencies, 3) giving social and nonsocial rewards according to established contingencies, 4) fading explicit contingencies and increasingly using spontaneous social rewards to maintain behavior. This training can usually be done as the behavior program progresses. The parent training can be conducted in a family session or in parent groups. Patterson (*3*) has used parent groups consisting of three to five families. Before entering the group the parents read the required text and attend an individual session with the therapist. The goals of this session are to specify a couple of the child's behaviors to work on and establish procedures for the parents to use in observing and recording the selected behaviors. Only after several days of collecting adequate data is entrance to the group permitted. In the group each family has 30 minutes to describe progress, plans, and data collected. A timer is used to determine the time; in fact, all discussion about one family can be limited to the 30-minute period. Parents who failed to collect data go last in discussion. This appears to be a fairly efficient approach to the training.

For some parents consistent data collection is difficult. As a third step in training, home contact by the telephone is usually desirable. This could be daily and routine at the start of the program even before group training.

For parents collecting good data this could be discontinued quickly. The parents who have trouble collecting data may need continued telephone support between group sessions.

An additional level of practical training can be arranged by staging family interactions in the therapist's office. Videotaped sessions (*32–35*) and radio signal devices placed in the parents' ears (*3*) have both been used to train parents to give more nonsocial rewards to support good behavior by their children (*1*). In some cases the radio devices or simple observation and discussion can be conducted by a trained observer during home visits. A home visit could consist of 20 minutes of observation of the child and 5 minutes of the parents, with this 25-minute cycle repeated twice at each visit. Dinner time is often a good time to sample the family patterns. Home observation is, however, obviously costly; with good telephone contact it may be superfluous except for research purposes.

A final step in training involves continuing contact after treatment is terminated. Most families can proceed through the steps in training within a rather short time, occasionally a matter of 8 or 10 weeks, although sometimes considerably longer. After treatment, follow-up contacts should be kept to assist the parents in maintaining social rewards. These can be telephone contacts with appointments made as needed. Patterson (*9*) reported that over a 1-year follow-up period, families required an average of about 2 hours of professional time for retraining and support. He noted that 3 months and 6 months appeared to be particularly difficult times during follow-up.

MAJOR PROBLEM AREAS

Negative Parents

Some parents have adopted such negative approaches to managing their HA children that there are few positive rewards they are willing or able to give. They view the child as bad and they have been confirmed in this view by reports from both school and neighbors. In such a situation the counselor finds he has to rely mostly on extinction and punishment contingencies to set the initial stage for behavior change. After some initial success he can attempt to point out to the parents the child's progress and work with them on the need for positive rewards. Some therapists have tried to increase the rewards the children give the parents in an attempt to increase the parents' use of positive rewards. This has met with mixed success (*17, 36*). With hyperactive children, particularly, this approach will be difficult and probably impractical.

If the school system provides programs and starts sending home positive comments, this can help improve the parents' orientation. Similarly, some short term success with stimulant medication can provide a positive aspect to the situation. In the long run, the treatment gains depend upon adequately training the parents to be positive and reinforcing for their child's good behavior.

Family Systems: Rewarding the Parents

In each family there is a system of reward and punishment contingencies which generally serve to produce stability. Altering the parents' reactions to one child also alters this system. For most families with hyperactive children the alterations will be automatically desired and reinforcing for other family members, particularly the parents (*36–38; m*). The techniques can often be usefully generalized to dealing with the other children in the family. For some families, however, the change can cause stresses. The counselor needs to be alert for these problems, particularly for the situations where the changes have mixed reinforcement and punishment values for the parents. Further analysis and intervention in the family system may be required to ensure that parents receive adequate reinforcements. In many situations, parents may profit from developing positive rewards outside of the family situation, including mutually positive experiences without the children. The counselor for the child's problem should be sensitive to these issues and, where appropriate, institute other approaches or refer the parents for other types of help.

Fading Nonsocial Contingencies

Perhaps the most difficult part of the home behavior program involves fading (gradually removing) the nonsocial contingencies (*3, 19*). The problem comes not so much in arranging gradual reduction of the nonsocial rewards as in ensuring the development of adequate social consequences to replace the nonsocial ones. The parents may have learned from past experience that they have relatively little social reinforcing value for their children. As was noted previously, if the HA child has been particularly oppositional, the data available indicate that the parents' social reward value was probably very limited (*26, 27*). However, when the token or point system is used, the parents' social reinforcing value is considerably enhanced (*24–27*). The parents may have had such limited success with social rewards in the past that they may not have discovered their new effectiveness. The parents need to be informed and encouraged to start increasing the use of social rewards.

As additional support for use of social rewards, home telephone contact or home observation would be desirable and, in some cases, necessary. The parents could be called and the day's behavioral program discussed, emphasizing parental response to good behaviors. Home use of a tape recorder could also be used to provide feedback for the parents regarding their success in giving social rewards.

Outcome and Duration of Effects

There seems to be little doubt that behavior therapy in the home produces significant change not seen in untreated controls (*39, 40*) or in a waiting list control (*41*). In one study with a placebo control group the behavior problems actually became "worse" (nonsignificantly) for controls and showed the usual improvement for the behavior group (*42*). The average decrease in amount of misbehavior for the aggressive and overactive children ranges from 40% to 60% of the pretreatment levels and are within the higher limits of the range observed for "normal" controls (*43*). About 75% of Patterson's (*9*) cases showed positive outcomes (30% or greater reductions in misbehavior), whereas about 20% became somewhat "worse." Moreover, Patterson (*9*) reports that 25% of his cases had been on medication for "hyperactivity" before treatment and all were off medication after treatment termination (involving school and home behavior therapy). Unfortunately, Patterson does not provide a breakdown of relative therapy outcome for this group compared with other cases, nor does he indicate type of medication and effectiveness of medication. In the three cases Patterson presents with a clearly defined symptom of overactivity, two showed improvement. This 67% positive outcome is similar to the 75% for the total sample and at least suggests that HA children respond as well as non-HA children to the behavior management.

Such clear evidence for efficacy is not available for any other form of nonchemical therapy with HA children. From a cost-effectiveness standpoint, it is encouraging to note that treatment time was relatively short, often only 8–16 weeks. However, the amount of professional time required for the families was noted by Patterson to be about 32 hours. This is more than usual for brief psychotherapy, but less than long term psychotherapy.

Although the behavior management is effective, the duration of effects after treatment can be a problem. Behavior therapies in the home explicitly aim at changing the reinforcement system so that social (natural) rewards will produce a durable change in the child's behavior. Thus, the emphasis upon transfer to social contingencies. The behavior therapies essentially anticipate that eventually informal contingencies in the home will maintain desired behavior patterns.

Do such lasting changes occur? Behavior management will speed developmental changes about to occur in any event, such as potty training (28). Reduction of misbehavior and restlessness in the HA child, indeed, occurs with age, but the change is painfully slow, so that even in their teens the HA symptoms often remain a problem for these children (44, 45). Clearly, then, behavior therapy in the HA child seeks to implement changes *not* expected in the near future of the child's development (*n*).

The other best data for long term effects of behavior therapy with misbehaving children come from a 12-month follow-up reported by Patterson (9, 43). For 14 families, there were no significant changes in the rates of targeted (undesirable) behavior during the follow-up; in fact, the data presented suggest, if anything, continued improvement during follow-up. Only 2 of the 14 families did show poor outcome in the last few months of the follow-up period. These 14 families were not, however, untreated follow-up cases. Patterson's team provided continuing behavior training as needed, and the observers who visited the home served to suggest obtaining further training during follow-up if it seemed needed. Thus, an average of about 2 more professional hours per family was used during the follow-up. Certainly, this is a minimal amount of professional time. Nonetheless, it indicates the need for continuing on-going support for some families.

Clearly, the data on the long term benefits of behavior therapy for home management of the HA child are severely limited. However, the data indicate that, although families will often need some form of continuing support, the behavioral approach is nonetheless the best alternate to the use of medication. More work remains to evaluate cost-effective methods for providing the assistance, and much more is needed to evaluate long term results of this treatment approach. The answers are far from obvious.

NOTES

a. Counseling with families can involve a large variety of treatment orientations. Aside from the behavioral approach, major alternatives have emphasized behavior problems in children in terms of: parental neurotic conflicts (46), problems with family roles (47), and disruption in family communications (process orientation) (48). Behaviorists have argued that available data do not support the view that anyone of these problems suffice to account for the development of deviant child behavior. In particular, the literature review by Fontana (49) has supported the view that family pathology is neither a necessary nor sufficient condition for behavioral deviance in children. Thus, correction of the reinforcement maintenance for deviant behavior in a child will not always lead to substitution of new symptoms of the family pathology (3, 36).

b. One of the major problems involves the inherently poor reliability of parental reports (4, 50). Even the validity of parental recollection of behavioral occurrences has been shown to be poor when compared with direct home observation (52–53). Thus, it seems that unless parents learn to record behavior events as they occur, they will not be able to give a good report. Indeed, many parents may be such poor observers of their child's behavior that they will not be able to even record behavior without training in observation procedures. These problems contribute significantly to difficulties in obtaining parental cooperation.

c. The principal reason for the once daily dose is to reduce risk of side effects. It deserves note that for some HA children medication effects on typical play behaviors at home will be so small as to go unnoticed by parents (6). For some severely HA children, however, medication becomes more important for home management.

d. Weiss and colleagues (7) showed that for the methylphenidate-treated HA children a positive family diagnosis was a significant predictor of good 5-year outcome for school achievement ($r = 0.36$, $p < 0.05$), delinquency ($r = 0.38$, $p < 0.05$), and emotional adjustment ($r = 0.48$, $p < 0.01$). The family diagnosis was, however, *not* related to outcome for the group *not* consistently treated with medication. The family diagnosis was based on rating items such as physical condition of the home, marital relationship, psychiatric illness in parents, deviant child rearing practices, and emotional climate at home.

It deserves note that another report (54) on a 5-year follow-up of HA children combining those using and those not using drug treatment failed to show any predictive relation between family diagnosis and outcome. This report did, however, note that good outcome was associated with significant *improvement* in family scores while poor outcome cases showed negative changes.

e. Home environments show considerable variability in contrast to the more uniformity in the school environments. The importance of home factors in predictive outcome may, in part, reflect the existence of this extreme variability.

f. Parents can even be taught to graph the rate of behavior occurrence (55). The graph provides a vivid summary of change.

g. It is not necessary that every action of a parent after a child's misbehavior be viewed as rewarding; rather the more significant (as determined by observation of the child's reactions) of the consequent parental behaviors are likely to be the reinforcers.

h. The essential difference between reinforcement and response cost involves expectancies. Thus, if a new positive consequence (C^+) is made available contingent on a behavior it is a reinforcement contingency. If the desired behavior is now done most of the time so that C^+ is commonly received, the C^+ becomes expected. When, on rare occasion, the behavior is not done, then the expected C^+ is not received; to the subject this appears now as a response-cost contingency. Thus, reinforcement contingencies with a high rate of C^+ may become perceived as response-cost contingencies.

i. Social reinforcers from parents (26, 27) and adults in general (23–25) appear to have relatively little effect upon deviant children. In contrast, less deviant children tend to be most influenced by these reinforcers. It deserves note, however, that by use of nonsocial reinforcers, the parent can considerably strengthen the influence of his social reinforcers (24–27). The reasons for this change are not obvious. Patterson (3) speculates that the limited efficacy of social reinforcers in misbehaving children reflects the general pattern of aversive interaction between parents (or adults) and deviant children. Altering this pattern requires some external event to create a change in the significance of social contact; thus, pairing social interaction with nonsocial reinforcers changes the expectations of social interaction.

j. One example that probably illustrates the model strength of parents is provided by delinquency. Robins (56) has reported that the best predictor of juvenile delinquency is the arrest record of parents.

k. Response satiation is not a commonly described behavioral procedure, but it can be loosely viewed within a framework assigning optimum occurrence frequencies to behaviors. The assumption is that over a short time there exists an occurrence frequency for a behavior which the organism desires to maintain. If deprived of the opportunities for the behavior, the chance to perform the behavior becomes a reinforcement (57). Obversely, if the behavior is forceably overindulged, the behavior will no longer be freely chosen.

The literature using response satiation in smoking treatment has tended to indicate that the effects largely stem from the "aversive" qualities of the forced behavior rather than simple satiation (58). It seems, therefore, that it would be most appropriate to view this procedure as a mildly aversive punishment contingency rather than as a satiation procedure. Its application is limited, but at times very useful.

l. Cueing parental behaviors by an experimenter has been done in a great variety of ways ranging from simple direction (19) and hand signals (59) to electronic signal lights (60) and walkie-talkies (34).

m. Minde and colleagues (54) have noted that positive changes in family interaction occur with good treatment outcome for HA children. They viewed this as a result of the child's improved behavior; a positive change in one aspect of the family system is seen as inducing further desirable changes in the total family.

n. Minde and colleagues (54) have argued for a critical accelerated social learning during medication treatment of HA children. They noted that an optimum treatment time is between 12 and 36 months; during this time changes apparently occur, removing the need for further medication. This is a poorly documented concept, but if true, suggests that rapid developmental changes can occur for school age HA children given the addition of effective treatment. Thus, in this view, once the changes are established they tend to persist. Perhaps behavioral therapy could be substituted for medication in facilitating this change.

LITERATURE CITED

1. Munro, D. M. G. An experiment in the use of group methods with parents in a child guidance clinic. Brit. J. Psychiat. Soc. Work 6: 16–20, 1952.
2. MacNamara, M. Helping children through their mother. J. Child Psychol. Psychiat. 4: 29–46, 1963.
3. Patterson, G. R. Behavioral intervention procedures in the classroom and in the home, in A. E. Bergin and S. L. Garfield (Eds.), Handbook of Psychotherapy and Behavior Change. New York: Wiley, 1971.
4. Haggard, E. A., Brekstad, A., and Skard, A. G. On the reliability of the anamnestic interview. J. Abnorm. Soc. Psychol. 61: 311–318, 1960.
5. Safer, D. J. Drugs for problem school children. J. School Health 41: 491–495, 1971.
6. Sleator, E. K., and von Neumann, A. W. Methylphenidate in the treatment of hyperkinetic children. Clin. Pediat. 13: 19–24, 1974.
7. Weiss, G., Kruger, E. K., Danielson, U., and Elman, M. The effect of long-term treatment of hyperactive children with methylphenidate. Presented at the American College of Neuro-Psycho-Pharmacology, 1975.
8. Williams, C. D. The elimination of tantrum behavior by extinction procedures. J. Abnorm. Soc. Psychol. 59: 269, 1959.
9. Patterson, G. R. Retraining of aggressive boys by their parents: Review of recent literature and follow-up evaluation. Can. Psychiat. Assoc. J. 19: 142–158, 1974.
10. Wahler, R. G., and Erickson, M. Child behavior therapy: A community program in Appalachia. Behav. Res. Ther. 7: 71–78, 1969.
11. Tharp, R., and Wetzel, R. Behavior modification in the natural environment. New York: Academic Press, 1969.
12. Patterson, G. R. An empirical approach to the classification of disturbed children. J. Clin. Psychol. 20: 326–337, 1964.
13. Lindsley, O. R. An experiment with parents handling behavior at home. Johnstone Bull. 9: 27–36, 1966.
14. Patterson, G. R., and Guillion, M. E. Living with Children. Champaign, Ill.: Research Press, 1968.
15. Becker, W. C. Parents are Teachers. Champaign, Ill.: Research Press, 1971.
16. Ray, R. S. The training of mothers of atypical children in the use of behavior modification techniques. Unpublished masters' thesis, University of Oregon, 1965.

17. Patterson, G. R., Ray, R. S., and Shaw, D. A. Direct intervention in families of deviant children. Oregon Res. Inst. Res. Bull. 8(9), 1968.
18. Hawkins, R. P., Peterson, R. F., Schweid, E., and Bijou, S. W. Behavior therapy in the home: Amelioration of problem parent-child relations with the parent in a therapeutic role. J. Exp. Child Psychol. 4: 99–107, 1966.
19. Zeilberger, J., Sampen, S. E., and Sloane, H. N. Modification of a child's problem behaviors in the home with the mother as therapist. J. Appl. Behav. Anal. 1: 47–53, 1968.
20. Wahler, R. G. Behavior therapy for oppositional children: Love is not enough. Presented at the Eastern Psychological Association, Washington, D.C., 1968.
21. Kaufman, K. F., and O'Leary, K. D. Reward, cost, and self-evaluation procedures for disruptive adolescents in a psychiatric hospital school. J. Appl. Behav. Anal. 5: 293–309, 1972.
22. Fox, R. M., and Azrin, N. H. The elimination of autistic self-stimulatory behavior by overcorrection. J. Appl. Behav. Anal. 6: 1–14, 1973.
23. Levin, G. R., and Simmons, J. J. Response to praise by emotionally disturbed boys. Psychol. Rep. 11: 10, 1962.
24. Patterson, G. R. An application of conditioning techniques to the control of a hyperactive child, in L. P. Ullmann and L. Krasner (Eds.), Case Studies in Behavior Modification. New York: Rinehart and Winston, 1965.
25. Perkins, M. J. Effects of play therapy and behavior modification approaches with conduct problem boys. Diss. Abstr. 28(8-B): 3478–3479, 1968.
26. Patterson, G. R., McNeal, S., Hawkins, N., and Phelps, R. Reprogramming the social environment. J. Child Psychol. Psychiat. 8: 181–195, 1967.
27. Wahler, R. G. Behavior therapy with oppositional children: Attempts to increase their parents' reinforcement value. Presented at Southeastern Psychological Association, Atlanta, 1967.
28. Fox, R. M., and Azran, N. H. Toilet training the retarded: A rapid program for day and nighttime independent toileting. Champaign, Ill.: Research Press, 1973.
29. Bandura, A., Ross, D., and Ross S. A. A comparative test of the status envy, social power, and secondary reinforcement theories of identificatory learning. J. Abnorm. Soc. Psychol. 67: 527–534, 1963.
30. Bandura, A., Ross, D., and Ross, S. A. Vicarious reinforcement and imitative learning. J. Abnorm. Soc. Psychol. 67: 601–607, 1963.
31. Patterson, G. R. Families. Champaign, Ill.: Research Press, 1971.
32. Johnson, J. M. Using parents as contingency managers. Psychol. Rep. 28: 703–710, 1971.
33. Bernal, M. E. Behavioral feedback in the modification of brat behaviors. J. Nerv. Ment. Dis. 148: 375–385, 1969.

34. Bernal, M. E., Williams, D. E., Miller, M. W., and Reagor, P. A. The use of video-tape feedback and operant learning principles in training parents in management of deviant children, in R. D. Rubin, H. Festerheim, J. D. Henderson, and L. P. Ullmann (Eds.), Advances in Behavior Therapy. New York: Academic Press, 1972.
35. Furman, S., and Feighner, A. Video feedback in treating hyperkinetic children: A preliminary report. Am. J. Psychiat. 130: 792–796, 1973.
36. Patterson, G. R., and Reid, J. B. Reciprocity and coercion: Two facets of social systems, in C. Nuringer and J. L. Michael (Eds.), Behavior Modification in Clinical Psychology. New York: Appleton-Century-Crofts, 1970.
37. Patterson, G. R., and Reid, J. B. Intervention for families of aggressive boys: A replication study. Behav. Res. Ther. 11: 383–394, 1973.
38. Eyberg, S. M., and Johnson, S. M. Multiple assessment of behavior modification with families. J. Consult. Clin. Psychol. 42: 594–606, 1974.
39. Martin, B. Family interaction associated with child disturbance: Assessment and modification. Psychother. Theory Res. Pract. 4: 30–35, 1967.
40. Martin, M., Burkholden, R., Rosenthal, T. L., Tharp, R. G., and Thorne, G. L. Programming behavior change and reintegration into the school milieux of extreme adolescent deviates. Behav. Res. Ther. 6: 371–383, 1968.
41. Wiltz, N. A., Jr., and Patterson, G. R. An evaluation of parent training procedures designed to alter inappropriate aggressive behavior of boys. Behav. Ther. 5: 215–22, 1974.
42. Walter, H. I., and Gilmore, S. K. Placebo versus social learning effects in parent training procedures designed to alter the behaviors of aggressive boys. Behav. Ther. 4: 361–377, 1973.
43. Patterson, G. R. Intervention for boys with conduct problems: Multiple settings, treatments and criteria, in Behavior Change 1974. Chicago: Aldine Publishing Co., 1975.
44. Mendelson, W., Johnson, N., and Stewart, M. A. Hyperactive children as teenagers: a follow-up study. J. Nerv. Ment. Dis. 153: 273–279, 1971.
45. Weiss, G., Minde, K., Werry, J., Douglas, V., and Nemeth, E. Studies on the hyperactive child VIII: Five-year follow-up. Arch. Gen. Psychiat. 24: 409–414, 1971.
46. Ackerman, N. W. The Psychodynamics of Family Life. New York: Basic Books, 1958.
47. Bell, J. E. Recent advances in family group therapy. J. Child Psychol. Psychiat. 3: 1–15, 1962.
48. Haley, J. Strategies of Psychotherapy. New York: Grune and Stratton, 1963.
49. Fontana, A. F. Familial etiology of schizophrenia: Is a scientific methodology possible? Psychol. Bull. 66: 214–227, 1966.

50. Yarrow, M., Campbell, J., and Burton, R. V. Reliability of maternal retrospection: A preliminary report. Fam. Proc. 3: 207–218, 1964.
51. Crandall, V. J., and Preston, A. Verbally expressed needs and overt maternal behavior. Child Develop. 32: 261–270, 1961.
52. Sears, R. R. Comparison of interviews with questionnaires for measuring mothers' attitudes toward sex and aggression. J. Personal. Soc. Psychol. 2: 37–44, 1965.
53. Smith, H. T. A comparison of interview and observation measures of mother behavior. J. Abnorm. Soc. Psychol. 57: 278–282, 1958.
54. Minde, K., Weiss, G., and Mendelson, N. A 5-year follow-up study of 91 hyperactive school children. J. Am. Acad. Child Psychiat. 11: 595–610, 1972.
55. Koenig, C. H. Precision teaching with emotionally disturbed pupils. Research training paper No. 17: Children's Rehabilitation. University of Kansas Medical Center, 1967.
56. Robins, L. N., West, P. A., and Herjanic, B. L. Arrests and delinquency in two generations: A study of black urban families and their children. J. Child Psychol. Psychiat. 16: 125–140, 1975.
57. Premack, D. Reinforcement theory, in D. Levine (Ed.), Nebraska Symposium on Motivation 1965, pp. 123–180. Lincoln, Nebr.: University of Nebraska Press, 1965.
58. Lichtenstein, E., Harris, D. E., Birchler, G. R., Wahl, J. M., and Schmahl, D. P. Comparison of rapid smoking, warm, smoky air, and attention placebo in the modification of smoking behavior. J. Consult. Clin. Psychol. 40: 92–98, 1973.
59. O'Leary, K. D., O'Leary, S., and Becker, W. C. Modification of deviant sibling interaction pattern in the home. Behav. Res. Ther. 5: 113–120, 1967.
60. Wahler, R. G., Winkle, G. H., Peterson, R. F., and Morrison, D. C. Mothers as behavior therapists for their own children, in A. M. Graziano (Ed.), Behavior Therapy with Children. Chicago: Aldine-Atheaton, 1969.

Chapter 9   Educational Management

The significant issue for the educational management of developmentally hyperactive children is *not* their hyperactivity, but the learning disability most evidence. For their learning difficulties, such HA children need additional educational assistance. Accordingly, this chapter emphasizes educational efforts for learning-impaired youngsters, highlighting problems of learning-disabled children who have concomitant HA.

Educational programs for learning-impaired children developed primarily under the aegis of special education, a specialty tailoring education to the handicapped. During the first half of this century, special education dealt exclusively with children who had severely handicapping conditions: mental subnormality, blindness, hearing impairment, cerebral palsy, etc. Since the late 1950's, their services expanded to encompass the needs of children with less obvious educational impairments, the specific learning disabled (SLD).

In the 1960's the thrust of special education efforts for SLD children was clear: self-contained, small classes; an individualized curriculum; remediation of "perceptual" and academic handicaps. In the 1970's, the direction of special education has shifted to focus on the integration of regular and special education programs for these children. To implement this change, alternative educational programs developed which included: mainstreaming, itinerant teachers, resource rooms, and bookless curricula. This chapter initially emphasizes the traditional self-contained educational approach. The latter sections deal with more recent developments.

LEARNING DISABILITY CLASSES

The SLD classroom is traditionally self-contained; that is, children stay in one room for the entire day (*a*). The class size averages 8–10 students (*b*). The room is staffed by a teacher with special education training who usually has the services of a half-time teacher's aide. Most commonly, the SLD class exists at the elementary school level. Such classes now serve about 200,000 children; this represents 5–10% of all children in special education classes in the United States (*1, 2; c*).

The environment of the SLD class is more routine, organized, and structured than is the regular classroom (*d*). The children receive fewer choices and their academic assignments are arranged in smaller units. The teacher closely evaluates the academic level and skills of each of the students and based upon this, supplies appropriate learning materials for classroom use. When the curriculum is personally tailored to the child's academic level, the educational method is referred to as individualized instruction.

Generally selected for SLD classes are children who are learning-delayed, nonretarded, disruptive, and developmentally immature (*1, 3; e*). Accordingly, most students in SLD classes have MBD (*4; f*).

The hope in the 1960's was that the specially trained teacher, the small class size, and the modified curriculum would lead to sufficient academic progress and behavioral changes, such that when SLD students returned to regular classes, they would have the tools to succeed (*g*). This hope remains to be realized. However, SLD classes have the following advantages: 1) they offer a supportive academic environment for learning-impaired children; 2) in SLD classes which utilize cubicles as study areas (*5*), the children can show less distractibility (*6, 7*); 3) the classes relieve the regular classroom teacher of a number of inattentive-disruptive youth, allowing her to spend most of her time with a more homogeneous group of children who respond better to group instruction; 4) SLD classes allow the public school to more functionally maintain some HA children who would otherwise be very poorly tolerated in the regular classroom.

Nevertheless, for all their educational appeal and waiting lists, special education classes for SLD children have clear limitations. Even with their small class size and teachers trained in newer remediation techniques, special education class programs in general have done little to reverse the learning impairments and prominent achievement delays common to HA children (*8–13*). The approach is quite expensive, costing 2–3 times more per year per child than regular education. After a few years in special classes, approximately half of the children still have, unfortunately, not matured or progressed enough to fit with some appropriateness into a regular school program (*8*). Other objections to special education classes are: 1) children placed there often feel the stigma of "mental" or "dummy" labels (e.g., "Sped" for special education) assigned to them by peers; 2) special education classes legitimize the exclusion of deviants from the regular classroom, rather than their integration there; 3) assigned children often have to travel quite a distance to the school which offers SLD classes.

THE RESOURCE ROOM

Because of these limitations, because specialized, full time, small classes cannot possibly be offered to all or even most SLD children, and because many learning-disabled students can make adequate progress outside a self-contained SLD classroom, special education administrations have been shifting to new methods of delivery of service, such as the resource room. The resource room is a designated school room staffed by a special educator and stocked with specialized learning materials. SLD children receive 1–3 hr daily of individual or small group remedial assistance in this room (1–3), but receive the rest of their instruction in regular classrooms. Resource rooms can be integrated into the regular program and theoretically, resource room teachers can assist regular teachers to maintain the same type of special education instruction for the child throughout the day. This collaboration has proven to be difficult, in fair measure because regular teachers (for adminstrative and/or personal reasons) guard their territory (the curriculum) from outsiders (h).

MODIFICATIONS OF REGULAR EDUCATION

It has been estimated that at least half of learning-impaired children receive no special education assistance in elementary school (2, 14, 15). Because of this gap in services, because SLD class and resource room programs do not reverse the handicaps of many SLD children, and because segregation is less and less a satisfactory social solution for the problem of deviance, more general, less exclusive changes are obviously necessary in the delivery of educational services to students who experience learning difficulty.

One major change which has been pioneered by special educators is individualized instruction (16). This has been implemented in regular classrooms and could be greatly expanded (16). To institute this, more manpower is necessary, which older peers (17), parents (18, 19; i), or community aides (20) can supply. Also necessary are special training for regular teachers and a broader range of classroom materials. Data show clearly that the more individualized the instruction, the better the academic outcome (17, 21) and that community aides can promote the academic advancement of pupils (20). In addition to organizing for more individualized student assistance, the teacher can "individualize" her method of group instruction. As an example, she can divide the classroom structurally into teaching stations and provide multiple varieties of programmed instruction at each.

A second change that is being increasingly utilized and which better deals with the learning impaired is the nongraded class system. When this approach is fully operational, students go from one elementary school classroom to another for instruction in academic subjects taught at their academic (although not necessarily their age) level. Nongradedness implies nonretention of students and classroom programming to ensure continuous academic progress.

A third consideration for change is to have more basic (or low track) education sections in the early primary grades so that rather than being failed, slowly progressing students can work at a more appropriate pace. In most urban areas, 15–20% of children are unable to read at the primer level at age 7 and it is these children who are frequently nonpromoted in early elementary school. (Some 60–80% of HA children are retained in grade during their first 3 years in school.) Since the number of children seriously behind at the end of first and second grade is so great, a transitional class could be set up for them in most elementary schools. Although the transitional class has drawbacks characteristic of low ability sections (j), it still represents a distinct improvement over the almost routine nonpromotion of HA children (k).

Another possibility for modification of the regular system partially overlaps the first; it involves a greater school system focus on the individual needs of children in the 3–6-year age range. Children at this age have such variability in their learning rates and styles that many need individualized assistance which utilizes their natural skills and focuses on their interests. Placement of *all* December 6-year olds into first grade academics and an emphasis on reading instruction for *all* first graders are antithetical to this concern.

REMEDIAL INSTRUCTION

Educational efforts to improve the academic skills and abilities of learning impaired children are commonly referred to as "remedial." One remedial approach for SLD children is the *developmental* method. It is based on the assumption that education can correct deficits in fundamental perceptual-cognitive skills and thereby assist academic learning. Developmental remedial instruction utilizes diagnostic tests, particularly the Wepman test of auditory discrimination, the Frostig battery, and the Illinois Test of Psycholinguistic Abilities (22), to evaluate the perceptual, integrative and expressive deficits of the SLD child (23). Such a diagnostic analysis provides the basis for prescriptive (or diagnostic) teaching, which is a systematic method of training to strengthen deficit information processing skills. After the "perceptual training," a better use and integration of these skills within an instructional format is emphasized.

A second remedial approach is what can be called the *task analytic* (or behavioral) method of remediation. This remediation approach focuses on the academic process directly, as for example, training for slow reader in phonics or in word recognition.

In practice, special educators tend to be eclectic and to utilize both the developmental and task analytic methods of remediation simultaneously. Furthermore, as they attempt to remediate the SLD child's weaknesses, they also take advantage of his natural strengths and interests.

Two basic remediation approaches for SLD children are: 1) find the functional ability level of the student and build on it; 2) reduce academic tasks to small bits so that success is more likely (24). In keeping with these supportive approaches, grades in special education are given more for completion of assigned tasks than for test scores. Frequently utilized also in remedial work are: programmed instruction (25; l), other self-instruction materials and equipment, oral examinations, and the combined use of more than one modality in instruction (as through the use of tapes along with a book).

The evidence from the literature is that students who receive special reading instruction are academically benefited significantly more than matched controls who receive no additional assistance (26). Unfortunately, after the special reading effort ceases, like most other therapy efforts, the additional gains following the instruction gradually fade (27, 28). (Thus, many who benefit from remedial assistance probably need continuing support.) A second important problem is that even though many special education (SLD) teachers used developmental remedial approaches which attempt to minimize perceptual deficits, the evidence strongly suggests that many such methods (e.g., Frostig, Kephart, Delacato) do not improve academic achievement (m). In fact, the evidence suggests that in general, to remediate the impaired reader, a phonic (linguistic) approach is the most efficacious method (26, 29; n). A third problem in remediation is that, at present, the vast majority of the instructional emphasis in special education for the SLD student is offered at the elementary school level (1). This distribution of services can be rationalized. However, it has been shown that many learning disabled children make sizable academic gains during their junior high school years (*30, 31*).

PROGRAMS FOR SECONDARY SCHOOL MISFITS

Although most nonretarded, learning-impaired children *ultimately* develop reading skills at or above the fifth grade level, many have a particularly difficult time in the public secondary schools. Their lack of competence in the language arts during the sensitive teenage years increases their embarrassment and frustration and commonly further lowers their motivation to try.

Nearly 5% of American *teenagers* with I.Q.'s above 80 achieve at or below the third grade level in reading. About one-third of these students (commonly those with developmental hyperactivity) have serious classroom behavior problems as well. Teenage students with gross problems in behavior and learning are the most ill-fit for the school system and are the most likely to drop out (*32*).

To enable such high risk students to better survive and be more effective in junior high and middle schools, the system needs to better accommodate their needs. Nontraditional approaches that have been tried to achieve this include: behavior modification programs, individualized curricula, career oriented programs, and bookless curricula. A token economy program in conjunction with individualized curricula has been reported to be successful for such teenagers (*33, 34*). Vocational programs by themselves are relatively ineffective for this population (*35, 36*). A bookless curriculum (*37*) is of interest, particularly for nonreaders, but it has not yet been tested. Utilizing a survival curriculum (*o*) is likewise attractive, but untested.

EDUCATIONAL OUTCOME FOR MOST MBD CHILDREN

If the hyperactive, learning-impaired child has average intellectual potential (or better) and is moderately motivated to learn, there is a great likelihood that by the time he is 18–21, he will develop adequate academic skills for customary adult functions (*38*). This is true in most instances even though the child was reading at only the second grade level at age 10. In his junior high school years and beyond, the average learning-impaired child is better able to learn language concepts and utilize compensatory techniques than was possible beforehand.

In practice, then, learning impairments in HA children of average ability generally result in a large initial academic deficit which, when the child is able to read, is followed by a mildly to moderately slower (than average) rate of academic progress. Thus, when followed up 5–10 years after childhood, most learning-impaired children are found to have educational deficiencies, but skills sufficient for most adult involvements (*38*).

NOTES

a. Often, older SLD class students go to regular classes for minor subjects (as music and art). Also, when an SLD child appears ready to return to regular classes, he is sent there part time for an evaluative (trial) placement.
b. Class size in special education is necessarily small to allow for individualized instruction by one teacher. It is of note, however, that studies in regular education have consistently shown no relationship between class size and academic progress (*39, 40*).
c. Most (*41*), although not all (*42*), of the funding for special education classes comes from federal and state funds. For this reason, special education staff tend to be fairly independent of local school authorities.
d. The effect of classroom structure on the activity level of students appears to be small. In ecological studies of heterogeneous classroom populations, Minuchin et al. (*43*) suggested that restlessness was less prevalent in "modern" than in "traditional" classrooms. Flynn and Rapoport (*44*), in a small, clinical study, found some data on HA children that supported this finding. They reported that teachers rated HA children on medication as less restless in an open than in a traditional classroom environment. However, independent classroom ratings did not bear this out. Furthermore, Solomon and Kendall (*45*) found no significant differences in student misconduct in open vs. traditional classrooms. Additionally, McParland and Epstein (*46*) reported that students in open school classrooms were reprimanded more for disciplinary problems than were students in traditional school settings.

  For HA children, the impact of classroom structural changes (such as the installation of cubicles) appears to be minor generally (*5*) and negligible academically (*6, 7*). At this time, then, lacking other information, one can assume that the HA student will exhibit undue restlessness in all educational environments when sustained attention for academic learning is required.
e. The emphasis placed on the I.Q. score in the placement of children into special education programs has been correctly criticized by Koppitz (*8*). In a mid-socioeconomic level junior high, 6% of the seventh grade population in regular classes who had I.Q.'s over 90 tested in reading at the third grade level or less (*47*) on the San Diego

Quick Assessment Test (48). Yet, in the seventh grade EMR classes in the same school, nearly 60% of the children with I.Q.'s in the 70–80 range read *above* the third grade level (by teacher estimate). Such information suggests that placement in special education classes would be more functionally served by greater attention to achievement than to I.Q. A statement by Dunn (1) echoes this point, ". . . the learning requirements of exceptional pupils—not their . . . medical classification—should determine the organization and administration of special education services."

f. Only about 35–40% of learning-impaired children are hyperactive, but 70–80% of learning-impaired children *with developmental behavior difficulties* are hyperactive. Since gross classroom maladjustment and misconduct are major criteria for the special class placement of learning-disabled children, there is a selective admission of HA, learning-impaired children into SLD classes.

g. This is like one mythical rationale that was used to support the development of child guidance clinics in the 1930's and 1940's: if we could only treat the emotionally deviant in their youth, there would be far fewer adult emotional deviants. The data that best refute the special classroom myth for the SLD child is presented by Koppitz (8).

h. Resource rooms, unfortunately, have some of the same limitations as full day, self-contained, special education classes. In themselves, they have not been shown to improve academic progress or the behavioral adjustment of SLD students (11).

i. School officials are often hesitant to have parents in the classrooms. As doctors never took the lead to alter the maldistribution of health care services, as lawyers did not lead attempts to reform accident and medical malpractice insurance abuses, so teachers have not supported the community school movement.

    One parent organization that is actively concerned about the difficulties of the SLD child is the Association for Children with Learning Disabilities (ACLD). This organization has a few hundred chapters across the country and has had some impact on special education funding by state legislatures. Although the domain of the ACLD broadly includes all children with learning disabilities, it is the largest parent organization to date to serve the HA child. The central office of ACLD is located at 5225 Grace Street, Lower Level, Pittsburgh, Pa. 15236. Other information on programs and organizations for the SLD child can be obtained by writing the National Special Education Information Center, Box 1492, Washington, D.C. 20013.

j. Grouping instructional sections at a given grade level by academic ability (e.g., section 7-A has the "dullards" and 7-M has the "brains"), known as tracking, is increasingly coming into question, in part because the process often winds up segregating children by socioeconomic level. Available data show that educationally grouping students by academic skills tends to mildly benefit the more able students (1) and disadvantage "slower" children (1, 12). The overall effects of tracking on achievement, however, are relatively small (49).

k. By retaining dull and uncooperative elementary school children, teachers can more appropriately use grade level, total group instruction. However, results from a good deal of research have consistently shown that nonpromotion is clearly disadvantageous academically to the retained student (50-52). Furthermore, when the student receives his second retention (or nonpromotion), usually in the secondary grades, it almost always marks his departure from formal public education. (Was this a dropout or a pushout?)

l. In programmed instruction, material is learned essentially without teacher assistance. By way of a special text or a teaching machine, the student attends to relatively simple bits of information which are sequenced in a highly systematic (often repetitive) fashion from the basic (or familiar) to the complex (or unfamiliar). At each step, the student is required to indicate his understanding of the material (25). Such a program supports the gradual acquisition of material, provides immediate feedback, and allows few opportunities for error, all of which serve to lessen frustration in the learning process.

m. Educators and researchers who trust primarily hard outcome data will find when they review the evidence that, with rare exceptions (53-55), there is virtually no support for the notion that developmental training programs aiming to remediate sensory, motor, or integrative "perceptual" deficits improve educational attainment (25, 56-71). Rather, reports in the literature stress that academic aid is more beneficial when it is directly related to the task to be mastered (29, 57, 59). Masland (72) states this succinctly when he says, "The more closely related to the ultimate task is the learning experience, the more direct will be the result." Cohen (70) similarly states, "In the reading field, the surest way to get urban ghetto kids to read is to teach them letters and words and do it thoroughly." Rosen (59), following a comparative study, concludes that it "... appears that additional time devoted to reading instruction [is] more important for reading achievement than time . . . devoted to perceptual training."

n. One could argue that programs aiming to motivate students to read are more basic and ultimately more valuable than formal remedial programs. In many instances, teachers indeed focus on motivation before remediation. The merits of a program aimed exclusively at motivation are promising (73) and deserve comparative studies.

o. A survival curriculum includes materials useful for life adjustment, such as auto mechanics manuals, the driver's manual, job application forms, income tax forms, etc.

LITERATURE CITED

1. Dunn, L. An overview, in L. Dunn (Ed.), Exceptional Children in the Schools: Special Education in Transition, 2nd Ed., pp. 3-62. New York: Holt, Rinehart and Winston, 1973.

220   Hyperactive Children

220   Hyperactive Children

2. Kirk, S. Educating Exceptional Children, 2nd Ed. Boston: Houghton Mifflin Company, 1972.
3. Senf, G. Learning disabilities. Pediat. Clin. N. Am. 20: 607–640, 1973.
4. Rogan, L., and Lukens, J. Education, administration and classroom procedures, in MBD in Children: Education, Medical and Health-Related Services, Public Health Service Publication No. 2015, pp. 21–30. Washington, D.C.: United States Department of Health, Education and Welfare, United States Government Printing Office, 1969.
5. Cruickshank, W., Bentzen, F., Ratzeburg, R., and Tannhauser, M. A Teaching Method For Brain-Injured and Hyperactive Children: A Demonstration Pilot Study. Syracuse, N.Y.: Syracuse University Press, 1961.
6. Somervill, J., Warnberg, L., and Bost, D. Effects of cubicles versus increased stimulation on task performance by first-grader males perceived as distractable and non-distractable. J. Spec. Ed. 7: 169–185, 1973.
7. Shores, R., and Haubrich, P. Effect of cubicles in educating emotionally disturbed children. Except. Child. 36: 21–24, 1969.
8. Koppitz, E. Children with Learning Disabilities: A Five-Year Follow-up Study. New York: Grune and Stratton, 1971.
9. Vacc, N. Long term effects of special class intervention for emotionally disturbed children. Except. Child. 39: 15–22, 1972.
10. Johnson, G. Special education for the mentally handicapped—a paradox. Except. Child. 29: 62–69, 1962.
11. Glavin, J. Behaviorally oriented resource rooms: A follow-up. J. Spec. Ed. 8: 337–347, 1974.
12. Haring, N., and Krug, D. Placement in regular programs: Procedures and results. Except. Child. 41: 413–417, 1975.
13. Christoplos, F., and Renz, P. A critical examination of special education programs. J. Spec. Ed. 3: 371–379, 1969.
14. Tarnopol, L. Parent and professional relations, in L. Tarnopol (Ed.), Learning Disabilities: Introduction to Education and Medical Management, pp. 41–63. Springfield, Ill.: Charles C Thomas, Publisher, 1969.
15. Silverman, L., and Metz, A. Number of pupils with special learning disabilities in local public schools in the United States, Spring 1970. Ann. N.Y. Acad. Sci. 205: 146–157, 1973.
16. Gronland, N. Individualizing Classroom Instruction. New York: MacMillan Publishing Company, 1974.
17. Jenkins, J., Mayhall, W., Peschka, C., and Jenkins, L. Comparing small group and tutorial instruction in resource rooms. Except. Child. 40: 245–250, 1974.
18. Ryback, D., and Staats, A. Parents as behavior therapy technicians in treating reading deficits (dyslexia). J. Behav. Ther. Exp. Psychiat. 1: 109–119, 1970.
19. Regal, J., and Elliott, R. A special program for special education. Except. Child. 38: 67–68, 1971.

20. Cowen, E. Emergent directions in school mental health. Am. Scient. 59: 723—733, 1971.
21. Mayhall, W., Jenkins, J., Chestnut, W., Rose, M., Schroeder, K., and Jordan, B. Supervision and site of instruction as factors in tutorial programs. Except. Child. 42: 151—154, 1975.
22. Frostig, M. Treatment of learning disorders, in J. Menkes and R. Schain (Eds.), Learning Disorders in Children, pp. 56—60. Columbus, Ohio: Ross Laboratories, 1971.
23. Peter, L. Prescriptive teaching system, Vol. 1. Individual Instruction. New York: McGraw-Hill, 1972.
24. Hewett, F. Strategies of special education. Pediat. Clin. N. Am. 20: 695—704, 1973.
25. Jones, R. Programmed instruction and teaching machines, in R. Jones (Ed.), New Directions in Special Education. Boston: Allyn and Bacon, Inc., 1970.
26. Silberberg, N., Iverson, I., and Goins, J. Which remedial reading method works best? J. Learn. Disabil. 6: 547—556, 1973.
27. Barlow, B. The long-term effect of remedial reading instruction. Reading Teach. 18: 581—586, 1965.
28. Silberberg, N., and Silberberg, M. Myths in remedial education. J. Learn. Disabil. 2: 209—217, 1969.
29. Bateman, B. Reading: A controversial view—Research and rationale, in L. Tarnopol (Ed.), Learning Disabilities: Introduction to Education and Medical Management, pp. 289—305. Springfield, Ill.: Charles C Thomas, Publisher, 1969.
30. Safer, D., and Allen, R. Factors associated with improvement in severe reading disability. Psychol. Schools 10: 110—118, 1973.
31. Birch, L. The improvement of reading ability. Br. J. Ed. Psychol. 20: 73—76, 1950.
32. Cervantes, L. The Drop-Out: Causes and Cures. Ann Arbor, Mich.: University of Michigan Press, 1965.
33. Heaton, R., Safer, D., Allen, R., Spinnato, N., and Prumo, F. A motivational environment for behaviorally deviant junior high school students (Unpublished manuscript). 1975.
34. Cohen, H. Educational therapy: The design of learning environments, in J. Shielen, H. Hunt, J. Matarazzo, and S. Savage (Eds.), Research in Psychotherapy, pp. 21—53. Washington, D.C.: American Psychological Association, 1968.
35. Ahlstrom, W., and Havighurst, R. 400 Losers, San Francisco: Josey-Bass, 1971.
36. Longstreth, L., Shanley, F., and Rice, R. Experimental evaluation of a high school program for potential dropouts. J. Ed. Psychol. 55: 228—236, 1964.
37. Silberberg, N., and Silberberg, M. The bookless curriculum: An educational alternative. J. Learn. Disabil. 2: 302—307, 1969.
38. Herjanic, B., and Penick, E. Adult outcome of disabled child readers. J. Spec. Ed. 6: 397—410, 1972.
39. Little, A., Mabey, C., and Russell, J. Do small Classes help a pupil? New Soc. 18: 769—771, 1971.

40. Morris, J. Standards and Progress in Reading. Slough, Kent, Great Britain: National Foundation for Educational Research, 1966.

41. Slater, R. Special services and trends in large city school districts, in C. Meisgeier and J. Kind (Eds.), The Process of Special Education Administration, pp. 358–365. Scranton, Pa.: International Textbook Company, 1970.

42. Reger, R., Schroeder, W., and Uschold, K. Special Education: Children with Learning Problems. New York: Oxford University Press, 1968.

43. Minuchin, P., Biber, B., Shapiro, E., and Zimiles, H. The Psychological Impact of School Experience. New York: Basic Books, 1969.

44. Flynn, N., and Rapoport, J. Hyperactivity in open and traditional classroom environments (In press). J. Spec. Ed. 1976.

45. Solomon, D., and Kendall, A. Teacher's perceptions of and reactions to misbehavior in traditional and open classrooms. J. Ed. Psychol. 67: 528–530, 1975.

46. McParland, J., and Epstein, J. Report to Howard County Public Schools on the openness of school programs (Unpublished manuscript). 1975.

47. Young, P., and Safer, D. Unpublished data, 1974.

48. La Pray, M., and Ross, R. The graded word list: Quick gauge of reading ability. J. Read. 12: 305–307, 1969.

49. Jencks, C. Inequality: A Reassessment of the Effect of Family and Schooling in America. New York: Basic Books, 1972.

50. Chansky, N. Progress of promoted and repeating grade 1 failures. J. Exp. Ed. 32: 225–237, 1964.

51. Coffield, W., and Blommers, P. The effects of non-promotion on educational achievement in the elementary school. J. Ed. Psychol. 47: 235–250, 1956.

52. Dobbs, V., and Neville, D. The effect of nonpromotion on the achievement of groups matched from retained first graders and promoted second graders. J. Ed. Res. 60: 472–475, 1967.

53. Elkind, D., and Deblinger, J. Perceptual training and reading achievement in disadvantaged children. Child Develop. 40: 11–19, 1969.

54. Serwer, B., Shapiro, B., and Shapiro, P. The comparative effectiveness of four methods of instruction on the achievement of children with specific learning disabilities. J. Spec. Ed. 7: 241–249, 1973.

55. Schiffman, G., and Clemmens, R. Observations on children with severe reading problems, in J. Hellmuth (Ed.), Learning Disorders, Vol. 2, pp. 297–310. Seattle: Special Child Publications, 1966.

56. Jacobs, J., Wirthlin, L., and Miller, C. A follow-up evaluation of the frostig visual-perceptual training program. Ed. Leadership 26: 169–175, 1968.

57. La Pray, M., and Ross, R. Auditory- and visual-perceptual training. Int. Read. Assoc. Conf. Proc. 11: 530–532, 1966.

58. Roach, E. Evaluation of an experimental program of perceptual-motor training with slow readers. Int. Read. Assoc. Conf. Proc. 11: 446–450, 1966.

59. Rosen, C. An experimental study of visual perceptual training and reading achievement in first grade. Percept. Motor Skills 22: 979–986, 1966.
60. O'Donnell, P., and Eisenson, J. Delacato training for reading achievement and visual-motor integration. J. Learn. Disabil. 2: 441–447, 1969.
61. Gorelick, M. The effectiveness of visual form training in a prereading program. J. Ed. Res. 58: 315–318, 1965.
62. Feldmann, S., Schmidt, D., and Deutsch, C. Effect of auditory training on reading skills of retarded readers. Percept. Motor Skills 26: 467–480, 1968.
63. Belmont, I., and Birch, H. The effect of supplemental intervention on children with low reading readiness scores. J. Spec. Ed. 8: 81–89, 1974.
64. Balow, B. Perceptual-motor activities in the treatment of severe reading disability. Read. Teach. 24: 513–525, 1971.
65. Hammill, D. Training visual-perceptual processes. J. Learn. Disabil. 5: 552–559, 1972.
66. The Doman-Delacato treatment of neurologically handicapped children. Develop. Med. Child. Neurol. 10: 243–246, 1968.
67. Robbins, M. A study of the validity of Delacato's theory of neurological disorganization. Except. Child. 32: 517–523, 1966.
68. Wingert, R. Evaluation of a readiness training program. Read. Teach. 22: 325–328, 1969.
69. Keim, R. Visual-motor training, readiness, and intelligence of kindergarten children. J. Learn. Disabil. 3: 256–259, 1970.
70. Cohen, S. Studies in visual perception and reading in disadvantaged children. J. Learn. Disabil. 2: 498–503, 1969.
71. Williams, J. Training kindergarten children to discriminate letter like forms. Am. Ed. Res. J. 6: 501–514, 1969.
72. Masland, R. Children with MBD–A national problem, in L. Tarnopol (Ed.), Learning Disabilities: Introduction to Education and Medical Management, pp. 67–94. Springfield, Ill.: Charles C Thomas, Publisher, 1969.
73. Fader, D., and McNeil, E. Hooked on Books: Program and Proof. New York: Berkley Publications, 1968.

Chapter 10 Coordination in Management

THE RATIONALE FOR COORDINATION

Some illnesses or biological deviations can be successfully treated in a unimodal fashion. These include bacterial pneumonia, which can be exclusively treated with medicine; hare lip, which can be adequately corrected by plastic surgery; and measles, which can be singularly prevented by a vaccine. Other medical ailments, however, cannot be so successfully treated in a unimodal fashion. HA is one such infirmity. Since, at this time, it cannot be cured, repaired, or for the most part prevented, it must be managed. Since the problems of HA are multifaceted, the management usually needs to be multimodal.

Although most professionals realize this, many in practice operate as if their generally undimensional approach provides the necessary treatment. Examples are: 1) the physician who views the child's office visits and the prescription of medication as central to treatment and fails to coordinate his management with the school; 2) the special educator who sees the new curriculum he has instituted as the vital part of treatment and doesn't encourage parent discussions and support; 3) the social worker who views his agency interviews with the parents as central to any change in the HA child's behavior.

Such limitations in scope characterize the specialty practice of many and are reinforced by technical, self-preservative, economic, and other considerations.

METHODS FOR IMPROVING
COORDINATION AMONG PROFESSIONALS

A number of approaches to increase the coordination and/or expand the breadth of professional services for emotionally deviant children are presently in operation. One major method of coordination is the *administrative staff meeting*. Usually, one staff member (e.g., within the school or an agency) discusses the case and receives input from others on the staff, although he retains primary responsibility for management. The staff meeting supports intra-agency coordination on the case, increases staff awareness of the problem, and provides administrative direction. Bringing the case to staff can, however, be time consuming (and thereby costly). Although it broadens the base of one system's involvement, it rarely serves to coordinate interagency efforts.

A second general method to promote the coordination of services is to *bring the needed professional support to the area of difficulty*. Instead of sending the child to an outside therapist, the therapist is asked to come to the institution which has the problem with the child (e.g., the school or the court). Such a move actively assists the professional (who heretofore was outside the institutional system) to become a part of the team. By sheer proximity, it increases interprofessional coordination of services. It also supports the school (for example) to become the major mental health resource for children with serious classroom emotional and behavior problems. (The rapid increase in number of guidance counselors and psychologists within the schools reflects this trend.) On the debit side, this approach could lessen the confidentiality between therapist and client, although probably not to any practical degree. Its effect on the cost of services is debatable.

To expand the breadth of services, one major historic effort has been the *collaborative treatment approach*. In collaborative therapy, involved professionals split the task by design. In child guidance clinics, one professional treats the parents and another treats the child (*1*). In medical circles, the allergist handles the shots, the pediatrician the colds, the child psychotherapist the psychic problems. Occasionally at regular intervals, although usually in time of crisis, the collaborating professionals share opinions and adjust their treatment strategies. The collaborative approach is usually expensive (*a*). It can unduly fragment treatment management and stir competition between the therapists (*2*). However, it provides more specialty assistance for case management, and in the right hands (and circumstances) can be very effective.

A second approach to expand the breadth of services is to train therapists to operate in a *multimodal* way. Examples are to train the teacher to counsel the parents, and the physician to consult with school personnel. The multimodal therapist might then provide most of the needed professional services for the HA child. This approach too can be expensive. Is it economical to train and utilize the pediatrician also as an expert in learning disabilities and behavior modification, and to train and utilize the educator also as an advisor to parents in the area of child rearing?

The multipurpose therapist would in addition need to be more accessible to all to maintain his one-man show. Private practitioners who do not charge for school contacts would have difficulty adjusting their fee and practice arrangements. Likewise, teachers tied to a full classroom schedule would have a hard time quickly mobilizing for a crisis interview.

The above listed methods of expanding coordination and the breadth of professional services for deviant children are not mutually exclusive. However, among the possibilities mentioned, there is a trend toward more services within the institution which has the difficulty, and for more multipurpose therapists.

In managing hyperactivity in children, the inter-relating of therapeutic efforts is particularly useful and is supported by a pattern of frequent communication among parents, teachers, administrative school staff, and health care professionals. Such coordination is desirable at all levels of service: screening, diagnosis, treatment, and follow-up.

COORDINATION IN DIAGNOSTIC
SCREENING AND TREATMENT PLANNING

Diagnostic Screening

The diagnosis of hyperactivity is made by a review of valid historical and classroom reports, and is supported particularly by an appraisal of the child's learning skills. It therefore can be made by anyone competent enough to obtain and understand this material. If the teacher obtains this information and knows enough about the subject, he can make the diagnosis. If the parent is a good observer and is also aware of the school maladjustment and learning disabilities of his offspring, he can as well.

Many teachers (and most parents), however, need help in this matter. For teachers, school psychological and medical consultants can organize their efforts so that needed data will be obtained. Because of the possibility of inaccuracy in a one-teacher diagnosis and referral arrangement, a second professional opinion *should* be obtained before a school official discusses his findings and recommendations with the parent. Also, for administrative reasons, the principal, school nurse, and guidance counselor should know about the teacher's impression and his recommendations. Such communications can be made conveniently at a school staff meeting.

School-Parent Communication

The next step would be for a school official (designated by the principal) to request a parent conference and inform the parents then of the child's classroom difficulties. If the parents choose as a result of the meeting to follow-up with a family doctor, local psychologist, regional mental health center, or the like, the parents should be asked to sign a form releasing school information on the child to the involved professional. (Alternatively, school personnel can wait for the receipt of a parent-signed form authorizing them to send their material to the involved professional. This is not the preferred route for school staff in these cases because not all outside agencies will initiate a school-"outside professional" dialogue.)

School-Therapist Communication

When the parents agree to initiate a particular diagnostic and possibly therapeutic course for the child, involved school officials should then convey (with parent consent) pertinent school information to the involved professional. Informing the professional diagnostician of the child's classroom maladjustment (the reason for the referral) fulfills (in part) the school's public health screening function (b).

The process also aids the professional for he is in a much better position to evaluate the child when he has the necessary school data. When this material (e.g., teacher check lists, school information form, etc.) arrives before the diagnostic appointment, it saves time in the evaluation.

In turn, the diagnostician-therapist should convey his recommendations to school officials. This does not mean, however, that sensitive items in the history (if there are any) should be included in a letter to the school. If a letter is sent to the school, only that information necessary to understand the recommendations should be included. Such written reports should then be placed by school personnel in a confidential school or health folder. Written correspondence of this sort may have minor disadvantages, but these are usually outweighed by the value of such reports for future educational planning.

COORDINATION OF MEDICATION TREATMENT

Medication Follow-up

Medication treatment particularly requires regular classroom reports for the physician. Based on these school reports, the doctor can then more knowingly adjust the dose or change the kind of medication to obtain the optimal therapeutic response. Clearly, good feedback improves the clinical results (*3*). (This process has been discussed in Chapter 3.)

The desired frequency of this reporting can vary. Always, the teacher's checklist should be sent to the physician initially as a diagnostic tool and baseline measurement. Next, whenever the medication is said to be less than optimally beneficial, follow-up checklists should be sent. If the therapy is proceeding smoothly, the checklists need to be mailed out routinely only once or twice yearly. An alternative (and probably better) method used by some is to have checklists completed and mailed before follow-up medical appointments (*4*). If weight and height measurements are made routinely by the school nurse, these can be added to the checklist form.

Noon Dosage

Many HA children on medication receive a noon dose of stimulant medication at the school (*5*). Such administration in the school requires a physician's written order. Drug administration is commonly performed by a school nurse. However, sometimes a nurse is not available at the school and someone else (as a school secretary or the teacher) gives the medication to the child. This is all right in most school areas (*c*) if the physician's order is broad enough to include administration of the medication by nonmedical personnel.

COORDINATION OF BEHAVIOR THERAPY

Home Reinforcement

Home reinforcement of good school behavior is most easily managed by a school coordinator, since he can be in contact with the HA child, his parents, and the teacher, and can, therefore, make needed modifications in the program (e.g., make sure that the teacher's signature or initials on the daily progress card were not forged). A guidance counselor is often excellent for this task and an interested vice principal can do the job. (A teacher can do it without assistance if he has the energy, time, and knowledge.)

When such a system is operating smoothly, a minute or 2 of discussion by the school coordinator with the child and with the teacher once or twice weekly, and a brief weekly or biweekly phone contact between the coordinator and the parent are all that is needed. If an outside behavior therapist is regularly involved with the parents and the child, he should be in touch with the in-school program coordinator at least every 2–8 weeks. However, in situations when an outside therapist is exclusively directing the home reinforcement of good school behavior *without* school staff involvement, he will probably need to meet more extensively with the involved parties for the program to succeed.

Outside professionals can easily have difficulty maintaining a home reinforcement program based on good school reports because crises come up often unexpectedly. The reinforcers weaken, the child is sent to the office for nonclassroom infractions, the parents or teachers by-pass the system, etc. However, with attractive reinforcers and a coordinated system available for crises, home reinforcement of good school behavior works for several months (or more) for most.

School Reinforcement

School reinforcement of good school behavior must be managed by a school official. If the child is to be reinforced at school *and* at home for good school behavior (always a good idea), then the same school official should coordinate both. Generally, the school reinforcement arrangement necessitates the active support of the classroom teacher. If the teacher persists in focusing on the child's misconduct and finds nothing to reward the child for, then school rewards (e.g., more play time) will never be offered.

SOME PROFESSIONAL ROLES IN COORDINATED TREATMENT

The School Guidance Counselor as Coordinator

The guidance counselor is in a unique position to aid the HA child's adjustment to school. He can coordinate a classroom contingency management arrangement, assist the teacher to modify the curriculum for the child, offer group counseling, do family counseling, etc. Generally, his efforts to assist the teacher in the classroom are more potentially useful to the child and to the system than seeing the child in his office for counseling. This is because the HA child's problems occur in the classroom and the more direct the focus of therapeutic intervention, the more likely it is to have its impact where it is aimed.

The School Psychologist as an Advocate and Facilitator

The school psychologist can influence mental health within the system by clarifying the needs of the learning-impaired child, by making others aware of the child's feelings of defeat and frustration, by suggesting options that remain for the school staff, by not validating the fears of some teachers, etc. He should be, more than anyone else within the school system, the child's advocate. He can take this role because he is both apart from (by training) and within (by employment) the inbred education system, and because he has the prestige to question the value of repeated suspensions and retentions, which have an adverse effect on most behavior-disordered, learning-impaired children.

Furthermore, by training, the school psychologist has more breadth than anyone else within the system. Therefore, he can readily advise teachers on classroom management, offer psychological assistance to the parents and the child, evaluate the child's psychological disability, evaluate a new educational method, etc.

The School Principal as Team Leader

The school principal has clear-cut administrative authority over other school staff and is the chief disciplinarian in the school. When students misbehave, he supports the classroom teacher routinely because the teacher observed the student's conduct infraction and runs the classes, and because an open (public) confrontation between them could jeopardize teacher authority and (thereby) student discipline. Whereas the principal is generally obliged to support the teacher and discipline the child, he should not in the process reinforce a pattern of repeated teacher referrals to the office, which can ultimately lead to a suspension for the child. In this broad task, he has to have the ingenuity, guts, flexibility, and intelligence to evaluate the long term consequences of the behavior of school staff to problem children. Did the discipline imposed stop the child's classroom misconduct? Did the suspension help the child, the parents, the teacher? Would a teacher-change, an itinerant teacher, or an incentive-reward system work better? How can he best use the counselor, pupil personnel worker, nurse, or psychologist in this case?

The principal's other major task for his HA students is to administratively set up a positive learning environment for them. This means that he should actively consider setting up in his school the following: ungraded classes, transitional classes, reinforcement contingencies, diverse minicourses, and a volunteer parent-tutor program (6).

COMMUNITY MENTAL
HEALTH-SCHOOL PROGRAM COORDINATION

Community mental health professionals such as the child guidance clinic (CGC) staff who give treatment to patients in their offices apply primarily the medical model of treatment. The patient has the ailment and comes to the therapist for rehabilitative treatment. This model for HA children has some appropriateness and applicability when the physician prescribes medication. Otherwise, it has many limitations. Outpatient psychotherapy with the HA child has only limited benefit (7), and counseling for classroom-related disorders outside the school setting adds unnecessary distance in problem solving.

Clinic procedure can be modified, however, for school-referred children so that the CGC staff member assigned to the case can serve as a consultant to the school. He can meet with involved school personnel at the school to set up a joint management program. The clinic staff member's role could include, in addition, meeting with the family to counsel them on issues not easily handled by school staff, and arranging for a trial of medication by a private or clinic physician.

A more profound CGC modification would be to set up a separate school mental health service within a community mental health center. This service would handle all incoming school referrals for mental health services and its staff would coordinate school, parent, and family doctor management efforts by way of counseling, consultation, and collaboration.

An offshoot from this modification would be a health department hyperkinetic clinic. School problem HA children would be referred by school staff to their usual source of medical care. If the family doctor felt he could not provide optimal care, he could formally route these children to a pediatrician or child psychiatrist in the health department. Such a clinic would provide specialty medical management for HA children who would probably not otherwise receive it through private channels and it could provide a unique degree of health profession-school staff coordination for those children (d).

NOTES

a. The collaborative approach is common in diagnostic as well as in treatment services. In some child guidance clinics, in a diagnostic work-up, the psychologist administers tests, the psychiatrist interviews the child, the pediatrician does a physical and neurological examination, and the social worker interviews the parents. The cost of this diagnostic examination alone is easily $250, which does not include the cost of the coordinating staff conference and the follow-up interview with the parents.
b. The school has the obligation to identify any handicap which clearly limits the child's functioning in the classroom, and to inform the parent of this. No doubt, school staff move most rapidly to inform

the parents that the child has an educational handicap when that child is disrupting the classroom. Furthermore, many administrators and teachers who have seen the dramatic effects of stimulants on HA children tend then to advise the parents to take the child to the family doctor. They would like the HA-misbehaving student medicated to improve the child's educational adjustment *and* for the sake of classroom harmony.

c. In New York City, *only* school nurses may administer medication to the pupils (*8*).

d. Such a hyperkinetic clinic was set up by Dr. John Krager within the Baltimore County Department of Health (Towson, Md.). It has been functioning smoothly and efficiently since its inception in 1971.

LITERATURE CITED

1. Szurek, S., Johnson, A., and Falstein, E. Collaborative psychiatric therapy of parent-child problems. Am. J. Orthopsychiat. 12: 511–516, 1942.
2. Berlin, I., Boatman, M., and Sheimo, S., and Szurek, S. Adolescent alternation of anorexia and obesity. Am. J. Orthopsychiat. 21: 387–419, 1951.
3. Weithorn, C., and Ross, R. Who monitors medication? J. Learn. Disabil. 8: 458–461, 1975.
4. Katz, S., Saraf, K., Gittelman-Klein, R., and Klein, D. Clinical pharmacological management of hyperkinetic children. Int. J. Ment. Health 4: 157–181, 1975.
5. Krager, J., and Safer, D. Type and prevalence of medication used in the treatment of hyperactive children. New Eng. J. Med. 291: 1118–1121, 1974.
6. Cowen, E., Trost, M., Dorr, D., Lorion, R., Izzo, L., and Isaacson, R. New ways in school mental health. New York: Behavioral Publications, 1975.
7. Eisenberg, L., Gilbert, A., Cytryn, L., and Molling, P. The effectiveness of psychotherapy alone and in conjunction with perphenazine or placebo in the treatment of neurotic and hyperkinetic children. Am. J. Psychiat. 117: 1088–1093, 1961.
8. Gittelman-Klein, R. Pilot clinical trial of imipramine in hyperkinetic children, in C. Conners (Ed.), Clinical Use of Stimulant Drugs in Children, pp. 192–201. Amsterdam: Excerpta Medica, 1974.

Index

definition of, 125, 137
home-school, 125
quiet-learning, 125
transfer to new situations, 126

Haldol, 64
Hyperactive child
activity level of, 6, 15
brain malfunctions of, 15–16
as a community problem, 3
discipline of, 101–104, 111
educational management of,
211–219
individualized instruction in,
212–214
nongraded class system in,
214
home responsibilities of, 104
I.Q. scores of, 19
management of, see *Coordinated
management of HA*
maturational lag in, 6
non-promotion of, 219
parental supervision of, 104–105
physical punishment of,
102–104, 111
problems in infancy, 15
problems in preschool years,
16–17
remedial instruction of,
214–216, 219
restlessness of, 106
social restrictions on, 105
Hyperactivity
age of onset, 5, 28
and behavior disability, 26–27
and brain damage, 6
clinical assessment of, 28
and complications of pregnancy
low Apgar score, 11, 15, 27
perinatal distress, 11, 27
prematurity, 11
definition of, 5–7
diagnosis of, 3, 16, 17–18
diagnostic evidence for, 27
diagnostic screening of, 227,
232–233
family history of, 16, 33

family influence on, 29
historical background, 1–2
and hypoglycemia, 31
laboratory measures of, 20–21
and lead poisoning, 31
major associated features of, 7–9
behavior problems, 9
immaturity, 9
inattentiveness, 7
learning impediment, 7
overlap of, 10–11, 14
megavitamin treatment for, 31
minor associated features, 9–10
emotional deviance, 9–10
impulsivity, 9
low self-esteem, 9
peer difficulties, 9
and mongoloid-related features,
19
and perceptual-cognitive disability, 8
prevalence of, 21
according to sex, 21
prognosis for, 21–22
as a syndrome, 24
Hyperkinetic behavior, 5
Hyperkinetic reaction, 23
Hypoactivity, 24
Hypoglycemia, 31

Individual therapy, 130
I.Q.
alteration by stimulants, 52
function in educational placement, 217–218
relation to restlessness, 30
use in diagnosis, 19–20

Lead poisoning, 31
Learning
influence of behavior therapy on,
133
Learning disability
and academic lag, 26
definition of, 7–8, 25
and hyperactivity, 25

DATE DUE			
MAY 15 '85	MAY 04 '90		
FEB 18 '87	MAR 0 2 1998		
911114			
MAR 11 '94	MAR 2 3 200		
MAY 2	FEB 13		
NOV 21 '94	MAR 2-7		
APR 08 95	NOV. 26		
MAY 15 '95			
MAY 29 '95			
JUN 03 95			
NOV 27 '95			
MAR 25 '99			